T0294925

THE
A-HA! METHOD

THE
A-HA! METHOD

Communicating Powerfully in a Time of Distraction

GABE ZICHERMANN

ROWMAN & LITTLEFIELD
Lanham • Boulder • New York • London

All figures in this book courtesy of the author.

Published by Rowman & Littlefield
An imprint of The Rowman & Littlefield Publishing Group, Inc.
4501 Forbes Boulevard, Suite 200, Lanham, Maryland 20706
www.rowman.com

86-90 Paul Street, London EC2A 4NE

British Library Cataloguing in Publication Information Available

Library of Congress Cataloging-in-Publication Data

978-1-5381-7221-6 (cloth)
978-1-5381-7222-3 (electronic)

For my niece, nephews, and godchildren—
Zach, Benny, Zoe, Izzy, and Maddy:
I am sure the world you'll build is better
than the one we leave behind.

Contents

How to Use This Book

QR CODES

Throughout this book you will find QR codes. These make it easy for you to snap a picture of the code with your smartphone and be taken directly to the link I'm referencing in the text. No one hates typing in full URLs more than me, so I hope you can appreciate this innovation.

To test your ability to snap a QR code, why not take a picture of the one below?

In case you don't have a smartphone (good for you, I guess!) you can also go to this URL and get access to the whole shebang in one spot.

That URL is https://whydontyou.com/haveasmartphoneanduseitforQRcodes/?UTM=youreallydidit.

I sincerely hope you didn't actually type in that URL. This is correct: https://speakersalliance.org/ahabook.

HOW TO MAKE THE MOST OF THIS BOOK

In addition to the practical and theoretical ideas laid out in this book, I believe you must build and practice your talk/pitch to get the full benefit of the A-Ha! Method. Furthermore, I think it's critical to engage with other speakers' content and understand how to develop your own voice on the platforms they've created.

To facilitate this, I've created a resource guide to accompany this book. It outlines a process you can follow to accomplish your goal of being a better communicator.

Snap the QR code below to go straight to the guide.

Resource Guide QR https://speakersalliance.org/ahabook

Introduction

I remember the first time I was invited to give a TED presentation. I received an email from a nice European lady that I met once at a conference, asking if I had any interest in coming to Belgium that summer and presenting at a new event they were launching called TEDxKids. It was going to bring together some of the best minds around parenting and child behavior, and they wanted me to come because of my work on gamification.

It was 2010, and gamification—which is the process of applying the design principles of games outside of pure entertainment—was beginning to blow up. I was writing about it daily, and my first book—*Game-Based Marketing*—had just come out. Over the twelve months prior to getting this email from the TED team, I had been getting more and more invitations to speak, and some organizers had even started to dangle small sums of money to entice me.

If you've been sentient over the last fifteen years, you'll recognize the immense power of the TED brand and the reach of their channels. Though the vast majority of TED Talks never vault their speakers into the top tier of the circuit, it is nonetheless one of the most prestigious platforms in the thought leadership world, and if you want to raise the profile of your work and research, nothing carries more cachet.

So of course, I turned the Brussels offer down. I would only have a couple of months to prepare, I didn't feel like I was at the level of a TED speaker, and I couldn't imagine how I'd be able to deliver it without messing up. Moreover, international travel just felt like a chore, and I had a lot of other stuff I had to do to build my business. Fin. End of Story.

Just kidding. The minute the invitation came through email, I started dancing around in my home office, and it took every ounce of my willpower to not write back within the first ninety seconds in all caps:

YASSSSSSSSSS!

Was I "ready" to do that talk when the email came through? Hell no. Despite having given many corporate and conference talks, there were good odds that I'd mess up my lines and embarrass myself on a global stage. Did I imagine that such a public failure would wreck my career—ending it in the first trimester? You betcha.

But I still said yes. And I knew that once I said yes, and my name was on the website speakers list that I wasn't going to be able to back out. I would, in effect, be forcing myself to face one of my great fears (international embarrassment) and to challenge myself to say something to the world that was different and imaginative enough that it would change history.

It was with this combination of fear and optimism that I embarked on my professional speaking career that day. I had been getting up and giving talks my entire life, and—for as long as I can remember—was willing to improvise in front of the class on a topic. In my junior year of high school, I even won the international DECA pitch competition. DECA was a kind of extemporaneous public speaking contest, and I came in first in the most challenging category from among eighteen thousand American and Canadian students.

You could read this part of my history and think, "oh, he has a natural affinity for public speaking; I don't have that," and you'd be at least 50 percent right. There's no question that I always felt called to the dais, but was that raw talent and drive enough to get me to the top echelons of paid public speaking, where companies routinely offered me $40,000 to give a one-hour talk? And would I be creating an entire course, book, and international training program for public speaking, working with some of the most exciting entrepreneurs and execs? No and no.

If I had just relied on my natural ability, this never would have happened. Making the shift from pinch hitter to major league batter doesn't magically occur, except in the rarest of circumstances. Moreover, people often look back and describe their career trajectory through a lens of predetermination ("it was meant to be") or by inflating their own agency ("I always knew it would turn out this way").

But in reality, taking the embers of an interest and turning that into a raging fire of performance takes a lot more than just natural talent. Practice is key, and coaching is super helpful, but mindset is what really sets us apart.

If you've picked up this book about a new way of public speaking and professional communication, you no doubt are thinking about the importance of this skill in your career. Whether you want to be a better teacher, raise that venture capital (VC) round, get that senior management promotion, or be a paid, public speaker—pulling off engaging talks and meetings will turbocharge your work life.

Let me repeat that a different way, because it's crucial.

No other skill will make you as much money, bring you as much power, or help you get what you want in the world (if not money and power), than public speaking.

This is true in politics, business, the arts, advocacy, and every other field of endeavor. Just think about the people you thought of *first* when I made that list of categories? For me, it was: Barack Obama, Steve Jobs, James Baldwin, and the Reverend Martin Luther King Jr. Your list may be less America (or male)-centric, but the point is likely the same.

What do each of them have in common? They were incredibly compelling communicators, able to persuade vast audiences that their ideas were worth pursuing. Each of their eras also had different attention and technology challenges. MLK often had to speak in places with no electricity—and to hostile audiences, while Steve Jobs had to command listeners who were—by his own design—deeply distracted by their phones. Obama had to reach across a swath of a highly divided nation, and Baldwin used writing and oratory together to intellectualize discourse that remained stubbornly feckless.

And this is the real reason many people find public speaking frightening. Sure, it can be embarrassing to forget your lines, and it can be intimidating to get up on stage with august experts and make your case. But what you're really afraid of isn't failure at public speaking, it's failure at the underlying goal that public speaking can help you achieve.

What you really need is a system: something that can help you bring order and process to the chaos that is learning something new and challenging. Combined with coaching and guidance, such a system can allow you to shift your focus from the mechanics of public speaking to the substance of public speaking. And in the process, you'll acquire the chutzpah to say yes to big career opportunities, even if they scare you to death.

This is the promise of the A-Ha! Method—and what animated my desire to teach what I've learned. If we want to unlock everyone's true potential, we need to make it possible for them to communicate the beautiful ideas locked in their minds to the rest of the world, and to allow those ideas to shift our understanding. In order to accomplish this, we have to overcome two great and scary forces: the audience's distraction and the speaker's fear of failure.

This book—and its accompanying workbooks, tools, and courses—is a step-by-step process for going from the earliest stages of speaking interest/skill, to the top echelons of your field, using professional communication (speeches, pitches, and meetings)—both virtual and real world—as the vehicle to get you there.

No matter how raw your skills, you can give a TED Talk. Even if you're an immigrant and/or this isn't your first language, you can still pitch and raise a ton of money for your ideas. And even if you're pretty junior in your company, you can lead meetings that will set you apart from your peers. You will be able to command the audience's attention, influence their emotions, and do that in a unique way that gives your distinctive ideas and style the oxygen they really need.

If you do the work of this book—that is, developing a short talk and iterating it using my techniques until you have something stellar with visuals and audio, I am confident you'll be able to leverage that into whatever personal and professional growth you seek.

And even if you just want to be able to give a wedding speech for your first—and hopefully last—walk down the aisle, this book can help.

Being good at public speaking changed my life and career, and it can yours too. Congratulations for picking up this book—it's a great first step. Now, let's do the work.

PS—if you want to watch the TEDxKids talk referenced above to get a better sense of who I am and how I like to communicate, scan the below QR code and watch me work. While you do, bear in mind that the room was really warm, there was a small technical fault, and my pants had ripped just before walking into the venue, so I had to scramble to buy a pair of slacks that would fit me in a small Belgian town at the last minute. I don't say those qualifiers to *excuse* my performance, I say them to boast a little bit about my confidence. See if you can tell that several things had just gone majorly wrong. If you follow the advice and steps in this book, you can get ice running in your veins, and overcome any obstacle thrown your way. Skål!

Fun is The Future TEDxKids Talk: https://qrco.de/bczBoG

1

What to Expect (When You're Expected to Speak Beautifully)

The first time many professionals start thinking about improving their communication skills is when they've been invited to speak, pitch, or lead a meeting that is high stakes. Because "public speaking" is so stressful and fraught at the beginning, it makes sense that many of us avoid it for as long as possible.

Perhaps you're staring down the barrel of a hard deadline or interested in self-improvement and leveling up your career. You've probably observed by now that most successful entrepreneurs have to pitch, most executives have to give talks, and the fastest career trajectories are the province of those who get up in front of others and lead.

But what may seem like fearlessly confident communication in our role models is almost always the product of a ton of behind-the-scenes work on both substance and style.

There are almost no examples of people I know who were true public speaking prodigies. Even in my case as someone who grew up speaking very early (9 to 10 months), in two languages (Hungarian and English), and who spent a lot of time with adults, getting good at public speaking took a while. Getting *really* good took a long while.

Yes, I had some natural ability and affinity for the craft, and I was fortunate enough to find gigs early on that wanted me to play the role of spokesperson. I joined my first "exited" startup, Trymedia, when two cousins raised pre-seed money to tackle the idea of security in video games. The CEO, who was otherwise extraordinarily competent and intelligent, had zero interest in being the "face" of the company. So I, at the tender age of twenty-five, became the chief spokesperson for our business—and without coincidence—the burgeoning casual games industry we were evangelizing.

Over my six years at the startup—and indeed peppered throughout my previous jobs—I had given over a hundred talks and media interviews. I also had the benefit (!!) of trying to raise money during the 2001 dot-com crash, which meant giving literally hundreds of financing pitches over the phone and in person. After we downsized in the crash, I was also the only salesperson, and gave our sales pitches until we could hire someone again. As the market rebounded, I leveraged my relationships to get us panel speaking slots and the occasional keynote, letting every event organizer in the games industry know I was controversial, competent, and always on time.

In retrospect, it might seem like I had a strategy—but I didn't. I just wanted the company to be successful and identified that these were opportunities for us to get in front of decision makers and establish our credibility. It was public speaking as a sales strategy.

I put a full court press on getting keynote-style speaking opportunities, and as I started to do them—getting better each time—more and more invitations were extended to me. Over the course of a couple of years, I went from asking for speaking slots at key industry events to being invited to them. And I went from the guy calling reporters to pitch them on ideas to the guy reporters called when they had questions about our industry.

Often in corporate communications, this kind of program is called "thought leadership" and is an investment companies make in their top executives to generate earned media. When delivered by true professionals, a thought leadership campaign can be highly effective, if expensive.

But do you need a PR firm, team, or even a deep-pocketed budget to accomplish the goal of raising your profile? Absolutely not. In fact, if what you really want is to be in executive leadership—and thus benefit from even more corporate support for your ambition—the surest way to push yourself is to improve your professional communication skills. You want to lead that meeting, pitch that client, raise that money, talk to that reporter, and build connections for your business. You need to take the chance on yourself, and the best investment you can make in your career is to communicate more beautifully.

This is even more important for people who want to lead their own enterprises. Everything from a startup's inception through its acquisition or public offering rests on the founding team's ability to evangelize their message. It may start as early as recruiting a co-founder (which requires a kind of highly specialized sales pitch), but certainly extends to fundraising, partnerships, business development, and marketing. Leaving your communication skills dangling until the last possible moment doesn't advantage anyone for success.

But, here's where most of us are. Intimidated by public speaking, but aware of its power and importance in our careers, we skirt the necessary investment for as long as possible, hoping our fears of public speaking will go away, or that we'll be just good enough to get that prize.

And everything has become even more fraught with the advent and meteoric rise of extreme social media, screen time, mobile devices, and the expectations of an always-on culture. As we'll discuss, even the idea of "audience engagement and attention" has shifted so much in our current tech-addled lives, that we fully expect conference attendees—online or off—to multitask while speakers are presenting. Sometimes we literally want them to also be on their social media (e.g., to promote our event or talk), and in other cases it's simply the demands of jobs, families, or minds that just won't stop—even for 20 minutes.

In this context, the challenges for effective professional communication have increased one-hundred-fold. In my school years, we were expected to sit and listen to a professor talk for 45, 60, 90, or even 120 minutes (n.b.). This is the place where you'd expect the "get off my lawn comment." I promise I'm a cool old guy). Their ability to deliver the material well and keep us engaged was mostly irrelevant. It was incumbent on us to pick up the information they were sharing, and to make the most of that opportunity. So we sat, often bored out of our minds, and absorbed.

It's hard to imagine our current generation of thinkers, doers, and team members being okay with that kind of communication. Forty-five minutes? We can't even expect unfettered attention for 45 seconds. We know that audiences certainly don't tune in to optional content (e.g., videos) that lack authenticity, connection, and dynamism. But we also must be conscious that in a world reshaped by Zoom even our compulsory communications are subject to vociferous audience multitasking.

Therefore you, as a communicator, need to be better than ever before. The bar is higher—and the expectations of the audience ever greater. You need to be able to grab their attention, hold on to it for an almost interminable amount of time, deliver your points to an open and absorbent mind, and then land the plane for the listener and bring them back to the real world. The foundations of good public speaking remain the same, but many of the methods and approaches have to shift in this era of distraction.

Rather than be discouraged by this inevitability, by picking up this book you've already signaled that you understand the value of the craft, and are at least a bit curious about how to make it work for you. That is the most important first step and (cue the horns) congratulations to you for doing that!

Now, what else do you need to be successful at improving your professional communications in this weird and wonderful time? Simply put, you need a process that is designed to help you get from wherever you are in your career now to mastery in this brave, new world.

This is that process.

THE BASIC FRAMEWORK: DEADLINES, ITERATION, PRACTICE, REVIEWS

I use a not-at-all cheesy acronym to describe the process I expect my coaching clients to follow as we work on their ascent:

D—Deadlines and Details (a target talk with a delivery date)
I —Iteration (the process of developing your content to achieve mastery)
P —Practice (makes perfect . . . ish)
R—Reviews (incorporating feedback and opinions to make everything better)

n.b. Just be glad it wasn't DIAPER (Deadlines, Iteration, Achievement, Practice, Evaluation, Reviews), as in "I'm going to need this DIAPER to do this keynote." It goes without saying, don't let the acronym drive the branding. Later in the book we'll discuss the pitfalls of deus ex machina acronymization.

Before diving into each of these, let's look at the overarching, Agile approach I'd like us to take.

AGILE APPROACHES

If you've worked in software in the last decade or so, you've undoubtedly heard the phrase "Agile development." Used to refer to the way that software is built, Agile posits that the best products come from an iterative approach, where development teams are constantly putting forward the smallest unit of acceptable product and testing it directly with users. Based on feedback, they then change, remove, or add a small unit of whatever is needed to improve user engagement.

Though Agile methodologies are highly logical and mostly successful in tech, they can also work wonders in any field where rapid skills acquisition is the goal. In my speaker coaching practice, I use a very successful agile approach to help aspiring communicators improve, and this book is based on that philosophy.

As we work through the process of getting you to mastery, you're going to create or modify a talk at every point. It is this talk—and your delivery of it—that we are going to use as the milestone to drive toward and measure against. If you keep track of (by recording and saving) your first deck and first run through, and then compare it against your twentieth or twenty-fifth, you're guaranteed to see some significant progress.

At the beginning, it's going to suck—even if you're pretty good at it. But over time, everything—the content and the delivery—will get better.

You can lead a horse to water . . . but you can't make them drink. In this scenario you are the horse and I am leading you to the water (which is knowledge). Or maybe I'm the water and you just want to take a long drink of me. Either way, I love this journey for you—as long as by the end of this book you've created an amazing talk and are able to deliver it beautifully.

DEADLINES AND DETAILS

In order to create the optimal process for improving communications, we need some deadlines and details. That is, we need to aim our efforts toward creating either a:

1. Talk (speech, keynote, or other pedagogical work), or a
2. Pitch (a specific kind of talk for raising money or selling something)

Which should you choose? Well, the best idea for making the concepts of the A-Ha! Method work for you is to ensure that you're working toward something you actually want to do and would like to deliver. So, this goal ought to be something practical that will help you level up in your career, and also provide the guideposts and structure for helping you get there. If you want to start a company or sell some product, a pitch is ideal. If you want to establish or grow thought leadership, let's choose a talk.

Now we also need to know more about the when and how of this talk. I recommend using an actual event that you'd like to speak at if you don't already have something booked. This could be an industry conference or pitch competition, or just an annual town hall meeting where you'd like the chance to make a great impression. Even if you haven't been invited to do this talk yet (and you will, I promise), you can use an event that is at least a couple months in the future as your target. If you do have an actual talk "booked" to work toward, all the better. This will definitely light an even bigger fire for you.

And it goes without saying that as you start down the path, you're going to take the concept of the talk we create here using the A-Ha! Method and pitch yourself as a prospective speaker for this event. The goal is, after all, to get you out in front of more people for your career. So, why not start once you've got something to confidently pitch?

So now that you have a talk and a deadline, what about the details? After all, things like timing and format are essential for building an appropriate deck and delivery.

If you've already booked this stage time, congratulations—this has already been decided for you. If we're working on a "spec" talk—one that doesn't yet have a home—you can work with some sample parameters so that the finished product has greater potential utility.

Take a look at the past (and future) versions of the industry conference, pitch competition, or town hall you want to speak at. See if you can gather this information:

- Type of talk (keynote, breakout, pitch)
- Length of talk (the normal length of talks at this event in minutes)
- Themes or topics (especially useful if you're pitching a future event)
- Live or virtual
- Dates

If you don't have this information, or haven't yet thought through where you should speak, now would be a good time to do that research. But even if there's not a clear-cut target, you can create something that might have more generic appeal and could be pitched later.

In that case, I'd suggest using this framework:

- Talk type: keynote
- Length of talk: 20 minutes
- Themes: a topic you care about and also helps your career
- Live or virtual: live
- Date: 60 days from now

Though it may seem weird to sweat these details so early in the process, I cannot stress this enough: knowing what we're aiming for—what goals are and when—is a powerful forcing factor.

A Note About Deadlines

Whenever you see a conference date published, you need to understand that a deadline exists *prior* to that date. That is, while you'll be working to practice and tweak your presentation up to the day you get on stage, you must have completed the basics some time before the day they go live.

Many industry events will have a speaker check in 2 to 4 weeks before the conference, and ask to get your slides a week or so before. These two milestones allow the organizer to know if you're actually on target and ready to present, or if they need to lean in (or, in the unusual and worst-case scenario, cut you at the last minute).

For this reason, and the need to practice, I suggest setting the deadlines of:

- 1 day prior: done, done, done, done
- 2 days prior: super confident, can deliver eyes closed
- 1 week prior: deck is "99 percent final" and talk is deliverable
- 2 weeks prior: talk can be given with notes

If you've ever done theater, the 1-week deadline above is the "off book, know your blocking" phase, and the 2 days prior is the "we need you to go on as the understudy for the lead" date.

ITERATION

As we'll discuss in a later chapter, I believe that mastery of presentation skills is best achieved by mastery of content/material. The more you know the content you plan to deliver, the easier it will be to deliver it well—largely because you won't be trying to remember what you mean to say, and will instead focus on the flow state of saying it.

This means that with few exceptions you need to create your own deck and material here. I know that it is tempting to say something like:

"I've got a deck and the material, and I just need to pretty up the images and memorize the script."

But if you're coming from this perspective, I want to disabuse you of this misguided worldview.

You cannot divorce the process of content creation from the process of delivering that content unless you are either a masterful creator (e.g., writer) or masterful actor, and another master is giving you the other side of your equation.

If you know anything about some of the twenty-first century's greatest political orators, you'll know that while Obama had a speechwriter, he extensively and comprehensively wrote and rewrote his speeches. To wit, the skill of being able to write speeches convincingly in another person's voice is itself a highly specialized skill that only the best writers possess.

So, forget about outsourcing. I don't care if you're the CEO of a public company and a pretty busy person yourself. You're going to need to build this deck by hand, from scratch, and use every milestone along the way as an opportunity to hone your craft of storytelling in concept and delivery. There are no shortcuts.

If you've already built a deck or have a presentation that you think is mostly OK, congrats. Now throw it out and start again.

A NOTE ABOUT SPEECHWRITERS

If you are indeed the CEO of a public company, you undoubtedly have several people on staff who are more than capable speechwriters and deck builders. And you should leverage their skills and expertise wherever possible. But unless you have mastery of this process yourself, your work will not feel authentic, and you will not be able to guide your support staff in the right direction. And if you're not the CEO of a public company, why—other than fear—are you outsourcing this in the first place?

PRACTICE

Simply put: practice, practice, practice.

By the time you've picked up this book, you already know this adage, and probably live by it in some aspects of your life. But now you're a busy professional or entrepreneur, and you don't have hours and hours each day to devote to getting better at speaking. You just want some shortcuts and simple tips and you'll be on your merry way.

Hold on to your hats, because this is going to shock you.

I don't believe this is possible or appropriate. You need to put in the work of practicing alongside the iterative creation of your content in order to truly master this process.

I am a very skilled public speaker, with over a decade of paid, international keynotes under my belt (and another 10 before that pitching and speaking my heart out). I practice a new presentation at least 25 times before giving it.

Yes, you read that right. A brand-new deck might take 20 to 25 sprints to get right. So if the talk is 20 minutes, that means I'm spending at least 400 minutes giving the talk out loud, plus 3 to 4 times that in the iteration and review phase. As we get further into the process, we can speed up the actual run throughs, but the basic framework is the same regardless.

I'll also let you in now on a secret of professional speakers: once you're established on the road to being an expert in your subject, it's unlikely that you'll be creating a large number of entirely brand-new presentations. You're going to start with a repository of slides and ideas you've given before, and add/subtract content to make it fit with the event and audience you are targeting. This will also accelerate your practice cycles.

But even with a talk that I know backward and forward (and I strive for this in every talk I do), I will nonetheless rehearse 5 or more times before the date to ensure I'm really and truly ready, and have tweaked it to perfection.

Consider the rehearsals of an actor or musician. A singer on tour, who probably has fully mastered their songs, nonetheless will do a run through before every major concert. Actors rehearse for months sometimes, and then "practice" by delivering their lines daily in the theater? The amount of practice that goes into performance cannot be understated, and the sooner you embody this idea entirely, the more successful you will be.

REVIEWS (AND FEEDBACK)

Generally speaking, feedback in public speaking comes from one of three audiences: the attendees (those who watch your talk), the organizer (the people who booked you), and your peers/family/friends who give you input. Sometimes, you'll also get feedback from your speaking agent, but this is much rarer.

Let's start with the most important category while you're building your presentation: peer feedback. Probably the most often used—and misused—during the gestational phase, peer feedback is important but must be correctly targeted and aligned.

When to Get Feedback

The best times to incorporate external feedback are when you've reached a milestone in the creation of your talk and are ready to do an edit/revision pass. Generally speaking, you should not do this until you have at least the basic framework of your talk strung together as it's not super useful for most reviewers to listen to you give them a set of bullet points. Unless they are professional speaking coaches (ahem!) you'd be well advised to give them something that at least resembles an actual talk or pitch.

So after you've done your first pass and have a talk you *could* give—even if it's very rough—it's time to do your first presentation to others to gather feedback. Then consider doing it at least two more times: when you've got a set of visual slides, and when you have a version of the talk that you feel pretty confident about, alongside visuals.

The same is true of a fundraising or sales pitch, though because you generally have more structure to follow, you may find yourself skipping the visuals feedback stage and instead doing several post-polish loops with different people. The amount of feedback necessary for a pitch is at least double that for a keynote-type talk, and you should plan on exposing your ideas and words to several folks in either case.

Choosing the Right People

It may be tempting to pitch the people right in front of you: your partner, family, colleagues, or friends. And while I am all for efficiency and an agile approach, it is important for you to closely consider whom you ask for feedback.

The people you ask should be as close to the demographics of the audience as you can find. This means that if you're going on *Shark Tank*—a broadcast show that reaches a fairly wide demographic—you want to make sure your rapporteurs are a good cross section of the audience (so your mom might be OK). If you're speaking to professionals, make sure they are of at least a similar background—and even better if you know people with the particular knowledge set of your audience. And when pitching your company or product, you should definitely try to practice with folks that are either investors or founders so that you can get the most relevant input.

Of course, you don't want to delay your process significantly to find the right folks, and you probably don't have unlimited time—so choosing from inside your circle is best for a first time go around. But feel free to ask your closest friends, family, and colleagues to refer you to someone with the requisite background. I'm sure you're no more than two degrees away from all the right feedback folks.

Limit the number of people providing simultaneous feedback to you to 3 per round, with an ideal goal of getting one person each time who is perfectly suited to playing the target audience.

Instructions

First and foremost, you need your reviewers to act impartially. They may really love you and think you are the best at everything you do (Hi, mom!), but in the case of a talk feedback loop, the last thing you need is empty encouragement. You need specific, actionable feedback—and you need it to be as honest, harsh, and brutal as possible.

If the person in question does not know how to provide honest feedback, either because they just avoid confrontation or are "too close" to you, they are probably not right for this ask. In general, I'd choose an asshole over a bestie any day of the week—better if your bestie is also—in a different life—an asshole. That's the ideal combination, and undoubtedly you know the right person.

In 2015, I co-founded a company and went out pitching for money from a major venture firm through a partner there who was also my friend. In the preparation process for the raise, my VC insisted on inviting over a couple of other folks to give us direct feedback. The people he invited were—to be charitable—asshole-ish in their approach and responses. My co-founder had never gone through this process, and he was initially offended by the tone of the reviewer. In our debrief, we explained the logic of inviting this guy over, and later my co-founder remarked on how valuable it had been. Find this person or people if you really want to be great at public speaking and pitching.

Before beginning any feedback ask or session, make sure to lay out the ground rules. Effectively, what you want is them to:

- Suspend disbelief—pretend they are the audience.
- Listen closely and take notes on anything that comes to mind.

- Pay attention to their own attention level, ensuring they note if their focus fades in or out and when.
- Ask questions and provide honest feedback to clarify what they did or didn't understand, and what they'd prefer you to change.
- Be direct but not mean. In the early stages, you're mostly looking for substantive feedback about the story, the structure, and what you have to say. As the talk development progresses, you should include more asks about presentation skills, especially with regards to tone and speed. Remembering a core tenet of A-Ha! is that the audience pays attention when needed, you can also inquire about their attention level as you progress into a more repeatable phase. And slides should be evaluated at least once for clarity and impact, though if you've done visuals a few times, and follow the advice in this book, you probably won't need much input there.

If your talk involves Q&A—such as in a funding pitch, you might want to also ask them to ask you some questions in the correct format. Those questions are also a type of feedback, so you should pay attention to the issues that are raised indirectly by this. It is exceedingly important to listen.

Listening

To get the most out of any feedback session, it's imperative that you pay close attention to what is said and what isn't said by your audience. Hopefully they will have done a good job of telling you directly what they think, but in every case, we need to listen closely.

Feel free to ask them follow-up questions based on inputs you receive. Queries such as "what do you mean by that?" or "can you say more about that?" will help you tease out what they are actually thinking. Again, if the audience is expert at providing feedback, you probably won't have to do this too often, but in every case consider how you can truly understand what they had to say.

Questions they ask can be especially instructive. As an example: you're pitching your company to raise money and trying to get some feedback. If someone asks you to explain your go-to-market strategy, they are signaling that you didn't do enough the first time around to explain your plans.

Also important is what they don't say. For example, if there's a particularly controversial or complex idea in your presentation but they don't comment on it either way (e.g., "I don't get it" or "that was a great point"), you might want to zero in on that and ask the listeners some questions about why it didn't resonate.

Given that your feedback session will likely be very small and intimate—with no more than three other folks in a room or on Zoom—you should also be better able to sense their nonverbal cues at high fidelity. For example, when does their attention increase, and when does it flag? At the beginning it might be hard to sense this, but you'll get better over time.

Recording

If you're interested in recording your practice sessions with others, I have a suggestion for you—instead of training the camera on yourself, as you might with a self-taped practice, I propose that the camera face your audience. You will still be able to hear yourself, but in this way, you'll be able to look closely at the nonverbal cues of your attendees. Of course, in a narcissistic fashion, you might miss seeing your cute face on the screen while you talk. But you have plenty of opportunities to create those videos on your own. In this case, it's best to see the crowd. And if you're on Zoom—even better. Configure recording when you start your presentation and you'll get a stream that includes both your face and the faces of your listeners.

AI-Based Feedback

An increasing number of startups and established companies are beginning to offer public speaking feedback via artificially intelligent (AI) software platforms. Even Microsoft is in on the act, offering a kind of computer-based pitch coaching for free in PowerPoint.

These tools have been developed to address the same problem you probably thought you had before starting this book: the "soft skills" of tone, pitch, and pacing. And to evaluate those, many of these products do an excellent job.

I would suggest, however, that if you're building your talk on a content-first approach, you need to get actual human feedback many times before hitting up the AI to help you tweak those more minor issues.

WORKING WITH A COACH, GROUPS

If you have the money or the time, you should strongly consider adding coaching or group presentation classes to your planned approach here. These can be very helpful with building confidence, and a coach trained in the A-Ha! Method will also help you develop content that sings and is optimized for your style and target audience.

One group you can take advantage of is Toastmasters—an international, volunteer-based organization that gets people together throughout the world to practice talks with each other in an effort to raise confidence and improve speaking skills. Toastmasters has helped lots of people, though it does come with some advantages and disadvantages.

My complaint with Toastmasters—and indeed most speaking education before building this framework—is that there is an overemphasis on minor details, and a lack of attention to the bigger picture. For example, Toastmasters' relentless focus on filler words ("umm, ahh, ya know," etc.) is wasted energy in my opinion. If your talk or pitch is inspiring and well-constructed, no one is going to notice how often you say filler words. To be sure, they are distracting and annoying when used excessively, but even top tier orators use filler words—and I'm sure you've never even noticed it in your favorite speeches.

The content is king—and your ability to deliver it in your own unique, authentic way, is queen. Together, these are the priorities that must be met first. Get yourself additional help as needed to accomplish this goal, a priori.

THE IMPORTANCE OF PROCESS VERSUS STRUCTURE

No matter how many tips, tricks, and hacks I show you, if you aren't willing to do the work, you will have difficulty being excellent at public speaking and pitching. The worst speakers can—with the application of effort—become highly effective. Those who are medium-skilled, but slightly lazy or impatient, run the greatest risk of failure here.

I suggest taking a moment now and deciding whether or not the A-Ha! Method is right for you. To be sure, you can learn something from just absorbing the wisdom and suggestions in this book, but if you're not willing to do the work—are you really trying?

What we want to teach you is a reusable process you can apply to all your professional communications in the future, but one that is tailored to your specific personality, goals, and objectives. We don't need to give you a proscribed structure to work from—we need a place to start, a vision for the future, and concrete steps you can take to get there.

That's what this book and its companion resources, including a course and supplemental training, are for.

WHAT TO EXPECT FROM THIS BOOK

By the end of this book, if you've done the work—including the exercises, practice, and so forth—you should have a talk you're proud of and are prepared to give. Ideally, this talk will be in your voice, on a topic that you want/ need to cover, and is something you can deliver with confidence and charisma. It will include slides and other supporting materials, and be a calling card for whatever career goals and aspirations you may have.

And that's the goal of the A-Ha! Method: to help you level up your professional life. This can include becoming a paid public speaker, if that's your career goal. But for most folks, professional communication is a means to an end—a way to get that promotion, raise that money, sell that product—and thus become more successful.

Because I don't know what you want to accomplish in your own life specifically as a result of this, I'm going to trust that you are pursuing public speaking in furtherance of something you really want to achieve. But I want to make sure you don't fall into the language learning trap.

If you learn a new language but never use it, eventually it will wither. Sure, if you go to French class every week until you die, you'll be using your French and it won't completely atrophy. But it won't grow and progress into a confident fluency unless you're forced to use it in practical situations—such as in the country of origin.

The same is true of public speaking. You cannot really improve your professional communication skills with a one-off presentation. That talk needs to be the gateway to a world where you imagine yourself in increasingly expository situations, and where it becomes a bigger and bigger—or at least more stably recurring—part of your life. That is, speaking beautifully is a skill you acquire, but must nurture for the rest of your life through practice.

But if you can't be a world-class orator right from the jump, why bother? Obviously, you know the answer to this rhetorical question is about the journey, ten thousand hours, etc., etc. While you probably can't go from zero to speaking hero on your first professional talk or pitch, I am very confident in your ability to go from zero to a competent and successful speaker by the time you finish this program.

That is the promise of the A-Ha! Method and this book. If you learn and do the work, you will be able to speak better, more authentically, and in a way that today's distracted audiences can truly absorb and get excited about.

But why is it that you can't just will yourself to be a great public speaker, and why doesn't the audience simply grasp your magnificence right out of the gate?

After all, didn't we evolve as a species to speak to each other, and haven't you been doing that since a tender, young age? By now, you've probably even managed to use your words to graduate from schools, complete key assignments, and to do a job. So what's the leap from that functional use of communication skills to commanding a room, and why is it so hard for so many?

Well, the answer lies at the intersection of the way we're taught to communicate, and the changing nature of the audience's attention span. Both have shifted away from each other in a dramatic, but entirely predictable way—leaving most speakers in the dust.

In the next chapter, we'll look at the context for this skills gap, but if you want to skip directly to the part where I explain the breakthrough methods outlined in this book and how to get started, you can go directly to the A-Ha! Method chapter. But set yourself a reminder in any event to come back and get some more context.

Remember that the resource guide accompanying this book is available to you and contains supplemental content that can help you dramatically improve your skills. Snap the QR code below to be taken to the resource guide.

Resource Guide: https://speakersalliance.org/ahabook

2

Everything You Know about Communication Is Wrong

EVERY TALK IS A PITCH

Whether you're giving a speech at TED, leading a meeting for your team on Zoom, pitching your company, or trying to win a nomination to public office, you need to persuade. At the core of everything you say should be a single-minded vision for persuading people in the room that they ought to follow your proposal or advice. Obviously, you won't get 100 percent of the crowd on your side, but the goal is to maximize the number of adherents, and drive them to further action—whether that action is to buy/invest or to change themselves/heal the world.

Think about the startup entrepreneur giving a pitch to investors on *Shark Tank*. The founders come in with props, samples, backdrops, and a carefully rehearsed spiel that always begins and ends the same way ("Our names are . . . we're looking for $$ investment for % of our company"). On TV, the deal needs to get done (or not) during that episode, so the whole thing is structured to jump from pitch to close in a single step. But if you've ever raised funds (or tried to sell anything large and complex), you'll know right away that first meetings rarely yield a closed sale.

Typically, the goal of a pitch is to get another meeting. The opportunity to pitch from a platform (TV show, conference, etc.) is a lead-generation tool for you, the startup founder, to find new potential investors. The rest of the job, including due diligence, meetings with partners, term sheets, legal and funding, cannot happen until after you get that first expression of interest.

So in this context, it's obvious what the speaker's *goal* and *persuasive approach* need to be.

Goal: Get another meeting
Persuasive approach: This is a problem worth solving and we are the team to do it (credibility)

If you're thinking about leading team meetings over Zoom, or doing a conference in front of your peers, this may not seem truly relevant to you. But it is—and it's crucial to note that all forms of public speaking trade on the same basic premise: that if your audience *believes in you*, they will believe in whatever it is that you're trying to sell.

We'll talk more about authenticity and charisma (the mechanics of personal persuasion) in a subsequent chapter. But if you still believe that pitches/sales meetings are reductive, and that you'd never try to convince anyone of anything, let me explain why you must shed this old-school way of thinking.

EVERYTHING AND EVERYONE
IS TRYING TO PITCH YOU

When you look around your world, what do you see? On every surface, someone, somehow, is trying to persuade you. These efforts to sell you can take many different forms, but one thing is for certain: they have become much less obvious over time.

Take the TV commercial for example. Commercials are obviously a snippet of video that is different from the underlying program and designed to sell. Different cultures approached this demarcation between "sales" and "non-sales" with varying levels of intensity. In many European countries, for example, commercials were not interspersed throughout TV shows, because that was seen as being too manipulative. They were in a big batch at the beginning—or end—of the programming block.

Think, too, of the news. The newspapers and TV broadcasts of our childhoods were fewer, more authoritative, and—we believed—impartial. Today, the media landscape is fractured and polarized, with news organizations competing to attract eyeballs by delivering "clickbait" headlines that rile up their audience. On networks like Fox News, the line between reportage and opinion has been irrevocably blurred, and this has reshaped our entire understanding of "content" and the "sales in between."

So where you used to know what was an ad and what was editorial, now those lines are deeply blurred, from product placement in movies to infomercials. But nowhere is this issue more pronounced and ubiquitous than online.

Online mega platforms, like Facebook, Instagram, Google, and TikTok make their money by getting you to pay attention for long periods of time. In exchange for using their platforms for free, they resell your attention to sponsors and advertisers. And if you look closely, you'll see "sponsored" in the Facebook news feed, but it's easy to miss. As advertisers have become savvier, their pitches look more and more like content created by your friends.

For tech companies monetizing attention, their platform exists only to serve ads. There is no higher purpose (despite what they might say), and no real effort to create great content. The more agitated you are, the more time you'll spend, and the more money they will make. And with each turn, they learn more about you and your interests, refining what content and advertising they show you to maximize their yield.

As a result, everything is persuasive, even if the receiver doesn't understand or acknowledge it as such. Every piece of content you see is put there by an algorithm these companies developed with a specific purpose.

So as you're contemplating your presentation, you have to understand that you are up against a backdrop of continuous distraction. But what are the impacts of that on public speaking and professional communications?

THE IMPACT OF TECH AND SOCIAL MEDIA ON ATTENTION AND COMMUNICATION

According to Microsoft Research, the average person has an eight-second attention span. This is just a fin-flip shy of goldfish, who can focus on new stimuli for a whopping nine seconds.

This data came from observational studies on people visiting unfamiliar websites. Within the first glaringly short seconds, they decided whether to read more or navigate away—leading to the eight second number. If you're a contrarian (or just love critical thinking as much as I do), a few objections might pop up for you right away:

1. You have examples of plenty of situations in which you've personally spent more than eight seconds on a topic that wasn't especially interesting (see: taxes).

2. Reaction times to new websites can't possibly be emblematic of all types of audience attention.
3. People everywhere seem to be gorging on social media content, sometimes for hours, even when there's nothing newsworthy to see.

If you thought of any of those objections—good for you. You're right that such a number, a distillation of all human attention capacity to a single digit, oversimplifies how people respond to unfamiliar situations.

But the underlying point is the important one here: technology systems are designed to capture attention within the first few seconds. To be sure, some companies are better at this than others, but for those with a particularly great engagement skill, the ability to drive eyeballs and hours is unparalleled.

I know this because I've been on both sides of this complex puzzle. For the past fifteen years, I have devoted myself to helping companies make their products more addictive and engaging using techniques I pioneered called behavioral design, or more commonly, gamification. These design patterns and tactics take the best ideas from games, loyalty programs, and the behavioral sciences and atomize them. This made it possible for companies like Instagram, Snapchat, TikTok, or even JetBlue to capitalize on the human desire for novelty, reward, and social reinforcement.

Major tech giants like Facebook, Google, Amazon, Apple, and Microsoft have all learned from me (and many other experts) how to make their products more addictive. For example, the Facebook newsfeed algorithm is constantly running experiments on you—hundreds per day, in fact. Every time you like/comment, scroll back up to read something, click on an ad, or even pause at a specific post, Facebook's AI is recording your behavior to develop a model that can predict what you will find interesting. It then serves up that hypothetical item to you next in the feed, all designed to keep you there so they can sell more ads.

And speaking of ads, you've probably had the experience where you were talking to someone about something (say a new mattress they purchased) and all of a sudden you see tons of ads for mattresses on Instagram. Many people assume big tech is listening to our conversations, convinced they have sophisticated voice processing that can parse what you said and serve up relevant ads.

But what most don't realize is that there is no magic or malfeasance involved at all. In addition to guessing which piece of content will keep you hooked, the Facebook algorithm also tries to figure out which ads you'll find most interesting. And one of the factors influencing "interestingness" is what your friends have been searching for or looking at. So each time your friend posted about, clicked on, or read something to do with mattresses, Facebook added up their mattress interest score, and some of that bled over to you. Guilt—or sleep—by association.

Understanding this early has put Facebook in a commanding position to capture attention. But the rest of the economy is waking up (as are regulators) and a mad scramble to identify, control, and compete with these powerful algorithms is afoot. The arms race to determine the "ownership" of your precious time has become expensive indeed.

Now, you may be asking yourself how this is relevant to someone who wants to communicate effectively with others. After all, if you're given fifteen minutes to present to your company's executive board, you expect to have fifteen minutes of their undivided attention. Similar expectations abound: for entrepreneurs pitching their companies, actors auditioning, teachers teaching, and professional public speakers pontificating.

But you know full well this isn't true. You yourself have been guilty—probably multiple times this week in fact—of multitasking when something else was going on. From picking up your phone in the middle of a conversation with your spouse to Googling Black Friday deals on Amazon during your latest Zoom call, this division of attention has become de rigueur. And since we've brought up Zoom, the COVID-induced orgy of virtual meetings has only made this that much worse. Perhaps it might be frowned upon to task over to your laptop during a one-on-one with your boss or clergy, but on Microsoft Teams meetings, no one can hear you scream. Or rather, no one is screaming to pay you their undivided attention.

You see, the main problem with Facebook's and Apple's control over people's attention is that it's *mobile*. Everywhere a person is, a distraction is right there—on their lap, around their wrist, or in their pocket. Anything that drags, becomes monotonous, or seems less than perfectly urgent, beckons the mind to wander . . .

"What was the name of those cute socks I saw Kylie Jenner wear?"
"Susan's trip to Cabo looks amazing, maybe we should vacation there."
"When *was* the last time I got an STD test?"

Once the mind wanders enough to prompt the audience to pick up their devices, it can be shockingly difficult to put it back in its rightful place—focused on you at the front of the room (or screen)—listening raptly to what you have to say. But even if they don't act on it, the incessant human need for stimulation can push people away from your message. We used to call this daydreaming, but now it might be more accurately called "futurebooking."

The wandering of human attention is so pervasive and universal that it forms a central plank of what people try to control in mindfulness meditation. Gurus will tell you not to fight your mind wandering, but rather to embrace it and "gently bring your focus back to your breathing." This is hard enough to do when you have a spiritual guide blasting out of your Sonos, lying on your back, lights low, candles flickering softly. How do you practice this gentle attention refocusing in the real world?

The seemingly simple solution would be to ban devices for important gatherings. But we tried that at the beginning of the mobile era, and it really didn't work. First off, people resented not being able to stay connected and bring their devices—and today it's almost a Sisyphean task to separate folks from their iPhones. But moreover, event organizers and employers realized that the audience's devices formed a critical part of how they achieve social promotion. That is, if you post about this interesting product launch or fascinating talk online, some folks might see it and ultimately buy the company's products or answer a recruitment ad. So rather than discourage devices and multitasking, many organizations require—or at least encourage—it.

So tech—and the psychological burden it's created—are here to stay. No matter what they claim, everyone in the ecosystem is now fully invested in the idea that devices form a natural co-pilot to our everyday lives, and that you should be "on call" for important messages as needed. Even disconnection gurus like Tristan Harris and Ariana Huffington can be interrupted by their phones.

At the same time, our need to get and keep people's attention with the spoken word hasn't changed. What has changed is that we can no longer depend on people to set aside a "reasonable" amount of time to hear us out before deciding if they care or not. And because the lure of distraction is omnipresent, even if you can grab people in those first eight seconds, who's to say they won't swim away at the first sign of boredom or danger.

The persistent demands of an always-on culture have also led people to be markedly more anxious and testier when receiving communications. This has subtly but importantly shifted the professional speaker's power dynamic relative to the audience's expectation.

Historically, audiences for professional communication (whether conference, sales meeting, pitch, or book report) give the speaker the benefit of the doubt at the outset of their talk. A source of authority (conference organizer, EVP, professor, investor) has vouched for the speaker by putting them "on stage," and the audience is willing to give them a head start even if they are unknown because of this endorsement. Plus, the audience is typically there because they want to be, and a curiosity to learn what you have to say can be a powerful incentive to listen.

Conversely, amateur stand-up comedians will tell you that audiences can be cruel toward an unknown comic. They are often the toughest critics, though that criticism fades as the comedian moves up the ranks of their profession. This is why stadium comedy audiences (such as those shown frequently on Netflix specials) laugh like hyenas at every joke made by the comedian. Beyond good editing, the viewers have self-selected as fans, and have a specific expectation of enjoyment up front.

To understand what I mean, let's take a look at the table below summarizing an audience's predisposition to a speaker:

	Audience Knows You	Audience Doesn't Know You
Stand Up	"I'll probably laugh at everything"	"Make me laugh"
Public Speakers	"I'm probably going to be bored"	"This could be interesting"

Audience Orientation

Qualitatively, I believe that professional and business audiences are trending more in the direction of stand-up than the other way around. That is, they are becoming more hostile or wary of unknown speakers, and more satisfied with established speakers. This raises the bar for everyone.

Putting together this propensity for more audience criticism and technological distraction, the need to carefully engineer your communications becomes even more acute. You must break through the initial resistance, keep digital use to a minimum, maintain audience attention for 5, 10, or 30 minutes, get positive social promotion, and simultaneously educate the receiver while striving for good reviews/a sale.

Accomplishing this is a Herculean task, even in relatively low-stakes settings. But by understanding the behavioral science that drives user distraction and hostility, you can engineer every interaction to both leverage and overcome those issues to your advantage. The A-Ha! Method is designed to help you do this, and once you understand it you will begin to see it being used all around you.

As in the stand-up examples above, we will draw on numerous fields to understand what they each bring to the table for professional communications. Every domain has already had to contend with this challenge in its own way, and top-tier practitioners have developed distinctive approaches to overcoming our modern attention challenges.

We'll explore the unique contributions of politicians, clergy, TV writers, improvisers, sales experts, educators, entrepreneurs, and, of course, comedians and professional public speakers. Rather than advocating for a one size fits all approach toward your communication style, the aim is to borrow the best techniques and to map those onto your unique voice, context, and objectives. What works for a Baptist preacher at the Sunday pulpit may have influence on how you structure your fundraising pitch, but copying them exactly is unlikely to net you the VC dollars you seek.

You are both a speaker and a receiver of communication. So one of the most powerful proof points is how *you yourself* behave. As part of this process, I'll encourage you to raise your awareness of how you give and divide your attention. Like method acting techniques, this will allow you to see what you have to say from both sides, and model how it may be received. This is critical because one of the blind spot biases of most professional communicators is their belief that what they have to say is original and interesting, and that the audience will simply see their brilliance shine through. I cannot count how many times a speaker I've coached will express shock that their speech actually created more confusion and less clarity than before they started speaking.

Putting yourself in the audience's shoes is a critical first step, and uncovering the cognitive biases and heuristics that drive behavior a close second.

Though social media and big tech have many advantages when seeking our attention, they also have some serious limitations of which professional communicators can take advantage.

For example, *flexibility*. While the Facebook algorithm is great at serving you the next most interesting piece of content, it isn't yet capable of creating content on the fly in response to the room's feeling or mood. The correct and timely use of improv will greatly benefit your communications, but requires you to be very comfortable with your material in advance (a core tenet of the A-Ha! Method's approach to making you shine in front of an audience).

Another advantage you have is *authenticity*. Your ability to transmit confident authenticity can be especially enrapturing to audiences who are sick of perfectly polished Instagram feeds, or double-speaking politicians. In an era characterized by the curatorial bias (the tendency for people to filter/edit what they show to project a specific image online), your true and honest self—geeky, exuberant, aggressive, or amusing—can be a breath of fresh air. But again, this takes practice.

The third leg is *empathy*. Your ability to put yourself in the audience's shoes, to consider how what you're saying may make them feel, is a powerful force in aligning your goals in communication with their goals in learning. Algorithmic news feeds don't exactly *feel* anything, and as a result cannot deliver the emotional release or support the audience requires.

Plus, you have the advantage of having something interesting to say. To be sure, Twitter and CNN attempt valiantly to get you interesting content to keep scrolling, but you are original—one of a kind. At the intersection of your personality, the topic, your point of view (POV) and the audience is a highly volatile and combustible mix that you can learn to blend masterfully.

All that is to say, you are not powerless to fight back against the devils of our distracted nature. By combining behavioral science with your own charisma, uniqueness, nerve, and talent (the RuPaul theory we discuss later in this book), you too can achieve communication nirvana.

Together, we'll engineer a talk and approach that will break through the noise, capture attention, and get you what you came here for.

Facebook be damned.

THE LIMITATIONS OF CURRENT PUBLIC SPEAKING EDUCATION

Like me, most of the professional speakers I've met did not complete any formal training in persuasive, public communications. In fact, most never attended a Toastmasters meeting, and rarely received any form of supplemental training at work on the topic. Consistently, the most prolific public speakers I've met tell the same story—that of being naturally predisposed to being open and communicative, and building their presentation skills over years of iteration in a professional and personal context.

This kind of "on-the-job learning" is a decent and powerful way to acquire a new skill, especially if it's paired with the opportunity to practice that skill regularly. As I discussed, this was my path as well, and through a combination of providence and persistence, I came to this level of skill and professional satisfaction.

But what if your natural tendencies don't lead you to explore public speaking of your own volition, and what if your career options don't really give you enough opportunity to practice today? These and several other questions can be answered with a simple mantra: you can learn the skills and processes outlined in this book, but you must do the work to put those skills into practice.

And indeed, you can save a lot of time and learn from others in the ways that I've advocated herein. A reasonable question you may ask, however, is: Why is this process—the A-Ha! Method—better than other ways of acquiring this skill?

To put it mildly, the traditional ways of teaching public speaking are simply no match for the always-on, algorithmically based attention span of the current audience. If we cannot connect and persuade, our efforts are for naught.

I think it's cute that people used to sit down without any distractions, and listen to a boring professor drone on for 45 minutes or more. I had to do this in school, though I do remember daydreaming and doodling an awful lot. This is, of course, no longer the case—many people can't even watch an engrossing movie or TV show without checking their phones and tablets. So any program that does not acknowledge this reality and use behavioral science to counteract it is not going to work anymore.

But also, authenticity matters a great deal. In our social media–driven age, careful control of messaging is still incredibly important—to be sure—but the overriding characteristic that makes people succeed or fail is their authenticity. That is, how closely they can connect to their audience and convey their unique perspective or voice. Authentic but terrible people are often famous and persuasive, just as much as authentic and lovely/motivated people are. But inauthentic communicators—no matter how skilled—face an uphill battle in today's world that I think is virtually insurmountable.

So public speaking education that emphasizes structure and conformity also doesn't work. One of my favorite examples is the admonition—popularized in books such as those written by Dale Carnegie—to open with a joke to break the ice. While this may be a good idea for some speakers, and in some situations, it is categorically not universally good advice. If you are not a naturally funny person, such a joke will appear forced and will actually drive your audience away. If the context for your talk is very short or very emotional, a joke may not be appropriate at all.

In Toastmasters and the Moth—as in most public performance groups—an emphasis on comedy is paramount. Novice speakers and storytellers see that comedic stories tend to outperform others, and so a tendency is to lean on humor as a means of winning the contest du jour, and to create audience alignment/affection.

Personally, I love comedy. But it needs to be authentic and appropriate. Any training that involves reaching for the joke will immediately fall flat. That's why I think improvisational skills likely hold the key to unlocking the funny in an engaging way—and we'll advocate for some approaches to use that here.

In short, the world has moved on from the 1950s, where a white guy in a suit could get up in front of a group and command their attention without having to consider their needs or the substance of their presentation. And that's not to say that every white guy since 1950 has been phoning it in—to the contrary. But rather it means that the ways *they* were taught to communicate need to be replaced with a process that creates space for a panoply of voices and experiences, that leans on authentic experience and relatability, and that is tuned for the reality of the audience today.

That's why I felt compelled to write the A-Ha! Method. Seeing the intense skills gap that exists, and knowing the power of being able to persuasively communicate, it became rapidly obvious that existing tools just weren't cutting it.

So how do we make this work today and achieve our goals? Let's tuck into the A-Ha! Method in the next chapter and find out how to use behavioral science and foundational techniques to unlock your true "shine."

3

A-Ha! The Behavioral Science of Modern Communication

You know that feeling where the hairs stand up on the back of your neck in response to something you just heard? Perhaps you have this feeling of an electric charge deep in your stomach, or even like butterflies of anxiety. This is your peak of intellectual or *emotional arousal*—a state of vibration high enough that it manifests in your body physically. And it doesn't really matter whether it's positive or negative, affectionate or nonsexual, the basic feelings in your body tend to be similar.

Now consider how much information you receive in a day and how many moments result in this experience in your body? Not many, I'd guess.

The ratio between data ingested and these moments of arousal is very, very large. And for good reason. If you were so moved by what you heard or learned at all times, you might find yourself in a state of emotional exhaustion—ping ponging from one moving idea to another. You can probably watch one or two videos featuring tearful marines-on-deployment reunions before it's emotionally just too much.

Your body and brain are selectively good at highlighting these moments of arousal. They occur as part of a deep, evolutionary relationship between your mind and your physical body designed to help you learn, get motivated, and stay safe. The best evolutionary theories suggest it is the human equivalent of the fight-flight-or-fawn response. The same thing that happens when a gazelle thinks it sees a lion across the savannah, may be happening in your brain in response to something that is *intellectually* important to your survival. How awesome is that?

There are many different ways to describe that peak of arousal, but when it comes to communications—and the received energy of a listener/viewer—I like to call these *A-Ha! Moments*. That is, those experiences that trigger an A-Ha! or confirmatory reaction in our bodies and minds, and that predisposes us to change our behavior/thoughts, build connection with the speaker, and really remember that moment.

In a world filled with noise, data, distraction, and clutter, these A-Ha! Moments are even more extraordinarily galvanizing and clarifying. The best public speakers know—intuitively or through A-Ha! Method training—how to include the right number of these points of arousal in a talk, meeting, or pitch. They know how to pace them, to leave time for emotional refraction and intellectual reflection, and how to slope them so the peak always happens at the right times.

You can build the capacity to communicate with the right A-Ha's through years of trial and error. Or, you can learn the behavioral science and cognitive biases that affect our memory and decision-making. Then you can program your talks, meetings, and pitches to elicit the reactions you need to be memorable, change hearts and minds, and get the results you want.

And now that we're in an era of unprecedented technological transformation—watching a generation's worth of digital change happen in a few pandemic years—this understanding of arousal is even more important. Many of the intuitive techniques people have learned in face-to-face communication (eye contact, body language, touch, for example) do not work virtually. Moreover, there are biases toward in-person communication that each of us have that makes us less predisposed to be moved when absorbing knowledge online. This means you must work even harder, and be even better, to cut through the noise. But you must do it in your own unique way.

That's why I call this approach the A-Ha! Method, and not the A-Ha! System. There is no one right or wrong way to develop, deliver, or engage using a talk, pitch, or meeting. But as illustrated in this chapter, there is a template for influence that you can adjust to your own unique style.

You may be tempted to take these ideas and blithely apply them to your next presentation. If you do, you will surely connect more deeply with your audience and increase your chance of success. But if you want to be a masterful communicator, one who can leverage these ideas even more profoundly, you will need to understand the science of arousal, the effect of cognitive biases, and the process-oriented logic behind the A-Ha! Method. Once you have mastered these, you can begin to construct a talk, pitch, or meeting that works uniquely well for you and your audience.

When you're ready, let's begin at the beginning.

THE SCIENCE OF AROUSAL

The behavioral sciences have always interested me because my own mind feels like such a mystery. As a young adult (and even now as a middle-aged adult) I experience many moments where I look back and reflect in one of these key ways:

- What was I thinking?
- What was I feeling?
- How do I improve my reactions for next time?

The behavioral sciences aim to understand, decode, and shape human behavior, so that people can improve themselves, our society, and the world. But *behavior* is itself an enigma, without a rock-solid consensus definition among psychological professionals. Overall, we know that behavior is a composite look or systemic view of how we conduct ourselves, particularly in relationship to others. But ask for one level of additional granularity, and there is little agreement on its meaning.

That is because behavior is complex, our understanding of it is changing, and the human mind evolves and responds so quickly that it can be nearly impossible to develop a unified theory of how it all works.

Where there is lack of agreement on what defines our behaviors and how to change them, there is general consensus about the purpose and scope of the behavioral sciences.

From the Behavioral Science and Policy Association, a definition of the field:

> [We] take a broad view of Behavioral Science, describing it as the cross-disciplinary science of understanding the causes of individual, group and organizational behavior across different levels. Behavioral Science encompasses the social sciences, and brings together insights and methods from a variety of fields and disciplines, for example *judgement and decision-making, behavioral economics, organizational behavior, neuroscience, and social and cognitive psychology*. Under the umbrella of Behavioral Science, these disciplines, which separately do not provide a complete picture of human behavior, offer a comprehensive toolkit to bridge the gap between economic models and everyday reality to shape both private- and public-sector policy and practice.[1]

The emphasized phrases above highlight the different disciplines included in the BSPA's expansive view of behavioral science. For you, a student of professional communications, the lesson is clear: if you want to effectively drive people's behavior, you need to understand what makes them tick—that is, how they are aroused.

PARASYMPATHETIC AND SYMPATHETIC NERVOUS SYSTEMS

The autonomic nervous system controls our unconscious actions, and is divided into sympathetic (SNS) and parasympathetic (PNS). The sympathetic side is our "fight or flight" system, while the parasympathetic side is our "feed and breed" system. They act in concert and in opposition to each other, helping regulate how we feel.

In well-functioning systems, our SNS reacts to external threats and opportunities, and the PNS then moves to calm us down. Our sympathetic nervous systems can accelerate heart rate, widen our bronchial tubes, constrict blood vessels, dilate pupils, and make us sweat. It can also cause "piloerection"—which is the scientific term for hairs standing up on your body (including your neck).

While most mammals react with piloerection only to major fight or flight moments (think of a cat or dog's hair standing up when stressed), humans can also experience this in response to something emotional or inspiring. The action is regulated in the hypothalamus, which exerts influence on the SNS.

In a subjective sense, the emotional manifestation of that response is often referred to as "chills or thrills," and this sensation can—and often does—operate independently of the physical hairs standing up. Nonetheless, the method of action is believed to be the same, and the two are inextricably linked,[2] even if not always seen together.

If you find yourself overreacting to unexpected stimuli, such as crying during emotionally manipulative McDonald's commercials (see: the author's life), you may have an overactive SNS or hypothalamus, or diminished activity in your PNS. Have that checked out. You're welcome.

The point is that humans are built to have significant physical reactions to emotional stimuli—whether heard or seen—that produces in us the same, involuntary, life-changing reaction that animals experience when threatened or excited. Understanding how to activate this psychological and physiological experience in your audience becomes incredibly important, and is an order of magnitude harder if you and your listeners are separated by a screen.

Over-Arousal

You'd be forgiven for thinking that simply putting as many A-Ha! Moments into a talk as possible will improve the audience's retention and satisfaction. But this is categorically not true.

An overuse of the arousal technique will likely cause one of two reactions in the listener:

A. A sense of discomfort
B. A desensitization to A-Ha's!

Neither of these is particularly good for you as a speaker or leader of meetings. And in cases where the listener can easily task away (or mute you), you can expect them to quickly do so.

Desensitization has many negative effects and has been studied both as a therapy (e.g., EMDR for people who experience trauma)[3] and as a negative influence on real-world behavior (e.g., for kids exposed to violent video games).[4] In both cases, desensitization is thought to be a significant factor in driving behavioral outcomes. Unfortunately, in public communications, the only likely outcome is that you will lose the audience.

So you must carefully manage the number, amplitude, and interval of peak arousal A-Ha! Moments to ensure that you're generating maximum impact without triggering an aversive response.

Arousal and Memory

Another reason you want to cautiously deploy these moments of arousal is the influence of arousal on memory. This is a very complex and relatively new field of research that is important for modern communicators.

Studies show that emotional arousal has a powerful, *selective effect*[5] on memory and retention. This means that when you're highly aroused, your brain increases the memory encoding for high-priority information and decreases it for lower-priority information. This is the memory-based analogue for that sense of tunnel vision you might experience when dealing with a dangerous situation. For example, in a near-miss traffic accident you may notice all extraneous information sliding away so that you can focus on evasive maneuvers.

The other side of the coin—high-arousal things which are processed later—are often considered the seeds of trauma in various aspects of behavioral research, such as the adaptive information processing (AIP)[6] model. AIP posits that when something is too traumatic or over-stimulating, it may become a buried memory that then creates lasting trauma. This is analogous to the common story of traffic accident victims not remembering the events of a crash. Clearly, the crash took place and their brains recorded some information about it, but the encoding is not something easily accessed.

As a speaker, you want to ensure that your most important points are those encoded into long-term memory. In the past, with a less-evolved understanding of psychology, speakers would try to accomplish this by saying "OK, this is really important." Such a call-out rarely has the desired effect and, if overused, simply trains the audience to consider everything else you say as unimportant.

By crafting your talks, pitches, and meetings with clearly defined emotional high (and low) points, you can influence when the audience will be most receptive to what you have to say, and control what data-point or idea is presented to them at that moment of greatest receptivity. As always, this "game" is played with *Price Is Right* rules: get as close as you can without going over. And if you answer correctly, the big prize wheel (communication excellence) is in sight.

Arousal and Multitasking

Another thing that arousal may affect is multitasking. When someone is both focused and alert, they are less likely to multitask.[7] By channeling this focus and alertness in our listeners, we can ensure minimal multitasking. This is especially critical because in the period immediately following a focused/alert state, research suggests, people are highly likely to multitask.

This connection is positive if your goal is to get that A-Ha! Moment followed by the audience writing down (or tweeting) what you said. In general, the perfect rhythm allows people to come to a point of focus, with maximal arousal and minimal distraction, and then feel free to encode or share those moments.

Arousal and Emotional Refraction

The time immediately after an A-Ha! Moment (or any meaningful stimulus) is called "emotional refraction." Its length corresponds to the amount of time it takes your brain to reset after you've encountered something new and meaningful.

By carefully separating your A-Ha! Moments, and explicitly giving people downtime to consider, process, and communicate what you had to say, you create more space for positive outcomes.

In a virtual talk/meeting/pitch setting, this is even more important because the users' device is their main point of focus, and so anything that beeps or alerts them can quickly become a distraction. Because you cannot control when they will receive a notification, your best hope is to provide time to build intensity toward A-Ha! Moments, so that the audience is cued in to pay more attention.

This can be done by the raising of your voice or tone, a change in the cadence of your speech, or by using smart pauses. We'll discuss each of these techniques in detail later in this book. But while it may seem like building in "downtime" in your talks and meetings is a waste of time, you must do this in order to foster the optimal outcomes.

Arousal and Connectedness

One of the outcomes that most speakers find complex to create is the fostering of connectedness. In our digitally distant world, people's sense of connection—however tenuous—is a powerful way to build and leverage trust. This can be as simple as someone having the verified checkmark beside their name on Twitter, a common alma mater, or even a bunch of mutual friends. Your connectedness to others is the core part of your social graph.

A-Ha! Moments can create powerful connections with your audience. This is accomplished through two different but important factors. The first is the "shared experience" that everyone in the room is going through. This can be particularly powerful when you are empathetic and vulnerable with your audience, but is useful in most contexts.

The second element of arousal and connectedness is what's called the "Separation Call Hypothesis." This is a theory that explains why humans have such a powerful physiological response to emotional stimuli. It posits that the reason we respond so strongly is because it is rooted in our protective reaction to becoming separated from our offspring. When we hear their call of distress, we are moved to take action to rescue them. So in a sense, your efforts at creating emotional arousal in your talk may be prompting the audience to want to save or protect you and the ideas you're putting forth.

And this is important on an even more tactical level. Ultimately, your power on social media (internal or external) can be highly influential in your future success. The more people follow and tag you in their content, the higher your influence score on most platforms, and the more opportunities that open up. Regardless of the context or content of your presentation, it is essential that you maximize the opportunities to get followers, tags, and positive feedback at every turn.

PUTTING IT TOGETHER: EMOTIONAL AROUSAL

By carefully crafting what you say and when you say it to trigger this SNS response, you can maximize a few key aspects of your audience's attitude toward you and your talk:

- Maximize social media promotion (e.g., tweeting about what you said).
- Improve memory and recall.
- Increase connectedness to you.
- Generate more requests for your participation/leads/follow-ups.

DESIGNING FOR A-HA! MOMENTS IN A TALK, MEETING, OR PITCH

The A-Ha! Moments of your talk, meeting, or pitch need to be carefully scripted and planned to produce the optimal reaction in your audience. This process should be modified for your topic, personality, and unique voice.

Let's take a deeper dive into the process of structuring with A-Ha's!

THE A-HA! PATTERN

In addition to an opening and closing statement—both of which must be evocative and powerful, you should plan on having approximately one A-Ha! Moment each 3 to 5 minutes of a talk or pitch. This is why well-structured pitches (which are usually less than 5 minutes) rarely have more than one or two A-Ha! Moments in them.

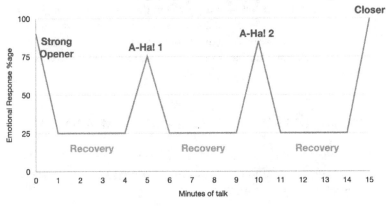

Ahas Per Talk

In the graphic above, you can see the pattern for a 15-minute keynote-type talk, with the main line representing the amplitude of emotional response. This amplitude measure is more conceptual than scientific, but it's designed to give you a sense of how to structure your points and the denouement between them. This in turn helps you achieve maximum arousal, memory, and connectedness from your audience.

TEDxFRA_Talk: https://qrco.de/bczBoH

Let's use one of my TED Talks as an example for how to design A-Ha's! You can see the talk at https://qrco.de/bczBoH or via the QR code above if you want to watch it and follow along. This speech is called "How to Win at Losing: A Failosophy for Innovation." Here are the crucial time codes:

> *0:00—Opener—I'm coming out of the closet—I'm a failure*
> 2:00—Kids/school—*key point*
> 4:45—Disney—*key point*
> 7:00—Silicon Valley's dishonest about failure—*A-Ha! 1*
> *8:00—Act II (Hero's Journey) Begins*
> 10:00—Portfolio theory—*key point*
> 11:30—Investor point—*A-Ha! 2*
> 12:30—What is failosophy? Summary—*key point*
> *13:00—Act III (Resolution) Begins*
> *15:20—Closer*

The first thing you'll probably notice is that I didn't hew precisely to the A-Ha! chart I presented above. The reason for this is that the process is a guide or conceptual framework rather than a dictum setting the precise timing of each A-Ha! Moment. Such a level of granularity would result in your talks sounding like my talks, and we want to find the best version of your individual communication that we can create.

I delivered a strong opener and closer, two major A-Ha! Moments, and four supporting key points, which are notable but not the emotional highlights. As part of my style, the high points are all accompanied by a mixture of humor and vulnerability, which works very well for my personality and speaking type. We'll talk more about speaker personality types in a later chapter, but you don't need to be vulnerable or funny to be successful with this method.

Before we get there, let's analyze some of the elements of this talk and check out the method behind the madness.

The Opener

I opened this talk with a strong statement and joke. This was designed to get the audience's attention and make them focus on what I was going to say next. The opening statement was specifically designed to elicit maximum impact— "I want to come out of the closet" makes most people pay attention.

Act I

In Act I, I cover my personal story and hypothesis about why we struggle so much with failure.

Our first major A-Ha! Moment comes when I discuss the dishonesty of failure attitudes in Silicon Valley.

Act II

In Act II, we take a look at companies, leaders, and individuals who approached failure in a different way. Our second major A-Ha! Moment occurs when we elucidate the key element of portfolio theory and how it applies to this problem.

Act III and the Closer

In Act III, we pull everything we've learned together into a cohesive idea, and leave the audience on a high by entreating them to push harder and to embrace their flaws.

Now that you understand the basic arousal pattern of the A-Ha! Method, go ahead and rewatch some of your favorite talks or pitches online and see how they do or do not conform to what we've discussed here. Also, observe yourself reacting. Do you pull out your phone and task away from the screen? If so, when is your attention flagging?

You can use yourself as a sample of one to help you understand the A-Ha! pattern and how to apply it in your communication.

Pacing

Within a talk's timeframe, the speaker must accomplish conveying all the core ideas to the audience that they intend. This means that the pace of information "reveal" must hew to the total talk/pitch/meeting's length.

So, if you have 5 key points that you want to make in a talk and 10 minutes to do it, you'll have to deliver a key point approximately every 2 minutes. In my speech above, I delivered 6 points and a closer in just under 16 minutes. This is a little over one point every 2 minutes even though they are not evenly spaced out so as to create a bit more drama in the pacing.

Many speakers are tempted to cram more points into their talk, with the idea that more data equals more persuasion. But this couldn't be further from the truth. As a general rule—and as we'll consider in a later chapter—the minimum amount of time for a given point is 1 minute, plus 1 to 2 minutes for setup and reflection. So any pattern that gives points less than 2 to 3 minutes is likely to create confusion in the listener.

You can also observe that I don't speak at a consistent pace—and neither should you. It may be tempting to speak at a uniform speed (say, 130 words per minute) when you're learning the lines for your talk and trying to remember every word.

But this rhythm, while helping you, actually does the audience a major disservice. They will not only find it boring, but varied pacing helps to provide a cue to the audience about when to pay attention. So even if they're face down or have tasked away from your livestream, picking up your speed will pull them back in.

I speak anywhere between 125 and 175 words per minute, depending on what I'm trying to convey. I do think that my pace is a bit "brisk" overall, but I modulate this for audiences that are not English speakers or those where technical details need absorption time. My pace changes quite a bit during the talk: there is a noticeable slow down when I'm referencing myself (coming out, lying about my resume, etc.). And I pick up the pace when coming to a key point.

This will all eventually come naturally to you through practicing the A-Ha! Method, but it's important to understand the mechanics that are deployed so you can be alert to how your audience may react.

Amplitude

Not every point is equally important, and many speakers don't fully understand the need to vary the amplitude of points in addition to their pacing and timing.

As a general rule (and as displayed in the referenced failosophy talk), the opener and closer should be the highest water mark moments, and the points should build in importance/intensity from beginning to end.

I would give myself a B+ for my amplitude management in the above speech. Although the second A-Ha! Moment has more oomph than the first, they are quite similar in overall intensity and clearly stick out from the rest of the talk.

You'll notice that as I come up to the A-Ha! Moment my tone of voice and speed of talking increase. These two signals also help audiences know when something important is about to happen and that they should pay attention. You must consider leaving "room" in both your tonal and pacing ranges to vary as required—so if you're turned up to an eleven the whole time, it will be exceedingly difficult to push past that barrier when needed.

Tone

My style relies heavily on humor and vulnerability, so I endeavor to use that as a secondary layer for getting and keeping the audience's attention. Knowing that viewers typically respond well—albeit differently—to vulnerable and humorous moments makes it easy for me to combine those with the A-Ha's!

In general, vulnerable moments are associated with a lower tone of voice than humorous ones. This is my personal style—and may not be yours—but it is part of a pattern I've seen among many top speakers. The change in vocal pitch acts as a signal both of importance and of emotional resonance. This is similar to the music in a movie scene delivering even more emotional power than the action or dialogue.[8] A faster soundtrack and higher pitch are more closely associated with tension, and slow music with a lower pitch is correlated with the process of discovery.

Your tonal style may not be the same as mine, and that's okay—vulnerability and humor are only two of the techniques that can be used to drive engagement. There are many others, and the most important thing is that these characteristics are aligned well with your intrinsic personality.

A-Ha! in a Speech

I am a proponent of scripting speech content with fine-grain authority. This allows you to more carefully lay out your A-Ha! Moments, when they'll happen, and what tone, amplitude, pacing, and so on you will use to get there.

Since most of the above examples concern an A-Ha! approach to talk creation, I won't belabor the point here too much—but think of the emotional journey you want your audience to go on as a roller coaster. There's a tense build up, a period of tremendous action, and then the relief of pulling into the station. Sometimes, a roller coaster opener is a surprise rather than a slow build of tension, but the underlying point is the same.

In order to effectuate the full experience of a roller coaster, you need to experience all three parts. If any of these elements is less exciting or relieving than the others, it creates a lop-sided user experience. Something like, "from the huge climb at the beginning I was expecting some really gnarly loops, but it just fizzled out." Even when the rider of the coaster knows what's going to happen next (e.g., because they are a frequent guest or RC nerd), they can still feel the emotional ups and downs of the ride and enjoy it just the same. Nothing beats novelty, but as long as the structure is right, you can entertain people of all ages, over and over again.

The same is true for talks. Consider the whole journey and each of its parts. Build them to be as comprehensive, focused, and effective as possible—and you will sell those books, build your brand, and book more speeches.

In a Pitch

The world of pitching has changed dramatically, both in terms of the local/ remote nature of teams, and in terms of the size, scale, and time allocated to pitches. In summary—pitches have gotten shorter, buyer (or investor) expectations are at an all-time high, and cynicism abounds.

If you correctly structure the A-Ha! Moments in your pitch, you can take the audience on a journey that will drive future sales, even if you only have a few minutes of their time. Some of the same rules apply to pitches as speeches, such as opening strong, pacing yourself, varying your tone, etc. However, you can dispense with some of the necessary framing in a pitch because the audience generally understands the context of the talk. For example, if you're pitching your company to a VC panel, they know—at minimum—you have a startup and are looking for capital. Similarly, if your ad agency is pitching a new client, they know you are an ad agency, they are shopping for services, and they likely know which of their products are being considered.

I recommend you do not do a preamble or introductions. Do not set a scene beyond a single sentence or two to set up the problem and your connection to it. Spend the majority of the time making 1 or 2 major points supported by A-Ha! Moments. In general, most of these points need to be framed as "problem-solution" and how you are the right team to solve it.

Remember always that the people in the room may (definitely) not have the same problems as the target customer, so if you need to anchor the problem-solution in the customer story or journey, you must set that up for the audience to understand. The more precise you are here the better, and while talks often focus on a more general "agreement" or "interest," your pitch conversation is undoubtedly oriented toward getting the sale or follow up meeting.

In my experience, most major deals or investments don't close on the first pitch—so it's unlikely that the first time you talk to a group you'll get the cha-ching right away. However, if you create enough interest and engagement, you can drive a follow-up meeting—and continue to inch closer to your close. That's the goal, and if you bring the A-Ha! energy to the experience, there's no way you can lose.

You can also add another layer of importance to this "get the next meeting" philosophy in remote work environments. Now, in order to proceed to the next step, you need to not only deliver your pitch perfectly, but you need to be good enough to warrant a trip into the office. This is what I call being "mask worthy" during a pandemic—justifying the personal risk folks may need to take in order to partner with you. The goalposts have never been further, and the target has never been higher.

All the more reason you need to master your A-Ha's!

In a Meeting

Leading a meeting or an internal dialogue (panel, etc.) can be more complex, because you do not have sole control over the content, tone, and pacing, and participants are expected to shape the outcome of the session. That is, they have voices, and unless you are all coordinated in advance—which becomes more like a pitch—you will be unlikely to know everything that can and will be said.

To use A-Ha! Moments in a meeting, you need to do three key things:

1. Think in advance about the goals and objectives, possible objections, and issues you may face during the meeting.
2. Plan a couple of additional A-Ha! Moments to support your point that you can pull out of your hat whenever needed.
3. Listen closely to the participants' A-Ha's! so you can capture that energy and reinforce what was said

Your tone, pacing, and inflection matter as well—particularly as the leader of the meeting. The participants will pay more attention when you're excitable, and less during dull moments. Prepare some bombs you can lob over the transom to recapture the audience's attention if you think it's flagging.

It is also powerful for you to use your personality as a speaker to drive the discussion, and you should leverage that unique perspective if you need to either cut through the noise (of a busy, distracting, or combative interaction), or cut through the fog and get/keep attention. The challenge is the same, and you must be able to deal with the participants' psychology.

COGNITIVE BIASES AND HOW TO USE THEM

Cognitive biases (CB) have always fascinated me. A common definition of cognitive biases is that they are the ways our brain responds incorrectly to the reality of the world. There are more than two hundred documented CBs that have been tested and proven through psychological experimentation.

While some of the biases correlate strongly with low intelligence or education, most of them are not exclusively the province of the under-informed. Even very intelligent people traffic in cognitive biases every day, often unwittingly. This is both due to our evolutionary biology—and how it affects the way the brain works—but also the way we're taught and learn to experience the world.

In my decades of work as a public speaker and behavioral designer, I've learned that systematically naming your cognitive biases—and actively working to counteract them—is one of the most powerful steps to improve yourself, your life, and your outcomes. The second step is to understand how others may be experiencing such biases and how to structure your communications to leverage/counteract them. Knowing what your audience is going through can be elemental in ensuring your communications are getting through, landing right, and having the desired impact.

Here are a few of the most important CBs for communication. I've taken care to give you a synopsis of the bias and how to use it, but the research that underpins each of these is deep and fascinating, and if you're interested in studying it further, I highly recommend doing so.

Agent Detection

Agent detection is the tendency to see the presence of an intelligent being or purpose behind what is otherwise a random effect. It's possibly connected to religiosity and conspiracy theory belief.

How to Use It

Most audience members likely have a "higher power" they ascribe to, be it god, markets, or science. When presenting information that challenges this, you will need to specifically call out their agent detection bias (perhaps using less complex language) and explain why your situation is different. Conversely, playing into your audience's bias here may make them more likely to believe you.

Anchoring Bias

Anchoring bias occurs when you rely too heavily on the first piece of information you receive about a subject or situation. This is frequently done in pricing theory to make sales seem more important than they are. For example, if the first price you see for a product is $50, a sale price of $20 seems like a steal, unless you know the usual price is actually $22.

How to Use It

The first piece of information you deliver about a novel subject will likely be the key detail that is remembered. When planning out your A-Ha! Moments be sure to place your strongest argument as soon as possible (either A-Ha! one or two).

Attentional Bias

Attentional bias exists when recurring information or thoughts have an out-sized effect on your audience's understanding of a situation. For example, if you are a regular alcohol drinker, you may be more likely to notice alcohol advertising around you.

How to Use It

The events around your specific talk can be part of setting the scene for the audience to really absorb what you have to say. This is commonly done by referencing some aspect of the event ("I'm so excited to join you for dinner tonight at Benihana!") or the world ("This situation is about as unfunny as this federal administration"), and so forth. This is especially powerful for imagery, if you can choose slide images that are connected to existing trains of thought.

Authority Bias

Authority bias exists when we attribute greater accuracy or importance to the opinions of experts. More often than not, such an opinion should probably be followed (wear your mask!).

How to Use It

From the moment you begin your talk, pitch, or meeting, you are taking advantage of the authority bias—you are the authority. The organizer of the meeting decided you should be one of the speakers, and this automatically confers some amount of credibility on you. Projecting that kind of confidence can be powerful in persuading others, so it's important for you to believe it. If you are running a meeting, pay special attention to the involvement of experts in your group, as their opinions will have an outsized impact.

Availability Cascade

The availability cascade is a social bias that can be best summarized by the propagandist's adage, "repeat something enough times and it becomes true."

How to Use It

You will undoubtedly notice that in many of the most impactful talks (especially those from the pulpit), speakers have a tendency to repeat themselves. Sometimes back-to-back. This technique both calls attention to the statement, and increases the likelihood that the audience will believe it. Naturally, your story or pitch may follow a cycle where you return to a central concept, narrative, or question. To maximize the benefit of the availability cascade, and to make it seem more natural, ensure that you're using *precisely* the same phrase each time.

Backfire Effect

The backfire effect refers to the idea that when someone's beliefs are challenged, they "dig in" and become even more adamant in their convictions.

How to Use It

Counterprogramming a closely held belief is a complex topic, and it is unlikely that you will know these detailed beliefs of your audience prior to your meeting, talk, or pitch. However, many experts believe that you can combat someone's deeply held—even conspiratorial—beliefs,[9] if you approach them with a desire to understand what they truly believe, recognize their emotions, establish common ground, and discuss facts while valuing their argument.

So for example, if you want to argue that capitalism should be abolished in favor of socialism, and you're giving this talk to the US Congress, you might encounter some aggressively negative reactions. Or, for example, if you're trying to persuade a consumer goods company that their hundred-year-old brand has lost its luster with millennials, and declining sales are not because of Chinese competition. The best thing you can do in these cases is to rope someone from the "true believer" camp into a public conversation, and use your persuasive skills to expose the contours of this belief system so others can learn from it. Don't fight on multiple fronts at once.

Bandwagon Effect

The bandwagon effect (also called groupthink) is the cognitive bias whereby one believes something to be true because of the number of other people around them who believe the same.

How to Use It

Though it may seem annoying or high-risk, Q&A with an audience or participants can be a great way of showing dissenters that they are in the minority. A poll in a digital meeting can accomplish something similar, as can explicitly calling out the number and/or credibility of sources when making factual points. The phrases "many people say" or "scientists believe" are ways of tapping into this bias without factual proof. Of course, giving an audience any opportunity to express their opinions has the potential of undermining your point, but if your conclusion or assertion is strong, this should pose no hindrance. Wherever possible, call on friendly participants first (and know who they are in advance).

Clustering Illusion

The clustering illusion is the tendency to see answers or trends in small subsets of data. It is related to the agent detection bias in that it encourages the observation of phantom patterns.

How to Use It

Especially in a talk setting, if you call out a cross section of information and draw a clear conclusion, you'll likely be able to take advantage of this bias. The number of data points necessary is non-specific, but an assertion of accuracy will likely hold sway. Just be sure your own conclusions are not subject to this bias, as it can—from personal experience—be a very costly mistake.

Confirmation Bias

Confirmation bias refers to our tendency to more readily accept data that confirms something we already believe.

How to Use It

If you can draw a parallel between the received wisdom of the audience and your point, you can take advantage of confirmation bias to increase your impact. As the opposite of the backfire effect however, you must avoid triggering an equal/negative response in the audience. One strategy for using this in a case where you are engaging in disagreement, is to explicitly call it out as something that will subvert the paradigm. You can also restate the belief and then pivot to the "but . . ." statement.

Dunning-Kruger Effect

The Dunning-Kruger effect is the tendency of individuals to overstate their abilities while those with the greatest skills and knowledge (e.g., experts) tend to understate them.

How to Use It

Dunning-Kruger is one of the most interesting and oft talked about biases, because it appears to happen so often—particularly in the political commentary sphere. When communicating with audiences, however, it's important to play into this belief set. If you're speaking to an expert audience, highlight how your approach/ beliefs help them improve themselves from their modest self-perspective. When speaking to low-skill audiences, flattery can be powerful and useful.

Framing Effect

The framing effect causes us to draw different conclusions from the same set of data, depending on how it's framed.

How to Use It

A classic example of the framing effect was the discussion about the risk of death posed by COVID-19. Some described it as "less than 1 percent, a fraction of the risk of Ebola, SARS, or AIDS," while others described that as "three million Americans might die." The underlying data is not in dispute, but the conclusions (and, ergo, what you should do about it) are different depending on how it's framed. As a speaker, consider how you're framing what you say to have the effect you want, but be sure to consider whether that framing is accurate, helpful, and something that will not be challenged extensively.

Chapter 3

Halo Effect

The halo effect refers to the tendency of one's positive or negative attributes to influence others' perceptions in an unrelated area.

How to Use It

If you believe that Bill Gates is a generous philanthropist, you may be disinclined to believe he was also considered one of the most ruthless and destructive CEOs in American capitalism. When discussing a particular person or movement in your talks/pitches/meetings, you can shift perception of that person by presenting them through their best—or worst—possible light.

Hindsight Bias

Hindsight bias occurs when we look at the past and say that we knew the outcome all along. It is a tendency to see the past as being a neat, predictable set of events—even though we could not have forecast the future.

How to Use It

The hindsight bias can be especially helpful if you use it to make a point to others about future possible choices. That is, analyzing the past but, rather than focusing on the knowability of a given outcome, distilling a set of lessons that the audience can apply in the present. Though we all do this, as a general rule, you should avoid making yourself look more prescient than you actually were. Unless you have some evidence that can be used to substantiate it, you may be perceived as talking down to your audience.

Optimism Bias

Optimism bias is our tendency to underestimate the chances of something negative happening in the future and to overestimate the chances of something positive occurring.

How to Use It

Though our tendency toward optimism may be culturally informed, in the US there is a definite bias toward an optimistic view of the future. In effect, if you position what you're saying to create the potential for future success, people will have a tendency to believe you, to feel inspired, and perhaps to put effort into that outcome. This is one of the biases that makes it very difficult to get people to change their behavior in the short term, as in climate change. While they may believe the enormity of the problem, they may also believe that it will not get that bad and will be solved regardless of what they do.

Parkinson's Law of Triviality

Parkinson's law of triviality refers to an organization's tendency to avoid making hard decisions or doing hard work but, rather, to focus on issues that are irrelevant or secondary.

How to Use It

This is particularly relevant when leading internal meetings or discussions, but can be applied to many forms of professional communication where tackling the hard problem is critical. You can call out the group's tendency to avoid or dodge, making the case for why the hard stuff needs to be tackled and needs to be tackled now. If you can, you may also turn the tough task into a series of smaller, easier, and more fun tasks that build toward the final goal, thereby using Parkinson's law to your advantage.

Pro-Innovation Bias

The pro-innovation bias occurs when we overestimate the importance or impact of an innovation and underestimate its weaknesses or issues.

How to Use It

Similar to optimism bias, pro-innovation bias creates blind spots that can prevent people from seeing things as they really are. Again, in American culture, making an appeal to innovation is likely to be viewed positively, and average audiences can be expected to overstate the potential for this innovation to make a difference. If you need to make the opposite case, be sure to call out the pro-innovation bias that you also share as a way of building rapport for persuasion.

Proportionality Bias

The proportionality bias is our tendency to believe that cause and effect share proportionality, so big things have big causes and small things have small causes.

How to Use It

In behavioral science, the proportionality bias is often something that must be counter-programmed when trying to affect behavior change. This is because some things (e.g., the power of compound interest) are actually small choices with outsized impacts. But people are bad at understanding this, specifically when contemplating the future. If you are dealing with a disproportionate cause-effect relationship, I suggest you call out this fallacy and actively program against it.

Reactance

Reactance occurs when we do the opposite of what we're asked to do because we perceive it as an infringement on our liberty or self-control.

How to Use It

The most important thing to prevent reactance is to avoid the use of directive language when presenting an entreaty. The words *should, must,* and *required* are often triggers that can cause an oppositional reaction in your audience. Just as you would never tell a prospective investor they "must" invest (or pretend that you have scarcity when you don't), you run the risk of reactance unless your requests are couched in the premise of personal (or group) agency.

Recency/Frequency Illusion

The recency illusion posits that we believe that something we observed recently also came into existence recently. The frequency illusion suggests that once we notice something, we tend to see more examples of that thing, leading to a false belief in its high occurrence.

How to Use It

Recency and frequency illusions (along with the Baader-Meinhof phenomenon) occur so regularly that even well-meaning and intelligent people fall prey to them. Common in linguistics, these phenomena also explain people's tendency to believe that Facebook is listening to their conversations. They are convinced that after a chat with a friend about mattresses, they're being shown a cavalcade of mattress ads, for example (though they are most likely just noticing them for the first time). As a speaker, I find this to be most powerful when called out and used to reinforce a point. For example, now that you know about A-Ha! Moments, you'll see them more often in the speeches and pitches you consume. Calling that out explicitly helps both reinforce that what you're saying is true, and primes the audience to understand your points better over time.

Rhyme as Reason Effect

The rhyme as reason effect suggests that people perceive things that rhyme as being more truthful or honest.

How to Use It

Advanced speakers often use rhymes to reinforce critical points in their presentation, and you can too. These can be spoken explicitly or placed on your slides as a subtle way of encouraging agreement. A similar, but less documented effect, is the tendency for people to perceive things with good acronyms as being more true or valid. You can use both of these approaches in your talks, pitches, and meetings, but be sure to modulate their use. If they appear too often, their effect is reduced and the technique starts to seem contrived.

Semmelweis Reflex

The Semmelweis reflex is our tendency to disagree with evidence that contradicts a paradigm we already believe without any conscious thought.

How to Use It

This is similar to the backfire effect and reactance, in that it predicts a negative reaction from people to new information. If you want to minimize the chances of a Semmelweis response, it may be useful to avoid placing the conclusion that causes the dissonance before the points that prove it. In this case, calling out the audience's reticence may be counterproductive.

Survivorship Bias

Survivorship bias is our tendency to over-focus on things that have survived a particular hardship, rather than those that didn't. Sometimes we refer to

"History Is Written by the Victors" as a kind of survivorship bias in literature and policy.

How to Use It

Depending on the kind of arguments you're making, survivorship bias can either be a positive effect or require some counter-programming. For example, if you want to press the notion that Amazon.com's strategy should be emulated for startup success, you'll likely find most people agreeing with you. Conversely, if you believe it should *not* be emulated, you may need to call out the survivorship bias of your audience and explicitly mention those other companies (perhaps deceased) that we should be emulating, and why.

Incorporating Cognitive Biases

We discussed cognitive biases as a way of understanding how people may be biased toward—or against—the things you have to say. Normally, we frame the importance of cognitive biases as elements of persuasion. That is, in order to persuade, you may need to defeat or leverage the target's cognitive biases.

But when considering the A-Ha! Moment structure, this may become a problem. If you pull the audience too close to conflict, they may use the refractory period after your points to make an argument against you. This is more likely to happen than not, if the cognitive bias is significant in their lives. While this is an absolute no-no for pitches (you never want to get a no if you can help it), in a talk setting this can be very valuable.

So while you want to avoid triggering cognitive biases in a pitch, in a talk, you may want to confront them head on. You can do this in the A-Ha! context by calling it out. In the failosophy talk referenced above, I do this with the point about portfolio theory, calling it out as something that only investors know, average people do not, and as an idea that is very complex. This anchors the listener in the idea that my simplification is important to them and also relevant to the conversation. Instead of rejecting the idea because it doesn't precisely comport with the way they think about investing, they are encouraged to assume it is simplified for their benefit.

There's no clear or specific way to implement the cognitive biases listed above, but as a general rule, your A-Ha! Moments shouldn't "poke the bear." That is, if you create a provocation that is likely to lie inside a cognitive bias— you probably aren't reaching the maximum impact of your talk.

Consider the closer in my failosophy speech. There, I delivered a provocation using confirmation bias, hindsight bias, optimism bias, and the hard-easy effect. It was intended to simultaneously challenge you on multiple vectors to do more, be better, and to see the future in a brighter light. Much like this book, success or failure depends on how well you lock into this.

And no greater challenge exists now than adapting to the rapid—and some might say technologically distracting—communications platforms of the future.

A NOTE ON COGNITIVE BIASES

When crafting your arguments and the flow of your talk, speech, or pitch, consider the different biases your audience may be bringing to the table, and use key techniques to ensure their impact is minimized (if counterproductive) or maximized (if useful). If you're not "poking the bear" at least a bit, you're probably not reaching your maximum A-Ha! potential.

4

The Tao of Zoom

Strategies for Meetings, Speeches, and Pitches

Now that we've taken a close look at the foundational reimagining of communication in an era of distraction, we need to begin thinking about our intended outputs. The strategy for any effective speech, meeting, or pitch begins by thinking through the whole thing from start to finish. Who will be there? What are we trying to accomplish? How do we structure everything for maximum impact?

This book will deliver its highest benefit if you have a specific output in mind. In this chapter, we'll look at some of the overarching and specific strategies for virtual/digital platforms in light of the new normal.

MAKING A GAME PLAN

Not all presentations you give will be virtual. But one of the likely scenarios you'll face going forward is that at least *some* of the people you'll be speaking to will be remote. Most professionals already have experience with remote "dial ins" to meetings. Those large starfish speakerphones and complex, self-moving video cameras have long been fixtures in modern offices. I'd venture to guess that for as long as there have been phones with an amplified speaker, people have been joining important meetings from afar.

What's different now is that many of the people joining from afar are not incidental to the meeting, but rather will have equal weight in determining whether or not you are successful with your efforts. Moreover, their expectations have shifted. In the past, if you were unable to attend a meeting (seminar, workshop, etc.) because of a conflict and had to dial in, you wouldn't expect to be catered to over the folks in the room. Expectations were lower, and callers/watchers were given wide latitude to participate or not. With these distinctions erased, it's even harder to know who you're playing to.

The COVID-19 pandemic and resulting effects on communication have changed this irrevocably. Perhaps we were always heading in the direction of purely virtual or mixed-virtual professional talks, but this transition happened faster than planned. Most of us and our organizations haven't fully digested the impact, even now.

Good communicators have always made a game plan for their talks beforehand. Every speech, pitch, or meeting requires a level of preplanning for maximum benefit, and the best speakers never really "wing it" without context. Today's circumstances require extra care and thought, but these are the things we ought to know before any talk:

- who and where
- what time is it
- meeting length
- polls, chats, and Q&A
- feedback mechanism
- who's running the meeting

Who and Where?

The first and most important question is: Who will be attending and where are they located? You want to know who you're talking to, to both tailor your message and also to perform a rudimentary prioritization as some meeting attendees are always more important than others. Request a list of all the people involved or at least get the basic demographic breakdown if the organizer doesn't know the details.

Next, you'll want to understand where the attendees are physically located and whether some are in a room together in the main event location and some are remote. For the remote participants, are some of them together (e.g., grouped by office) or is everyone at home? This will help you understand the emotional context of the people in the meeting, and the likelihood of multitasking and interruption.

If even some of the attendees are grouped together, their energy will be different than folks dialing in alone. While this may make it harder for you to see what's happening in the other space (due to the possibility of a single, further-away camera) you can assume that in-room participants are feeding off each other's energy. If the event is intended to have interactivity, clusters should be called on together by referring to the office location and inviting feedback. If everyone is independently remote, it is impractical to call upon attendees directly for conversation and you'll have to depend on other approaches, such as passively inviting feedback or polls/Q&A mechanisms.

An equally important question is: Where are *you*? If you are presenting locally, you must take all the steps necessary to ensure you're in position well before your meeting and fully ready. It may be tempting to not do the same level of pre-meeting prep when presenting remotely, but this would be a mistake. Whatever you'd wear for a live presentation you should wear for the remote one. Avoid the temptation of leading the meeting from your car or a city bus, and make sure you have a quiet, well-lighted physical space (and emotional wherewithal) to do your best.

What Time Is the Meeting?

Always double check a remote presentation's time zone and meeting time a day or two before the event. While a live meeting in the office is unlikely to face this issue, remote attendees (including you, your team, or the inviter) may make time zone mistakes that could leave you scrambling at the last minute.

Equally important is what happens before the meeting. I like to block the entire day before an important presentation. This allows me to focus only on the talk at hand and to get it ready. If this is impractical, I recommend blocking at least an hour.

A good "run down" of the time before an important remote presentation looks something like this:

    2 days: double-check timing, requirements, etc., and reconfirm.
    2 hours: showered and in position. Rehearse.
    1 hour: get dressed. Rehearse again. Do tech setup.
    30 minutes: log on to the platform, test all equipment.

Concomitantly, you want to know what time the meeting is taking place for the participants and what their day looks like before and after your talk/pitch. Will they be hungry or tired, near the end of their day, or under pressure to complete a task? This information can help you modulate your tone and gives you an opportunity to compensate for anything dragging on the other end.

Meeting Length

As a general rule, virtual meetings seem less time constrained than in-person events. Perhaps this is because of the reduced pressure on participants to rush to the next thing. Whether or not this is true in your particular situation, I highly recommend that you treat the timing as absolutely sacrosanct and be prepared to run your complete presentation in the time allotted.

Because virtual meetings also often have a bit of setup time at the beginning (with participants logging on, adjusting devices, dealing with interference, etc.), if you are leading the meeting, be sure to have a little bit of small talk or other delaying tactics at the ready to fill the space until everyone is on board.

Discuss the meeting's sub-timings with the organizer before as well. Find out what specific things are going to happen (e.g., Q&A) and build a little run down—if none is provided—that you can share with your team or anyone else attending from your side. This is particularly crucial if you are leading or presenting in the middle of a longer meeting.

Polls, Chats, and Q&A

All meeting technologies have some combination of interactive features to help facilitate communication among a diffuse group. These tend to include a polls (or questions) feature, a chat feature, and a mechanism for Q&A—either structured or unstructured.

Before the meeting, you need to decide two crucial things about interactivity—either alone or, if appropriate, with the organizer:

1. When is interaction allowed?
2. Who is running the interaction?

Polls need to be created and developed beforehand, and can be useful as a way to get answers from attendees about topics related to your meeting. If you conduct a poll during your presentation, be sure that the poll is relevant enough to warrant distracting the audience from whatever you have to say, because that is precisely what will happen when the poll is launched. It's also good practice to feed the poll results back into your presentation along the way. This justifies the audience's time commitment and demonstrates that you care about your attendees.

To be ready for chat during your meeting, you'll need a sense of how the attendees usually use the feature (heavy/medium/light). Additionally, you should designate someone from your side to monitor the chat for relevant questions and, potentially, to moderate content. Unless you are a very seasoned speaker or pitcher, I strongly recommend against trying to multitask during your talk. I've seen plenty of speakers do this with generally poor results, and the experience is especially painful when rewatching recorded meetings where the speaker is multitasking.

Whoever ends up moderating the chat needs to be able to field questions, offer resources (e.g., URLs you may have mentioned) and to invite participants to chat further after the talk. Any questions asked in chat should be answered or explicitly kicked down to a later date.

If your meeting has a structured time for Q&A, you'll want to know that and include it in your rundown of timing. I recommend that most virtual meetings allocate a time for Q&A rather than encouraging it to be spontaneous in the middle of a presentation. This will help make the meeting seem smoother, and allow you the mental energy to just focus on your communication first, questions later. Of course, if you are more seasoned, you may be comfortable with interruptions, but again I recommend that you use an interactivity feature (e.g., questions or chat) to obtain those queries during your talk.

Expecting people to interrupt you is both disruptive and unlikely to happen. The audio processing technologies at work on most virtual meeting platforms like Zoom prioritize a person's voice to rebroadcast at the expense of other participants. By design, this means that only one person can clearly speak at a time, and during their speech, other voices are potentially muted. As you've undoubtedly experienced, the algorithms for voice processing can seem arbitrary, and sometimes mistakenly prioritize the barking of a dog or a side conversation among viewers as important. Don't invite this chaos into your life, and mute everyone until it's time for folks to speak.

Feedback Mechanism

Of course, you want to know how your meeting, pitch, or talk was received, and you should ask the organizer how they will obtain this feedback. Sometimes, the feedback is done in real-time (e.g., using the polls feature), but typically events will try to survey after the fact. If you have the opportunity, you can also invite feedback directly in the chat ("How are we doing?") or as part of your follow-up with attendees. Obviously, if you're doing a fundraising pitch or other competitive speech, you are likely to know what the judges thought of you right away—even in a virtual setting.

Who's Running the Meeting?

You need to establish, up front, who's in charge of running the meeting. This person will typically have administrative access to control the meeting functions, and will be the one that opens and closes the room. You should ensure that you know how to privately chat with this person during the session (in case something goes wrong) and spend some time with them prior to the event, going over the process. If you're not the organizer, remind them to make you a co-host prior to the meeting's start so you can share your screen.

If you are the meeting organizer, you will need to build in additional time to do your meeting's setup, including technical requirements, roll call, and audience rule/expectation setting.

TECHNICAL CONSIDERATIONS

Because virtual meetings, pitches, and speeches are—by definition—happening over software, and are often run without the assistance of professional A/V teams, there is an additional technical burden for the meeting organizer and presenters. Some of these considerations include:

- meeting configuration
- webinar versus meeting mode
- computer setup
- network connection
- screen sharing
- video and audio sharing
- audio and lighting setup
- virtual backgrounds
- how to handle technical faults

Meeting Configuration

Each online meeting platform has configurations that need to be set, typically prior to the meeting. These include the meeting room ID, passwords, and participant limitations, recording, "webinar mode," and polls, questions, etc.

Platforms such as Zoom are often referred to as "frankenproducts," because they've added many functions in a haphazard way over time, usually in response to customer requests. This means that key meeting functions are often not where you'd expect them, and buried deep in the bowels of the settings feature. Moreover, many features must be set up prior to the meeting and cannot be configured on the fly.

For example, if you want to have a "practice session" prior to the start of a webinar in Zoom, you must configure this in the presentation settings from the Zoom website. You cannot configure this from the app, and you cannot change this setting after the meeting is set up. If you don't set up a practice session, your pre-meeting "chat" with the panelists will be visible to everyone watching. I highly recommend that all events have a practice session, either with the practice feature enabled, or by using a different meeting ID.

This is why it's also imperative that, if you're going to be giving presentations virtually, you familiarize yourself with the features available and how to configure them up front. Most platforms have tutorial videos you can watch and step-by-step meeting configuration instructions. If you are doing this for the first time (or the first time in a long time), leave yourself the space to set up a fake practice meeting with you alone prior to the event.

Webinar versus Meeting Mode

Webinar mode allows a larger group of people to watch the event in a passive way. Attendees cannot be seen on camera unless the organizer invites them on, and they typically must communicate with the panel and each other using the chat/Q&A/polls feature. In a regular meeting, each attendee has a camera/ microphone and can be visible in a grid during the talk.

If you're presenting in webinar mode, you need to make an extra effort to interact and engage with the audience, because webinars make it much easier for them to multitask. This is when inviting questions, moderating chat, and setting up polls are most valuable.

Conversely, if you have a relatively large group of people in a regular meeting, you need to take other technical precautions. Make sure (or request) that everyone be muted prior to start, and tell them explicitly how to unmute themselves if and/or when necessary. The global mute controls are powerful, so be sure to familiarize yourself with them beforehand.

In addition, if your meeting is large, you won't see everyone on the grid of participants, as only a certain number can be visible at one time. You can, however, pin certain people to the view, so if there are some critical attendees (e.g., decision makers or organizers) in the chat, you may want to identify and pin them so you can interact with them more directly (and monitor their feedback).

Note that in some apps, "pinning" an attendee actually makes them the focus of the video everyone sees, and not just in your grid. Sometimes this is referred to as "spotlighting." Try not to confuse the two.

Computer Setup

In order to ensure that you do not get any unwanted notifications—visual or auditory—while you're running a meeting, I recommend you create a new user on your computer called "meeting." This user should have everything disabled except for the tech required to run your meetings (camera, recording, platform software, etc.). Notifications should be turned off, but having a clean user profile will also minimize your tendency to multitask or launch computationally intensive programs (e.g., email) when you need to conserve computing power for maximum broadcast quality.

So when your meeting is about to start, log in as the meeting user, and run the meeting from there. Ensure that you have all the necessary links and documents in that user profile by sharing those via system filesharing or in the cloud. It's okay for you to be logged in to your cloud accounts under the meeting user, just don't run any programs that are not absolutely necessary.

If you are giving a major presentation or pitch, such as a keynote, I also highly recommend rebooting your computer at least ten minutes prior to the session. This has a tendency to "clear out the cobwebs" in your operating system and streamline performance. And yes, this includes Mac users—like me.

You may also want to take an eyeglass cleaning cloth to your webcam once in a while, as no one likes that halcyon look when trying to focus on your face. While you're at it, if you're wearing glasses, clean those as well. You'd be surprised what all gets picked up in an HD broadcast.

After your last meeting of the day, log out of the meeting user and return to your regular workspace. And it goes without saying, but be sure to silence your phones and any other devices during a meeting where you are presenting.

Network Connection

Platforms will often tell you that a wired connection is best for presenting, and they are correct. If it's feasible for your computer to be wired directly to your router, you will benefit from setting it up accordingly.

However, if that's not possible, you can take certain steps to ensure maximum quality and minimal latency in your presentations.

First, by logging into the "meeting" user described above, you will generally be minimizing network demand from your other applications. Some apps, such as cloud syncing and email can consume vast amounts of network bandwidth even though they don't appear to be doing anything. Rebooting and changing users is your best insurance against such degradation.

Another key strategy is to ensure—wherever possible—that others in your household are not performing network-intensive tasks during your presentation. To be sure, this can be complex depending on who is working from home and the time of day, but a simple request to not do any major tasks from 3:30 to 4:00 p.m. on Tuesday will add additional insurance.

Finally, I think creating an entirely separate network connection for meetings isn't a bad idea—and it's how I've configured my home office. Connected to my modem is a wireless router whose only device client is my presentation computer. This definitely doesn't alleviate any network congestion issues from the modem to the ISP head-end, but it does work wonders at removing network congestion over your local Wi-Fi, which can be prone to all kinds of drop outs and interference.

You do not need hundreds of megabytes of bandwidth to do high-quality presentations from home, you just need to ensure that you have the computational and network resources available to avoid any lags from either. This is doubly important if you're going to be doing multimedia tasks, such as screen sharing.

Screen Sharing

Another lovely benefit of using the "meetings" user account for your presentations is the reduced likelihood of an error or embarrassment while screen sharing. With fewer open windows, you'll be less likely to choose the wrong one to share, and you'll have more bandwidth and computing resources to deliver a higher-quality experience.

Remember that screen sharing often does two things to your attendees. First, it takes over their whole screen (though they can control this configuration option). Secondly, it will minimize the size of your face video, making it harder for them to see your facial expressions, and to react accordingly. Despite the larger-than-normal screen size, it can still be wickedly hard to read someone's screen share, so I recommend using the techniques we describe later in this book to ensure the right minimum font size and speed from page to page. Suffice it to say that bigger—and slower—is better.

To ensure you have the maximum usable real estate on your side of the house, I recommend configuring your presentation software (or whatever you're screen sharing) to present from a window, rather than full screen. This is a new feature in Keynote (and in some versions of PowerPoint) that will allow you to present what appears to be full screen to attendees, while maintaining screen space on your desktop. Make sure to take best advantage of this feature by avoiding sharing your entire monitor, and just sharing the application window or tab necessary.

Remember that most embarrassing screen sharing mishaps happen to people who are sharing their entire computer desktop. The less you can do this, the better.

A last pro tip: have all your sharing windows and/or presentations ready to go before beginning your talk so if you need to activate screen sharing, it will require minimal effort and disruption on your part.

Audio and Video Streaming

Zoom itself is quite good at streaming audio and video from your device to meeting attendees. In order to make this work well, however, you'll need to ensure certain configurations are optimized. First and foremost, make use of the strategies described above to boot into a meeting user, get everything ready and preserve computational and bandwidth resources.

Next, familiarize yourself with the controls for optimized video and audio rebroadcast from within your chosen platform. In Zoom, these controls are visible at the bottom of the screen when launching screen share, or in the menu after screen share is live. For example, if you do not check the "share audio" and "optimize streaming" boxes on Zoom, the audio will likely not play for your attendees and the video will be choppy. You cannot globally set these options, so they need to be configured each time you launch screen sharing.

Furthermore, if you are going to be screen sharing a presentation (e.g., from Keynote), and also have audio, video, or demos to perform, I highly recommend embedding those in your presentation file to minimize the amount of navigating, configuration, and screen management you'll have to do in the middle of your talk, pitch, or meeting. By compiling everything into a keynote, you can access these resources more seamlessly—and in a single window.

As always, make sure your audio and video are good quality, and that your computer volume is set to the level you want for your stream.

Audio and Lighting

If you're going to be presenting off a late model Mac, you probably do not need to buy an external microphone. External mics can be very useful and produce excellent sound, but are not absolutely necessary if you have the right computer. An external mic can provide some significant benefits and, if you're going to do a lot of meetings or recordings, you should definitely invest in one. I recommend the Blue Yeti series and have compiled a list of preferred home presentation tools you can access at the end of this chapter.

More important than even your microphone is the acoustics in your room. If possible, present from a room with many soft—not hard—surfaces. During the COVID-19 pandemic, a common strategy was to repurpose a walk-in closet or small utility room for presentations. Minimizing the size of the room as well as the number of hard, angular surfaces will reduce echo and make your voice sound more pleasant.

Lighting also makes a huge difference in presentations, particularly as most computers are designed to automatically try to compensate for changes in distance (auto-focus) and light reflection (auto brightness/white balance). If you don't have strong, appropriate, and consistent lighting, your image can change in a highly distracting way, and simply will not present you in the best light (see what I did there)!

A simple and cheap solution is a clamp-on ring light that you can purchase at your preferred online retailer for $30 or less. These LED lights plug into your USB port and provide enough bright or soft light to keep you looking good and in focus. Always test your lighting setup prior to the event to ensure you know what to expect—as fiddling with the lighting during a presentation is distracting visually and auditorily.

Another good hack is to ensure that your computer faces a non-direct lighted window, and you can take advantage of the natural light where you live/work. This will make you look your best and the audience will notice. However, you want to take care to not be in the direct sunlight—this is a case where less is more. If the sun is shining directly on you, your color rendering will be off and it will be as difficult to see your face as it is without light. Close the blinds to filter the light if needed before your meeting begins and use artificial light to supplement.

Getting the lighting right is especially important if you're going to use a virtualized background.

Virtual Backgrounds

Virtual backgrounds allow you to superimpose yourself over an image that appears to be the backdrop wherever you're presenting from. This can help cover up a messy or otherwise unattractive room, and/or provide a consistent visual regardless of your location.

It's important to note that you should have your virtual backgrounds setup and loaded in your app well in advance, and if you have an older computer, you should probably avoid using them entirely as they are computationally very intensive. The most crashes I've ever seen in presentation software seem directly related to virtualized backgrounds, so act conservatively.

Choose a background that represents you, and if you're pitching a company or project, I recommend using the real estate of your virtual background for branding—include your logo or a relevant image.

You'll probably also notice that virtual backgrounds are imperfect, sometimes hiding parts of your body or face, and revealing what's actually behind you if you move quickly. This is because the virtual backgrounding is using computer vision to find your face in the image, and to replace everything else with your chosen background.

But deciding which pixels are your face and which aren't is an imperfect science, and this is extra visible if you are using a prop or there is a second person in your camera view. Using a virtual background in either of these settings is generally a bad idea, as your object/the other speaker may be hidden arbitrarily by the software.

And as always, you need a backup plan in case something goes wrong. Sometimes, the virtual background doesn't work or there's a hiccup or bandwidth problem. So wherever possible, configure the space behind you to be a suitable—if imperfect—alternate. Put a plant or a piece of art on a wall in your camera's eye and you'll be fine.

> n.b. What do you think when you see someone presenting with a non-branded virtual background? I automatically assume they are in a very messy room, especially if they choose the "blur" effect. For a curious audience, this can be a distraction as their mind wanders to the horrors your blurry outline is concealing. Again, a neat, clean, and live view is ideal for almost every scenario.

How to Handle Technical Faults

Murphy's law posits that anything that can go wrong, will. And nowhere is this a more appropriate truism than in streaming virtual presentations, pitches, and meetings. And the more technically complex—or important—the element, the more likely the problem is to multiply.

Demos failing, videos crashing, audio too quiet, presentation files corrupted—the list goes on and on. Professional speakers know that they need to have a backup to the backup of the backup, and always have a few alternatives ready to go—just in case.

First, if you have a presentation—save it in a PDF and send it to the meeting organizer or admin beforehand. You can also put it in chat or use the cloud presentation features in Keynote or PowerPoint to make a link available to the attendees. You can use this option in the event your presentation fails, offering the viewers an alternative so they can continue to follow along.

If you are presenting with others, ensure that they have a mirror configuration of your presentation materials and tools available so they can take over if you suffer a technical outage or fault. You should also pre-discuss the scenarios where this might happen (not unlike a pilot and co-pilot gaming out possible issues before a flight) and when the alternative speaker should take over. Most critically, if you experience a major outage during your presentation (which happens more often than you might think), you should empower the alternate to proceed seamlessly, anticipating that you'll rejoin when possible. They should not call attention to the tech issue and, instead, ensure the presentation continues.

This is a kind of backup, and you should consider backups for all your presentation's "risky" elements. For example, if you were planning to do a live demo, I recommend you make a flat, image-based, video or PDF version of your demo that you can simply "click through" if the real thing fails. If you've got audio or video that glitches, be ready with a verbal description of what the audience would have seen/heard if everything had worked.

Most importantly however—you need to be decisive. If you encounter a technical fault, know what your alternatives are, and make a choice quickly and without fuss. For example, make an agreement with yourself that you'll cut your losses (and switch to a canned version) if your demo doesn't work properly after the second attempt. The worst experience for attendees is to watch, dying silently, as you fumble with your tech trying to make things work. It's embarrassing and a waste of time. No matter how good your presentation or demo, if it doesn't work, move on quickly and decisively. Your audience will appreciate it more than you realize.

And as always, having a sense of humor and self-deprecation works wonders at moments like these. Every professional speaker or communicator can tell you horror stories of the time an earthquake struck during a meeting, the power failed, someone had a heart attack or A/V folks started to play a rock song by accident. Famous incidents of people accidentally showing porn from their computers or incriminating/embarrassing notifications abound.

Minimize your risks, have a backup plan, act quickly and with good humor—and soon you'll be doing this effortlessly.

Now let's review some of the specific tips and strategies you should use in different communication settings.

TACTICS FOR LEADING A MEETING

If you're running a meeting in the virtual era, there are some unique considerations that should be front and center.

First and foremost, you need to have a good picture of everyone who's attending, and whether they are local or remote. If remote, you should understand whether they are grouped together by office, or independently remote. For any internal meeting—particularly those under fifty people—it will behoove you to have a detailed understanding of the specifics of each attendee's situations.

If your meeting is occurring in many different places at once, be sure to use the mute function judiciously during different phases of the conversation. Also, you'll need to call on people specifically, and I find it useful to have a few ideas of who you'll call on beforehand.

Crosstalk using digital meeting software is often impossible and always frustrating. So you'll need to establish yourself as the leader, and develop an approach for ensuring that everyone who wants to participate (and some who don't) get an opportunity. All the usual meeting issues still apply (e.g., the people who crowd others out), but in the virtual setting you actually have more control than you realize.

Attendees are also generally comfortable with the establishment of ground rules, and I suggest you spend the first couple of minutes in any meeting going over these. Explain how to handle questions, what the purpose of the meeting is, its timing, and anything else relevant to the audience. The first few minutes of the meeting should probably be spent doing a little bit of small-talk or pre-establishing to ensure that everyone has the necessary transition time from their previous event.

It is common for larger-scale virtual presentations to delay the start by a few minutes to specifically ensure everyone can log on and get their tech configured. This is especially important if folks need to be admitted to the meeting or use a password or other token to enter. That all takes time, and for many folks moving from one meeting to the next, there is often a few minutes delay in reconfiguration. This is especially important for meeting attendees who may be interacting with external partners using different technologies.

Given the need to create a bit of a buffer up front, you must also account for that in the length and scheduling of your meeting. A 45-minute meeting suddenly becomes 39 minutes if you spend the first 6 waiting for everyone to get online. And wherever possible, you (as meeting leader) should be set up and in position to start the meeting at least 15 (30 if you have tech setup or external participants) minutes before the event.

If your meeting involves a senior executive or sponsor who is critically important, there is no point in starting before they arrive. So you can engage in conversation of a different kind until they are online and ready to listen. You will avoid having to do any rework in the conversation and actually is more coherent for other attendees. Avoid the impulse to just caterwaul forward without ensuring that your minimal "launch" checklist is complete.

When you're leading a meeting where most of the participants are in the same room, you also get a lot of nonverbal feedback from attendees. This can be valuable to understand—for example—when everyone's energy is flagging, or if there is strong disagreement about something. Moreover, depending on your team's policy of device multitasking, you might be able to impress upon the audience the need to focus. In a virtual meeting, these are not readily possible, so I recommend some strategies to ensure optimal outcomes.

Plan on some interactive elements even if the meeting is mostly presentations or status. Create a poll question, ask folks something in chat, and don't be afraid to act as moderator and schoolteacher if needed to encourage participation. Ask people direct questions if appropriate, and solicit input. While the virtual presentation environment can be a boon for certain kinds of introverts, it can also give them an even easier excuse to not participate. Your job must be to tease them out of hiding and engage them as appropriate in the conversation.

I often find it helpful to open the meeting with a thought, question, or other provocation that we're intending to resolve or answer. Include this question in the chat and be sure to leave time to circle back to it later and evaluate whether or not it has been solved/answered.

TACTICS FOR GIVING A SPEECH

This book includes many chapters devoted to creating speeches designed for our new era of distraction and asynchronous communication. But there are a few crucial elements of giving a virtual talk that you must be able to marshal early and often.

First and foremost, you must get comfortable—really comfortable—with speaking to a blank, unfeeling black void. Namely, your webcam. This is a really different skill from speaking to a room full of live humans, where you can extract some nonverbal cues from the audience. For example, the nodding of heads in a room can be an encouraging sign to a speaker, and if you're accustomed to looking for affirmation that you're doing a good job, you may feel panicked when talking to the camera.

The best way to prepare for this, I've found, is to give your presentation to a wall. Yes, just walk up to the wall, stand six to twelve inches away, and give your presentation. Allow your focus to soften, and just keep staring straight ahead. You can move your head or use your hands, but learning to override the visual cues anxiety loop requires extreme measures.

Don't feel bad though, as this is a skill that is very difficult for a lot of people. Many of the most seasoned lecturers, presenters, and even actors have trouble talking to the camera. Over the years, most of them have developed techniques for helping to alleviate this. Some of these techniques include:

- Looking at yourself in the video feed. Yes, pinning yourself to the video feed can help you feel more comfortable with presenting because it's a familiar face (at least I hope it is) and gives your brain some of the visual cues necessary to feel like you're making progress.
- Look at a friendly person in the video feed. Instead of letting the platform decide which person you'll be looking at, pin a particular person to the feed, move the window as close to your webcam as possible, and look at them. If you know the person and can alert them to the fact that you're going to be looking at them, all the better. This role is best played by a compatriot and one that can be briefed, but I've seen speakers do this with unknown audience members as well.
- Place a photo of someone you like just above the camera's eyeline. To ensure that you're looking at the right place, but also to give you something familiar to focus on, you can post a cutout (or image if you have the monitor space) of someone familiar right above the camera.

As with everything performance related, practice makes perfect. Though I am an old pro at virtual presentations, I still get nervous without the audience's feedback and the nonverbal cues I've learned to pick up over the years. Give yourself time to adjust and practice this technique over and over again.

I also recommend that most virtual speakers give their presentations while standing. Using a standing desk, you can raise your webcam so that it centers perfectly on your face. Standing up, moreover, tends to give speakers more energy, and will help you enliven your talk. The secondary benefit of standing is that it actually makes you look better and your clothes more neat and unwrinkled.

Another area to pay attention to as a virtual speaker is your personal "head-space" prior to your talk. We've devoted an entire chapter to speaking hygiene later in the book, and I highly encourage you to read it and follow the guidance. You want to be well rested, properly fed and caffeinated, and not rushing to organize things at the last minute. Whatever techniques you normally use to get yourself "in the zone" of some calm and focus can be deployed here as well. For example, if listening to a guided meditation or thumping rock song helps you focus, build in time in your day to do that before the speech.

And speaking of time, ensure you're not rushing before your talk. As described above, it's incredibly important to make sure that key timelines and milestones are in your calendar: when to shower, eat, dress up, practice, and launch your talk.

In general, speeches have been getting shorter—and the pressures of distraction, online streaming, and event schedules have compressed these even further. Whereas it might have been normal to deliver a 60-minute keynote just a decade ago, today most event keynotes are scheduled for less than 30 minutes, and sometimes this includes 5 to 10 minutes of Q&A. Shorter is better, and in the virtual presentation space, this aphorism could not be more true.

Though you must leave enough time for listeners to absorb what you have to say, process it, and perhaps take notes—you also want to ensure that the length of your talk itself does not predispose the audience to tuning you out. That is, don't make it more likely they'll change the channel. As a general rule, I recommend keeping your talks under 30 minutes and make sure you leave time for Q&A.

Also ensure that any Q&A, feedback, or input from the audience, can be handled by someone other than you—but the more interactive you are, the better your talk will be received and the longer folks will pay attention. There is an interesting phenomenon of audiences being better able to tune out rehearsed, consistent speech versus the ups and downs of interactivity. The unpredictability can be enticing, and a great way to get attention from your audience. So if you have the advanced skills necessary, make Q&A and interaction a core part of your talk.

Lastly—and this is universally true—making yourself available to the audience will make it more likely that you'll close business and get future opportunities out of this talk. Include your contact information (have an associate post it in chat if possible) and make yourself available to attendees with questions, comments, or interest after your talk. Encourage people to reach out to you and give them a reason to do so. Hopefully, you'll get an opportunity to pitch your services, company, or ideas.

TACTICS FOR PITCHING

Back in the early 2000s, after the dot-com crash, startups had to run their first fundraising conversation over the phone. Investors were doing so few deals, and their existing companies were struggling so seriously, that they didn't want to waste time with initial look-sees. You had to develop the ability to pitch on the phone (this was well before video calling) with an eye toward getting an in-person meeting thereafter.

I was right in the thick of this trend, raising money for my startup Trymedia after the crash. This was one of the hardest things I ever did, and I must have done one hundred plus initial meetings with venture capitalists before getting a few second meetings.

Presenting yourself and your company over the phone was extra hard, because there was no way to control the visuals or even to project yourself beyond your voice. And while there is much more information carried in a Zoom presentation, the basic premise of the phone pitch is as true as ever: you need to be concise, collaborative, and clear.

As we've discussed, being concise and efficient with your time is critical in this virtual pitch era. Fundraising pitches, for example, have been on a long-term trend toward incredibly compact—with various accelerators limiting founders to 5 minutes or less. Many of the biggest startups in existence today—such as Airbnb—raised their first round off a 5-minute pitch presentation.

Of course, it's highly unlikely that anyone will write you a check based on what you have to say in 300 seconds, but it is still true that if you can use that time to get them excited, you can parlay that into a second (and third, fourth) meeting where you *can* raise those funds. So for an initial pitch, anything that's worth saying should be deliverable in 5 to 6 minutes—maybe 10 with a detailed demo.

And as we'll discuss later in this book, while it's important to open strong and get to your "hook" early in the presentation, it's also important to not give everything away in the first 20 seconds; you should leave some mystery. Both of these strategies are designed to ensure that you don't lose the audience—something even easier to do if they are hidden behind their video cameras.

Similarly for non-fundraising pitches, I recommend breaking the conversation into two or three segments. The first is always a 5- to 10-minute pitch that runs the gamut of setting up the challenge, the learning, and the conclusion (why they should partner/buy your product). Then, you can offer a second section for elaborating on those initial points. This allows you to deliver the meat quickly and while you have everyone's attention, while also creating space for further questions or deeper dives that can help reinforce the sale.

Another feature of remote pitches that differs strongly from those in person, is the challenge of a "reveal," particularly those where you might want to hand something to the audience. Think of the stage on *Shark Tank*, when the founders walk around to the sharks and pass out a sample of their product to touch and feel. That moment—the product reveal—is important for establishing excitement and rapport with the target audience.

But if you can't do that virtually, what do you do for tangible product connection? There are a number of strategies I've seen successfully deployed. First and foremost, if your product is virtual or digital, the audience will probably not expect anything physical and will be okay with an excellent digital presentation, deck, and discussion. But even if it's not expected, you can create extra impact.

For example, get your audience's address ahead of time and send them each a box with a reveal item. Be sure to include a note in the meeting invitation and on the box to not open it until told to do so—this will create some suspense. Then when it's the right time, you entreat everyone to open their boxes, and enjoy the drama of folks on camera each doing it. This will heighten everyone's collective emotion and create a moment of surprise and delight that will be memorable. Consider giving everyone time to digest what you've given them, and—if appropriate—create a space to discuss what they're experiencing with each other. If you have a sponsor or patron on the prospect side that you can include in the mix, you may want to tell them what to expect in advance, so they can be primed to react as you'd wanted.

You can also create digitally interactive experiences that go beyond your demo to convey important points to the audience. This is the right time to test out technologies like augmented and virtual reality, and artificially intelligent interactions that create the wow factor. Even a simple interactive website with some kind of prize feature could be a powerful way to create connection and excitement.

And a final note about tone. In an in-person pitch, we are often taught to ask for the sale. But in a phone or virtual pitch, it is highly unlikely that you'll be able to actually get the sale—particularly if it's a larger-sized ask. So your goal is to get another meeting, and therefore the ask needs to reflect this. A "pitchy" tone can also come off the wrong way in a digital or phone chat. Because people have trouble reading each other's non-verbal cues, it's too easy to turn off your prospects. Every pitch-like tactic you take will be amplified for the recipient, and so it's crucial to aim for a more conversational, friendly, peer-like tone.

Try to build rapport and engagement, and focus your energy on getting and keeping the audience connected to you. It's only through this kind of effort that you'll be able to persuade them to then move forward in the process, and take an in-person meeting. For however long the pandemic (or other restrictive macro conditions) recur, and the virtual/in person gap continues, you'll need to prove that you're worthy of the time and risk for an in-person meeting, more so than ever before.

PUTTING IT TOGETHER: THE TAO OF ZOOM

Being prepared and briefed is always critical to having a good meeting, but even more so when your meetings are remote. You need to know what to expect and to have yourself and necessary resources in place with plenty of time to spare. Ultimately, treating every virtual meeting, talk, and pitch like a heightened live event—while observing some of the unique quirks and approaches recommended in this chapter—will deliver optimal results. Remember always that the goal is another meeting, sale, or investment—so use this opportunity to build engagement and rapport, and get that follow up.

For a list of suggested equipment and supplies to make your home setup sing, snap the QR code below.

Materials Resource Guide https://qrco.de/bczBoF

5

The RuPaul Theory of Personal Style

RuPaul Charles is the host of the eponymous *Drag Race* series of shows, arguably one of the most famous people in the world and its most renowned drag queen. Starting from humble roots, RuPaul discovered the lure of performance early on—first in Atlanta and then in New York. In the 1980s he was a well-known and beloved fixture in NYC's underground music and dance scene, but most people first got to know Ru from his breakout single "Supermodel (You Better Work)" in 1993. From there, he's had two distinct career arcs—first in the 1990s as a host, artist, and celebrity, and again in the mid-2000s, reprising his hosting, music, and performance excellence.

Along the way, RuPaul has also had a tremendous impact on the personal style of millions of people. At the beginning of the first episode of *RuPaul's Drag Race*, Ru laid out his vision for what it takes to be a successful drag queen with this exhortation for the series' hopefuls:

Show us your

- charisma
- uniqueness
- nerve
- talent

The basic premise was that to succeed as "America's next drag superstar" the winner needed to demonstrate these four attributes and be measured on them in total. It turns out, this is good advice even for non-drag queens.

Time and again in my professional life, pundits and experts have weighed in on what makes a public communicator stand out from the crowd. Thousands of words have been written on the subject, and myriad theories proffered. But, on further analysis, I believe that RuPaul summarized this better than anyone before him.

Let's break these elements down a bit further:

Charisma

Charisma is a word with some religious overtones, but has transcended its origins. Today, we think of charisma as the compelling charm that inspires followers, and most people believe you either have it or you don't.

In her book *The Charisma Myth*, author Olivia Fox Cabane talks about the basic fallacy around charisma:

> Contrary to popular belief, people are not simply born charismatic—innately magnetic from birth. If charisma were an inherent attribute, charismatic people would always be captivating, and that's just not the case. Even for the most engaging superstar, charisma can be present one moment and absent the next. Marilyn Monroe could "turn off" her charisma like flipping a switch, and go completely unnoticed.[1]

In her book, Cabane makes the cogent argument that charisma is not intrinsic, but something that can be taught—and she lays out a strategy for doing just that. Even if you view yourself as generally uncharismatic, perhaps you can think of a time you were able to connect with others and persuade them to listen to you. Even the smallest moments of this magnetism—when amplified—can be powerful tools in the hands of a great communicator.

Uniqueness

Uniqueness refers to what makes you different or special, as compared to others. To be sure, standing out too much from the crowd can be traumatizing—particularly in childhood. But as we grow older, being quantitatively or qualitatively different generally serves us well in our professional endeavors.

Being unique may seem like a tall order, but there's a seminal book on marketing for business that I believe we can learn from as individuals. In *Blue Ocean Strategy*, authors Kim and Mauborgne argue that the most important thing in a startup's strategy is to redefine the market in a way that excludes competition. They write:

The only way to beat the competition is to stop trying to beat the competition
. . . imagine a market universe composed of two sorts of oceans—red oceans and
blue oceans. Red oceans represent all industries in existence today. Blue oceans
denote all the industries not in existence today. This is the unknown market
space. In red oceans, industry boundaries are defined and accepted. As the market
space gets crowded, prospects for profits and growth are reduced. Blue oceans,
in contrast, are defined by untapped market space, demand creation, and the
opportunity for . . . growth.[2]

In effect, Kim and Mauborgne are arguing that in order to be successful,
you need to define your market as a blue ocean, and expect that over time it
will become a red ocean space (as more competitors enter).

When we think about our personal expression and professional communication, I believe many of the same lessons apply. You're not just a personnel
manager, you're a personnel manager with refugee parents and a lot of empathy. You're not just a startup founder with a great idea, you're a startup
founder on a mission deeply connected to your faith.

The goal and idea is to stand out without being a completely unknown
quantity. My friend and long-time (un)venture capitalist, Geoff Lewis, often
describes this as "finding the thing you're best at in the whole world (no modesty allowed), and the thing someone will pay you to do, and to exploit that
intersection." I think this is good advice as you consider your personal brand
and how to maximize your uniqueness. I promise, it's in you.

Nerve

Nerve in RuPaul's context means taking risks. That's the way you fearlessly
approach challenges, stick your neck out, and try your best. Of course, when
choosing the best drag queen, this characteristic is obvious—as the profession
is one of performance. But public speaking is also a kind of performance. In
fact, as I'll argue later in the book, you'll have the most success once you start
thinking of yourself as a performer and taking the basic steps performers do
to ensure they give their all.

Nerve—or risk-tolerance—will vary from person to person. Perhaps one
is willing to take a big risk on a new startup's success or failure, but someone
else feels concerned their job is too important/irreplaceable to truly stick their
neck out. The critical thing is that you take the maximal risks that your situation allows, and that you use your nerve to make the world stand up and
acknowledge you.

Talent

You have to be good at the core talent elements of your career. The same is true in public speaking and professional communications. If you're an accountant, a proficiency with numbers and deep knowledge of bookkeeping rules is necessary. If you're a baseball announcer, you need to know the teams, players, and stats like the back of your hand. This is no different in professional communication.

Our "talent portion" is the ability to craft a unique narrative, whittle it down to its essence, deliver it clearly and charismatically, and on time. Too often, people new to public speaking and pitching believe that this too is either genetically expressed or not. But the reality is that anyone can develop the talent and skill necessary to be a great speaker. Of course, you may—like me—begin with a natural propensity for verbosity. But even if not, you can follow the steps in this book, practice extensively, and achieve your goals.

One of the most interesting things about RuPaul's philosophy on personal style is that it's not prescriptive. That is, unlike a Dale Carnegie or Toastmasters's approach, there's a clear understanding in drag that every person is going to come with their distinctive combination of skills to be judged. Of course, there's still a hierarchy (someone has to win the competition), but the diversity of thoughts, ideas, and expressions among winning drag queens demonstrates clearly that it is the maximization of your abilities in the four categories that creates the potential for success.

That is, by bringing the best of your charisma, uniqueness, nerve, and talent—and not backing down from the challenge to be your best self—you too can achieve greatness in communication skills.

Now let's explore the layer below this personal style—persuasion.

THE ELEMENTS OF PERSUASION

All professional communication is persuasive, and all persuasive communications are inherently pitches. The sooner you think of it this way the easier it will be to understand what you must do in order to connect with your audience in today's world. And it's a tall order. You must be:

- authentic
- knowledgable
- accurate
- economical
- self-aware

Authentic

First and foremost, you must be authentic. That is, audiences must believe that the persona you're conveying is the real you. With the number and level of fakes delivered and (ultimately) exposed over social media, it's no wonder that listeners expect you to be truly authentic. That doesn't mean you can't be the best version of your authentic self, but it highlights why most speech coaching and speaking education fail the first test: because they prescribe a "right" and a "wrong" way of speaking. Ultimately, this overreliance on irrelevant details scrubs your originality down to a perfectly packaged and shiny nub, and leads to the same-same-ness of so many speakers and leaders today.

Take the semi-annual Apple product reveals as an example. When Steve Jobs pioneered this model, bringing the iMac on stage in 1998, he was breaking the mold of previous product launches. Clad in his trademark dressed-down attire, putting the product front and center, and telling a story of tech innovation and triumph, he made audiences want to be part of the "movement" he was leading.

Three years later, by the time of the announcement of the iPod, iTunes, and macOS X, he had refined the pitch so well that these Apple events became media moments in and of themselves, and people would fall over each other to be in the room to be the first to hear the latest and greatest. His keynotes, legendary as they are, are colloquially called "Stevenotes," a reflection of his iconoclastic style.

One can argue that his reveal events are derivative of car show model announcements, except without the scantily clad women. But over years of practice, he made it his own. In fact, this desire for a better, cleaner, and more impactful form of presentation led him to push Apple to create Keynote—effectively a better PowerPoint originally designed for Stevenotes, and now the de facto standard for truly beautiful, professional slide decks.

But in the decades since the first reveal, the Stevenote style has lost its luster. And as more and more of the company's executives are called onstage to talk about their part of the ever-growing Apple empire, one cannot help but notice how there is absolutely no individual character, quirks, or language expressed by anyone (except, perhaps, previously by Jonny Ives). By enforcing a very strict carbon copy of Steve's style on the whole presentation crew, Apple inadvertently removed one of the main features of persuasive pitching—the belief in the speaker.

Now, this makes sense for Apple, as it is perhaps the most tightly controlled marketing company in the world. But having an entire team that communicates in the exact same way isn't exactly memorable. Sadly (or rightly), Tim

Cook et al. have chosen the banal side of public communication. It may ensure uniformity, but it certainly doesn't groom a worthy replacement for Steve. Who are these execs, anyway?

Now, unless you are the executive team of the world's most valuable company, you don't have the luxury of sounding like every other speaker in the world. Sure, borrowing stylistic examples from your organization when presenting internally is a good thing—flattery of the CEO has its benefits. But generally, it's preferable that you be your own person. Sounding like everyone else just won't cut it, especially in this era of social media.

Knowledgable

Another impact that social media has had on our communication culture is that it seems to make everyone believe they are an expert on every topic. There's no question that this cannot possibly be true, but as fact and opinion have blurred, so too have the lines between expert and armchair expert.

Unless you are specifically communicating to a room of people with a great deal of humility, everything that comes out of your mouth will be subject to the audience making a snap judgement: yes or no. I agree or I disagree. And this will happen throughout your talk, not just at the end, once you've had a chance to make all your points.

As we know from company pitches, you are trying to avoid as many noes as you can, while trying to tease out the yeses in the room. Again, you won't be able to please everyone all the time, but unless you have real knowledge of what you speak, and are willing to share it, it will be difficult to persuade people that you are worth listening to over their objections.

The noes are more powerful than the yeses, and this often bedevils folks early in their public speaking career. Obviously, it would seem, you're trying to get to yes with as many people as possible. But this misses the point: in a first interaction, the goal should be to get as few noes as possible, frequently because the yeses can't be given outright.

For example, when you're leading a meeting at work, with your team and your executives, and you're trying to persuade the company to invest in a new product line or marketing approach. In that first meeting, you may not be able to get to yes with the executives immediately. They may need to discuss it in another meeting, look at budgets, and so on. But you know this, so in your conversation you focus on being knowledgable and patient, with an eye on your big picture goal.

You can also see the difference between truly knowledgable speakers and those with a house of cards connection to their material clearly on *Shark Tank*. Each one of the sharks asks questions or makes statements that position them as experts. The founders are profoundly unsure how to respond in many cases—should they argue, agree, pivot? Truly knowledgable founders, those who know their material, do not get flustered during Q&A, and are able to sell in most circumstances.

Accurate

While it may seem like it's enough to know your material and to be an expert in your subject matter, you must also be accurate. That is to say, you must speak the truth in your public communication and—at minimum—avoid ever telling a lie.

This is because almost every talk you'll give will be recorded. And with the ubiquity of technology, it's trivially easy for people to check up on what you've said. As soon as people find a single untruth in your dialogue, they will discount everything else you have to say.

This problem also often bedevils people new to persuasion or sales communications. When you're up in front of a prospective client (and even if you're giving a conference talk, the room is filled with prospective clients—either for you or your company) and they ask you a question about who's currently using your solution, don't lie. It doesn't take much effort for your prospect to pick up the phone or shoot an email to their friend at your other customer and ask them what's going on.

You may be tempted to exaggerate, to oversell, and to make yourself and your ideas seem bigger and more real than they are. I encourage some of this bluster, particularly in situations where you need to persuade people on a completely new idea. But your bluster must never result in an outright untruth, or you will simply unravel all the good work you put into things.

Economical

> *"The secret of being boring is to tell everything."*—Voltaire

If this era of distraction has taught us anything, it should be that people can—and will—change the channel at the drop of a hat. That is, creating even the slightest frisson of boredom will cause your intended audience to go do something else—whether on their devices or simply in their mind. And, with digital and virtual events, the problem is even more acute, as you frequently cannot tell if the audience is multitasking.

One of the main ways you accomplish effective persuasion in these times is to be economical. By saying less, and more efficiently, you ultimately say more.

In past history, overwrought and florid oratory had a positive, not negative effect. It made the speaker sound more intelligent and could convey a sense of intellectual mystery that gave everything else gravitas. Consider the famous opening line of Abraham Lincoln's Gettysburg Address:

> Four score and seven years ago, our fathers brought forth on this continent, a new nation, conceived in liberty, and dedicated to the proposition that all men are created equal.

It is beautiful and evocative text, but probably wouldn't work today because it is much too long and convoluted for audiences to follow raptly. The lack of economy in saying what he means to say here can only be negative, even if the words are perfect in and of themselves.

People appreciate the economy of language, which results in saved time and less chance of distraction. The length of a speech has continued to decline, as has the target length of a meeting (though there's no accounting for why meetings go on so darn long). The standard conference talk used to be closer to an hour, and with the influence of TED, social media, and distracting technologies, today's talk timing average is closer to twenty minutes, rather than sixty.

This is not to say that you can't be stylistic or that you should just get to your point immediately. In fact, this book advocates that you do precisely the opposite: discover and promote your personal style, and carefully structure how you get to your point for maximum effect. But that still requires a certain economy of language. Less is, as ever, more.

Exercise: I'm sure you have your own thoughts about how to rewrite the Gettysburg Address for today's audience. As a thought exercise, why not

Gettysburg Address: https://qrco.de/bczBoJ

rewrite it now the way you would say it for today's audiences and see how long it takes you to deliver the structure of his points.

Self-Aware

One of the most tiresome aspects of bad professional speakers is when they lack self-awareness. Someone who is low-energy pantomiming a high-energy person, or someone with a nonexistent sense of humor trying to tell jokes tends to fall flat, regardless of the context. This is why it is extremely important for every speaker to understand their own personality, skills, and orientation and bring that to the party.

In my work with aspiring public speakers, one of the first exercises I have them do is a little self-analysis process—considering their inherent skills and beliefs on vectors relevant to great communication.

I've identified four different quadrants for speaking styles that recur across the board: funny, serious, vulnerable, and academic.

Of course, these types are both in opposition to each other and complementary, so when thinking about yourself on this chart, I believe it's important to

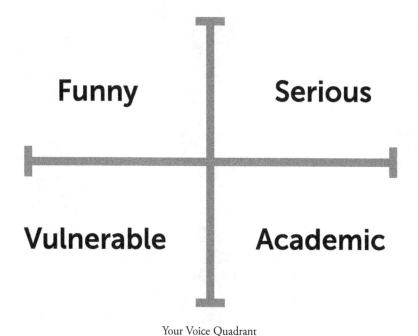

Your Voice Quadrant

consider each of the four characteristics independently and to place yourself on the grid where you feel you belong. For example, if you were in the dead center of the chart, your voice would be a perfect balance of the four dimensions.

This voice exercise is not exhaustive, and I don't represent it as a scientific approach to analyzing yourself. Rather, it's an opportunity for you to honestly reckon with what you've got going on, and create a "blue ocean" personal speaking style to maximize persuasiveness. If you're not funny, I don't want you to try to tell jokes. If you're not academic, lecturing may not be your best foot forward. Periodically in this process, I recommend that you reassess your self-identified skills and see how your finished speech, presentation, or pitch maps to how you see yourself. You just might find it shifts a little bit with practice.

Once you've brought together the core elements of persuasion and your voice, the next step in communicating beautifully is to have—and tell—a great story.

6

I Have the Best Stories

Act I

A BRIEF HISTORY OF STORYTELLING

Humans love stories. From the earliest human records, we find that story-telling—in all its forms—has been with us for as long as we've been human. In fact, cave drawings from two sites in France—Lascaux and Chauvet—appear to show visual storytelling as far back as thirty thousand years ago.[1]

Because the earliest forms of storytelling were visual and oral—rather than written—various conventions arose to help people remember what had just transpired. It is very difficult, after all, to go back to the beginning of an oral story and ask for character or plot clarification. So stories had to work in a semi-linear fashion before the written word—accounting for the rise and fall of the audience's emotional attachment.

No one ever really wrote down a guide to storytelling until the modern era, but by observing the patterns inherent in classic stories, such as *The Iliad* by Homer, or the Bible, we can see a kind of storytelling pattern emerging. By the time literature reaches the era of Shakespeare, these conventions had become de rigueur, amplified by the trend toward storytelling from the stage. The vast majority of Europeans at this time were still illiterate, so the oral conventions of storytelling worked well for the theatrical boom of the sixteenth and seventeenth centuries.

n.b. I recognize this is a very Eurocentric view of the history of storytelling, but it is the experience I'm steeped in. Other cultures have
developed their own unique story frames, and those deserve your understanding as well, especially if you're going to work there. That research
task however, falls to you.

Suddenly, storytelling was being "manufactured"—in the sense that theatrical
and published works were being created rapidly to satisfy the hunger of the
masses for entertainment. During roughly this same time, the novel emerged
in Western culture. Cervantes's *Don Quixote* (1605) is widely considered to be
the first novel in the West, and the first English novel was *Robinson Crusoe*,
in 1719.

As the Enlightenment spread and literacy increased, the number of theatrical and written stories exploded. Storytelling thus became a heralded profession that one could—with some financial success—make a living out of.

It is at the nexus of these conditions—the rise of literacy, the growth of
storytelling as a profession/industry, and a growing hunger/demand for stories
of all kinds—that we find the conventions of storytelling codified for students
and professionals alike. By creating a framework for stories that could be repeated and compared, the bards of their times could increase their output and
economic rewards.

Thus, in Western literature, the "common" story structure is born. Though
by no means exhaustive—many stories don't conform to this linearity—standard story structure is the amalgam of thousands of years of human storytelling and roughly breaks down into three discrete acts as follows:

Act I—The Challenge
Act II—The Hero's Journey
Act III—The Final Battle/Conclusion

Can you veer away from this structure? Absolutely. Nothing in the history
of story structure consigns you to follow it slavishly into the future. But by
understanding the foundations of storytelling, we can develop communication
that is both interesting and easy to parse/understand for our audiences. Just
like a playwright in the seventeenth century, you don't have much to lose by
understanding and following story structure.

The key is to adapt what we know of stories to professional communications.

THE PROTOTYPE TALK

To fully understand this chapter, it would be beneficial for you to watch Johann Hari's very powerful and influential TED Talk "Everything You Think You Know About Addiction Is Wrong," from 2015. You can view this and all the talks referenced in this book at:

Talks Reference List https://qrco.de/bczBoL

While you watch the talk, pay attention to the three acts. How does Hari set up the conflict in the beginning, how does he go on a journey to resolve it, and when does he shift into "final battle" mode to arrive at his main conclusion? More granularly: Does he announce the changing of the acts explicitly, or does he do it with tone, pauses, and pacing?

ACT I—THE CHALLENGE

The first act of any story sets up the challenge inherent in the piece. You will meet the protagonist and antagonist(s) and understand how they are going to be challenged to accomplish their goals. Though you may not understand all the issues and conflicts, before the conclusion of the first act, you undoubtedly know a great deal more about all the players and what you can expect.

From a professional communication standpoint, there are several best practices to be aware of and to pay close attention to.

The First 10 Seconds Are Crucial

Our attention spans are short and getting shorter. Even while you're giving a talk or making a key presentation or pitch, the lure of distraction is everywhere for your audience and we cannot depend on their undivided attention to ensure the success of our efforts. That is, we need to adapt to this reality rather than pretend it doesn't exist.

People are likely to start drawing conclusions about you from the moment you walk out onto the stage. For this reason, it's essential to take control of the narrative about you within the first 10 seconds.

This means adhering to a few critical rules of engagement.

First Impressions Matter

Because the audience will be judging you from the moment that they first see you on the stage or in the Zoom feed, it's crucial that you manage that first impression. The standard advice here would be to dress up in a suit and project the most professional appearance you can. But a lesson we can take from successful entrepreneurs—such as Steve Jobs—is that sometimes the optimal first impression isn't "business suit," even if the topic is hugely important financially. Though we'll talk about this in greater detail in a later chapter, it is essential that you look the part: if you're trying to convey nerdy technical knowledge, wear a turtleneck. If you're endeavoring to declare your athleticism, show off your body. Be the best version of whatever person will have the greatest credibility delivering the message.

Control the Narrative Before the Talk

In some settings—such as industry conferences—your first impression will begin prior to your appearance on stage. Often in those settings, your photo will be projected onto a screen at the front of the room and an MC will read a version of your bio to the audience. If you are being introduced by someone else, I highly recommend you sync up with that person prior to your talk. Ensure they are using the most up to date bio on you and that such a bio is short, concise, and presents only the most important highlights that are critical for you to get your message across.

I can't count how many times an MC will have my entire long-form bio in front of them to read before I get up on stage. Because I have significant professional history, publications, and awards, this long-form bio is looooong—and almost never appropriate for someone to read out loud. Be sure to have a short form of your bio ready to go (50 to 100 words) and always sign off on how your info is being presented to the room.

And it goes without saying—make sure your photo is attractive and professional, conveying the energy you want to project. Even if you don't have a lot of money to spend, you can get a professional headshot. If your company doesn't have a good one in the archives for you—I highly recommend getting one at your own expense and using those wherever appropriate. Understanding that your first impression may begin before you get up on stage can be crucial for creating trust and connection.

Do Not Waste Time

A common misconception proffered by old-school public speaking guides is to open with a joke or other comment before beginning your talk. This is almost never a good idea, and usually acts at cross purposes. If it makes you feel more comfortable making the transition from behind-the-scenes to the dais, I won't stop you from doing it. But because of the limited amount of time and attention that your audience is likely to offer, you are chewing up valuable first impression time. We'll talk about this throughout the book, but I also want to discourage you from telling jokes at the front end of your talk unless you're a very funny person and jokes are appropriate for the message you're trying to convey.

Even saying "thank you so much" to the MC wastes valuable time. In a more casual environment, it is perfectly natural and appropriate to thank the person who introduced you. But if you are in a high-pressure, high-stakes presentation, it's critical to stay focused on the power of your opening gambit in your material.

You would be better off opening directly to the establishing statement of your talk up front, and choosing which approach for this first statement is critical.

Trains—Planes—Rockets

I use a transportation metaphor to describe three different paces for opening gambits in presentations, roughly corresponding to how long it takes them to get up to speed. When thinking about the opening of your talk or pitch, consider not only the length of the overall session (shorter talks require more brevity, in general), but also the tone/approach/strategy you're pursuing.

Trains

A train—or "soft"—opener is designed to ease the audience into the conversation. Typically, this is a maximum of a 60-second "preamble" to your talk that is designed to accomplish one of three possible goals:

1. Charm the audience. If charm is a key component of your persona and what you're trying to convey, you might want to do a slow, charming introduction that lets the audience get to know you before they get stuck into the material you have to present. Brené Brown's "Power of Vulnerability" and Sir Ken Robinson's "Do Schools Kill Creativity?" TED Talks are good illustrations of when the speaker takes their time to establish rapport and convey their charm.

2. Win over a hostile audience. Though this scenario is rare in keynote speaker land, sometimes you have to give a talk to a relatively hostile audience. In business, this is more common—for example when bringing an idea to your management team that you know has already generated some push back—or even giving a presentation to investors to raise capital. A slower start may help the audience ease into your style before being confronted by what you have to say (and jumping to "no").

3. When you have time to kill. As a general rule, if you're blocked for any presentation longer than forty-five minutes without Q&A, you should consider giving that time back to the audience in the form of an early finish. But if you need to stretch your content to an expected minimum talk length, the preamble can be a good place to add a minute or two of extra content that pads your talk.

Typically, as in the talks from Brown and Robinson referenced above, this will begin with an anecdote or story that connects the audience to the material or the speaker. For example, if something recently happened in the real world that reinforces your point, this may be a good time to share it. ("I was walking down the street on my way here and . . .")

If you're not familiar with her oeuvre, check out Abraham Hicks's lectures on the law of attraction, all over YouTube or Spotify. She sometimes uses a personal anecdote to begin her answer to an attendee's question, helping the listener understand the concrete example underlying her theory.

Planes

The plane type of opener usually takes around 10 to 15 seconds, and sets up a contextual case for the talk to come in the form of "let me tell you about . . ." Two TED Talks that exemplify this are Julian Treasure's "How to Speak So That People Want to Listen" and Chimamanda Ngozi Adichie's "The Danger of a Single Story."

The latter, in her breathtakingly great talk from 2009, opens by stating that she is a storyteller, and her intention for the talk is to describe the problem with single-story perspectives.

Generally speaking, there are three scenarios under which you want to use this form of opening:

1. Establishing authority. Sometimes you want to have your bona fides established up front. Obviously, this isn't necessary if you're being introduced, and generally speaking most event organizers will conclude that the audience has already read your bio prior to your talk. But in situations where that credibility is crucial to getting the audience to listen to you, this can be very valuable. In Adichie's TED Talk referenced above, she begins by explaining that she is a storyteller. I've often seen this used to great effect when doing company pitches, in the form of "I'd been a chemical engineer for twenty plus years and suddenly I realized that . . ." It's a subtle/not-so-subtle way of reinforcing for the audience that you know what you're talking about, and may help pave the way for greater confidence in your material.

2. Shifting context. In some talks, you will be following someone with a radically different subject. Imagine hearing a lecture on the power of vulnerability followed immediately by one about the future of clean nuclear power. The transition would be so bumpy as to throw off the audience's ability to context shift from one topic to another. This is frequently true of pitch competitions as well, where company after company give 3- to 5-minute pitches, often from thoroughly different domains. A plane-type opener works here to shift everyone's sense of what's coming next.

3. Literary work. Generally speaking, if your presentation is about something you've written, created, or performed elsewhere, you may want to take some extra time to build up to the points you're endeavoring to make. Do this by contextualizing your content for the audience to view as a whole, rather than just the specific topic you're covering right then.

In any case, the plane type of opener can be useful for many different contexts, but one should nonetheless consider the downside: that it still takes the first chunk of the audience's attention away from the material of your talk to an establishing premise. If you want to jump right into the modern audience's attention as quickly as possible, a rocketship opener is for you.

Rocketships

Rocketship talk openers are exactly what they sound like: opening gambits that move very quickly to gain altitude and present their most dramatic side first. A rocketship opener can be said to establish the conflict immediately, and to engage users with a provocative statement or idea right off the bat. In literature, examples such as Dickens's famous opening line of *A Tale of Two Cities*—"It was the best of times, it was the worst of times"—gives you the flavor of a rocketship opening, and have become iconic in their own right.

Indeed, if you look at the fifty most popular speeches of all time (particularly in the TED-type domain), you'll see that the majority use rocketship openers. Often, the speakers will open with a single, provocative question designed to jolt the audience out of its complacency or stupor, and to immediately pull focus to what they have to say. The talk referenced at the beginning of this chapter (Johann Hari's) is joined by other super popular reference speeches, such as Jill Bolte Taylor's "My Stroke of Insight" or Simon Sinek's iconic "How Great Leaders Inspire Action."

In each, you'll see that the first words out of the speaker's mouth immediately establish a mildly shocking provocation that the audience probably doesn't see coming. So when should we use the rocketship opener?

1. Any talk that is under 30 minutes. If you are giving a talk blocked under 30 minutes, I want to encourage you to think about the rocketship as the best approach to opening. Don't waste any time setting up the scene, just get right into it. You'll be glad to have conserved every minute available. And if you are doing a 3-minute pitch, a tight and concise opener becomes all the more critical.

2. Big picture talks. If your talk is designed to present a big picture thought—something perhaps inspiring and oriented toward generating action, motivation, and excitement in the audience, the rocketship opener will add emotional heft to your point and clearly signal the kind of ride that attendees are in for.

3. Always, if you can. It's probably not surprising that I have a strong penchant for the rocketship opener, though I have used all three kinds at different times. The rocketship however is the most consistent with the frameworks of the A-Ha! Method, and—I believe—the realities of the audience's attention span. There is rarely a downside to grabbing the audience's attention right off the bat, and mostly upside to doing so.

Because rocketship talks focus heavily on the provocation presented by their speakers, it's also important to observe a few critical rules about those provocations to ensure you don't take it too far. And remember: the provocation can be used in any style of opener, but has its greatest impact if you hit hard with it.

Provocations

The core tension of your presentation, as expressed in your provocative opening statement, isn't a throwaway. In fact, the intensity and clarity of this provocation and framing is among the biggest determinants in how successful your presentation will seem to have been with the audience.

So what is a talk's provocation? Generally speaking, this is the point that the whole talk hinges on, and is usually in the form of something that *is, has, or should have happened.* The corollary to this is that there is something wrong with the way in which these things happen today that requires fixing.

In every company pitch, this is the essential tension: that there is a consumer or business behavior or process that exists today that could be made much better, or a future vision of something we should have as a society, but need leaps in technology to accomplish. Though it may be obvious that a VC would want to invest in something that promises a better future, I'm also here to tell you that most kinds of professional communications are improved by understanding and framing what they have to say in this way. It is not merely your job to present the facts as they are—this isn't a courtroom—but rather to persuade or influence the audience to do—or not do—something.

n.b. Trial lawyers, of course, also do this.

So if you think about it in this way, as a general rule, we want most of our provocations to paint a picture of a better future that can be ours if we . . . do what you're suggesting.

But provocations can easily be taken too far. First and foremost, anything you suggest in the opener must be resolved by the end. Setting up a conflict that ultimately isn't resolved will not do you any favors, and audiences may feel cheated, disturbed, or conflicted about what you have presented.

In the competitive cooking reality TV show, *Top Chef*, one of the most common ways for contestants to fail a challenge is to present their dish's title—for example, "Duck Three Ways"—but to have only plated two ways. If they simply reframed their dish as duck two ways, the judges would have compared the finished product against the setup.

Or consider a startup pitch for fundraising. The first slide/part of a pitch is typically the establishment of the problem, for example, "Gas is too expensive." Now if the rest of the talk is about your idea for the use of psilocybin in treating depression, no matter how good your talk, your prospective investors are likely to rate you poorly. You get to set up the problem, but whatever you say will be the context that you'll be compared against—and in turn, the problem must be resolved by the end.

To be sure, sometimes audiences will disagree with the fundamental premise of the talk in the first place—and challenge the problem laid out up front. But if you experience this kind of push back on the regular, you'd be well advised to reimagine the problem definition so that it's more consistent with what the audience can tolerate, and then take them to another level entirely by proposing an even bigger outcome.

Lastly, when considering your opening provocation, it's generally good practice to not directly insult your audience. If you're speaking to a room full of insurance adjusters, it might be a good idea to not begin with the statement "insurance is a scam," even if that would get you maximum attention (and probably a lifetime ban from their conferences). One of the first lessons in stand-up comedy school is to not directly insult the audience, or you tend to lose them. You can insult another group, or provoke a particular reaction, but a straightforward insult is rarely smart.

Once you lose the audience, it's exceedingly difficult to get them back where you want them.

The Fourth Wall

The fourth wall is a reference to the relationship between a performer and their audience. If you think of a theater stage as having three walls—back, left, and right—the fourth wall is the invisible barrier at the front of the stage, separating the audience from the players. When someone has "broken the fourth wall," they have brought the audience's attention to the fact that they are performing for them on stage, rather than re-enacting something that is meant to be a world in and of itself.

The corollary—and goal of most performance—is to create a world that you briefly forget isn't real—or what's called *suspension of disbelief.* The same is true of public speaking and professional communication, though usually on a less prosaic level than the theatre. Once we establish the provocation (or problem we're trying to solve) in the opener, it's essential that everything from that point onward live inside the world we're claiming exists.

The most common ways that speakers break the fourth wall involve referencing the hosts, other speakers, or a circumstance happening in real life. Later in this book we'll discuss in greater detail how to prevent yourself from responding to audience distractions, but an example of this fourth wall might be instructive.

Recently, I gave a speech in Mexico City at an industry event that was taking place in a big convention hall. The organizers had decided that everything would be in one big room—the stage and presenters, the expo floor, and the dining area. Things were separated a bit, to be sure—but we were still in one giant room.

I got up on stage to present around 1p.m. The audience was wearing headphones, to both facilitate translation and to block out the relentless din of a trade show floor running just behind them. About 5 minutes into my talk, a mariachi band—at full volume—began to play in the dining area approximately twenty-five yards from where I was performing. I noticed that the audience could hear—despite the earpieces—that there was some disturbance going on, and a couple of attendees briefly removed their headsets to see what the fuss was all about.

I had a choice to make in that moment about whether I'd call attention to the mariachi band playing in the room. It could have been humorous or frustrating, but either way—I'd be calling the audience's attention to what was happening in the room. Ultimately, I resisted the temptation, and made a little joke about it during the Q&A, once the talk was completed. Had I said something about it directly, I'd have been breaking the fourth wall.

Even without a technical disruption, speakers tend to break the fourth wall during Act I by making reference to the other speakers, the hosts, or a circumstance related to the conference. That is, they are bringing the audience's attention to something that is explicitly *not* the talk they are giving. Though it may seem impersonal to not thank the MC or speaker who came before you, I highly recommend avoiding this as much as possible to allow your audience the full range of suspension of disbelief during your presentation.

Even thanking the audience for having you—and I've been guilty of doing this dozens of times—wastes attention and affection on something that is fundamentally irrelevant.

The Rah-Rah Exception

So are there times when breaking the fourth wall is warranted in a speech, pitch, or meeting? The one exception—and I present it with significant qualifications—is when you want to get the audience ramped up. For example:

"How are you doing, Peoria?" Followed by, "I can't hear you, I said how are you doing, Peoria?"

This convention, borrowed I think from rock concerts, is usually done by the speaker at the beginning of their talk. However, if you've been to many rock concerts, you'll immediately recognize that the performers usually do this—if they're inclined to at all—after the first song or two. More sophisticated performers will also recognize that there's no need to amp an audience up if their energy is already quite high—such as at the beginning of the first day of an event, or right before a much-anticipated person's keynote. Adding energy then is a waste of an opportunity to engage with the audience.

Expert MCs generally do this audience amping when they see the energy in the room begin to flag. The scenario I've most often seen is right after lunch, when audiences tend to get sleepy and lethargic after eating all those delicious cellophane-wrapped sandwiches or fists of chicken.

But therein lies the rub, it is really the province of the MC to take care of this for you. The best convention is that when the MC hands the audience over to the next person, viewers are receptive to what the next performer has to say. Watch an expert at a comedy show do this, and you'll see exactly what's meant. The MC closes the previous session, engages in a transition, brings the energy up (or down if needed), and hands off to the next person. So unless you are the MC, this really isn't your job.

However, sometimes it is left to the speaker—either because the organizers haven't thought this through or because they simply didn't pay attention to the room's energy. We'll talk more about semi-conscious crowd assessments later in the book, but go with your gut. If you think the audience is flagging (again, consider time of day and prior activities) and the MC/host hasn't done a good job of getting them excited, you can deploy a tactic to build some energy.

I'd recommend against using the Peoria example above unless you're in Peoria. But you can certainly try various approaches, such as:

- Asking the audience to stand up and shake off their lethargy: "OK, can I ask everyone in the room to stand up for a second? Let's get the blood flowing . . ."
- Asking the audience to yell out the answer to a question or two: "OK, before we get started, I'd love to hear from you what your favorite event so far from the conference has been."
- Playing a short game such as: "OK, everyone please stand. Now, I want you to sit down if you've never eaten a bug before."

Now that I've mentioned these, you're probably thinking back to some comedy show or other event where a speaker used one of these conventions. And—in fact—as we'll discuss, there are lots of things to learn from comedians about how to engage audiences (even if you're not funny). In comedy circles, another strategy is to use *crowd work*—that is, asking some members of the audience questions and bantering with them. Unless you're a skilled comedian—and know how to control the A/V to make this work—I recommend against doing direct crowd engagement one on one. But the other strategies can be effective.

Now you know, it's all about changing the energy in the talk. Though we want to maximize the chances that the audience will be excited by what you have to say, it may be necessary for you to use some of your precious upfront time to work on their energy. It goes without saying, however, that this needs to happen at the very beginning—breaking the fourth wall 20 minutes into your talk to do a bit of audience rah-rah generally isn't a good look. And as we'll discuss later, asking the audience to do anything is fraught.

For now, add this to your arsenal of tips and tricks, and be prepared to take matters into your own hands, if needed.

Referencing Other Speakers

As a general rule, you should probably not reference other speakers that have gone before you, unless there is some specific tie-in to a previous talk that you'd like to make. The problems with doing this are many, including wasting your precious engagement time, distracting the audience from what you want them to be excited about (you!), or even provoking questions from audience members (or future video viewers) that didn't see the aforementioned talk.

Most often, when I've seen a previous speaker referenced, it's to either establish agreement with something they said or to disagree with the same. As a general rule—and we'll discuss this in the section on being a good panel guest—vociferous agreement is wasted energy. No one cares about something that everyone agrees on. It is disagreement that is the engine of compelling stories.

The converse is equally problematic. If you invite conflict with another speaker in the first few moments of your talk, you're also ceding some important ground in the problem-solution setup we discussed earlier: you'll allow the previous speaker's point to pollute your world building. That is, the audience will now tie together what they said and what you're saying to try to create a composite assessment of the situation. You're diluting your authority and points, and should generally avoid this if possible.

Are there some scenarios where it's worth calling out previous speakers? I remember once giving a talk at a major European tech conference where the organizers had programmed a talk with a similar topic—but a different conclusion—right before mine. As I watched from the wings with dread, the previous speaker made many of the same foundational points I was trying to make, stealing the thunder of the first act of my talk.

Because I'm a good extemporaneous speaker (a skill you can learn), and I know my material (something you must master), when I got up on stage, I started by referencing the previous speaker, complemented her thought process, and launched into my talk a bit further down the timeline, picking up at a point in her discussion and moving forward. I didn't need to repeat what she had already said, but also didn't want to leave future viewers in the dark, so I summarized her (and indeed my) opening gambit, and then moved forward full speed ahead.

I think of this scenario as having an inevitable need to reference other speakers. This will come up anytime there are two people programmed on the same topic, or where you have a significant disagreement with a prior speaker about a topic of great importance. You might—especially if you're in academic circles—even get called out directly for making points that someone else doesn't agree with. However you may feel about this, I want to recommend that you not reference other speakers. Let them to do that work and waste their time name-checking you.

Establishing Vulnerability

Before we move on to setting up the scenes and conflict in Act I, there is a further point about tone that needs to be addressed at the beginning: vulnerability. I've made reference to Brené Brown's work on the topic, and her blockbuster TED Talk about the same, and hopefully by now you've watched it (or read her books) and understand the basics about vulnerability and its place in the discourse.

Generally speaking, if you're going to be vulnerable in a talk, pitch, or meeting, you'd be well served to bring this into your opening gambit. Let the audience know up front that you are going to be baring your soul and treading on topics that might be a bit sensitive for you (and, likely, them). By doing this at the beginning, you will elicit empathy from the audience, and are likely to temper any harsh judgement you might otherwise receive for your assertions.

For example, if an entrepreneur with cerebral palsy is getting up on stage to pitch their company for funding, ignoring their CP is a counterproductive strategy. It would be better to highlight it up front, without connecting the dots about how obviously heroic it is that you've gotten to this point in your career despite the obstacles. You can let the audience draw their own conclusions, but you *should* help them understand what they're seeing, and take advantage of whatever empathy they can muster. It will only help you be successful.

In my TEDx Talk about failure, I opened by making a small, on-topic, joke about coming out of the closet as a gay man. The context was to establish that I was about to come out of the closet about other things (my failures), but also to connect with the audience and to build a world in which I'm being open about the most vulnerable sides of my journey. Coming out at the start of your talk may not be appropriate if you don't have something to express along those lines, but if you can connect the dots between what you have to say and some part of your individual experiences and challenges you've faced, you will improve your connection with the audience for sure.

Now, I'm sure some of you reading this are thinking about ways you can insert "fake" vulnerability into your talks/pitches to improve your chances of success. I want to encourage you not to think about vulnerability as a tactic but, rather, as a context for connecting with the audience. As we'll discuss in a later chapter, the important thing about being successful with finding and elevating your voice in public speaking is to be truly authentic to yourself. That is, if you're a highly emotional and vulnerable person, now's as good a time as any to embrace that. Conversely, if you're highly analytical and eschew emotionality, don't try to pretend you're an empath. Work with what you have, and present the best possible version of yourself to the audience.

If you are going to pursue some amount of vulnerability and bring it to the fore in Act I, remember this important rule: you'll need to weave it throughout the piece and circle back to whatever challenging emotional state you lead with to help create a resolution for the audience. That is, if the talk begins vulnerably, it needs to maintain that emotional energy throughout. This is another endorsement for authenticity, as it might be possible to make a small play for a vulnerable state at the beginning, but it's an entirely different thing to make that work over 30 to 45 minutes. Stay in your lane.

SCENES AND CONFLICT

The heart of Act I is the scene you present and the conflict you highlight (and ultimately, resolve). To create the best opening third of your presentation, it is important to focus on setting scenes and managing conflict to achieve your ends.

Scene Setting

There's a reason why "It was a dark and stormy night," the opening line of *A Wrinkle in Time*, is so iconic (and derided). It uses overly florid and melodramatic language to convey a melancholic opener to the novel. At the same time, it's memorable and highly effective at evoking the image of a dark and stormy night and the novel's context.

Rather than suggest you find a single statement that sets the scene perfectly, I want to encourage you to set the scene as economically and assertively as possible. Again, I'll reference Johann Hari's excellent TED Talk as a perfect distillation of this idea:

> One of my earliest memories is of trying to wake up one of my relatives and not being able to. And I was just a little kid, so I didn't really understand why, but as I got older, I realized we had drug addiction in my family, including, later, cocaine addiction.

In a few short seconds, Hari has created a visual/empathetic reference (being a young child unable to rouse an adult and how frightening that must have been), and a contextual statement about how and why we find him leading this charge in his life now. The crucial detail is that it is quick, it contains just enough context and visuals to elicit a desired response in the viewer, establishes empathy with the speaker, and frames the conflict—we know he's going to want to try and do something about the addiction that is plaguing his family. In short, this is a nearly perfect opening for this kind of talk, and while I don't expect you to be able to replicate this right out of the gate—and indeed it's not appropriate for every form of professional communication—it is instructive to understand both the economy and impact of his language.

So when you're thinking about the opening scene, it's worthwhile asking yourself a set of questions that might help you focus on what you should be saying to your audience:

1. Who am I and what is my relationship to this story?
2. Where are we and when is this taking place?
3. Why do I feel compelled to tell you this today?

Crucially, I recommend against spending a lot of energy setting a deep visual reference a la *A Wrinkle in Time*, unless your talk has a strong visual component. Rather, set the visuals in the context of the human story or connection you're trying to make, as in Hari's establishment of finding drug addiction as a young child.

A tendency of many speakers in this context is to try to use the slides to support the scene setting by employing visuals that will add flavor to the statements being made. This is the classic way to use slides, and a good idea here. However, don't feel the need to make the slides a literal interpretation of the story—and don't feel compelled to even have slides at all. If you're making a very emotional appeal in the first 60 seconds, you might find that *not* putting up a slide will actually make it easier for your audience to relate to you—and for you to deliver your material. A lot of this depends on your comfort level and what you're trying to say, but the bottom line is that, in this case—as in most—slides support what you say, not the other way around.

And crucially, don't do any scene or conflict setting that goes beyond the absolute minimum you need to do in order to establish your connection and bona fides to the subject matter. Again, notice the economy of Hari's language above. He could have added more detail ("I remember crying that my uncle wouldn't wake up and the wail of the sirens as the ambulance came to get him"), but unless that additional detail helps make the point he's trying to convey, it doesn't serve a purpose. You don't need to beat the audience over the head with the emotions you want them to experience. Rather, you want to do as little as you can—as authentically as possible—to provoke the reaction you need to tell your story.

The Conflict

Compelling content requires conflict. Even if you are loath to endorse conflict for conflict's sake—especially given our fraught political climate—I hope you can nonetheless understand why it's important for advancing understanding and connection with audiences. First and foremost, agreement is bland—if everyone agrees something is true, why would I want to spend 45 minutes hearing about it? Second, it is through the process of conflict that we learn the most about ourselves and others, weighing and considering differing viewpoints until an answer becomes clear.

Whatever your goals with your professional communication—it's imperative that you find the conflict so that you can connect with the audience and then resolve it. Moreover, the faster you get to the conflict of your presentation, the more likely your audience is to want to follow you through the rabbit hole, if only to see how the conflict is resolved.

Therefore, it's imperative to set up the conflict in your presentation within the first 60 seconds, if possible, though in some slower presentations a bit more exposition is fine.

There are many different kinds of conflicts, but as a general rule, your content will probably hinge on one of these:

1. Conflict between or among people (including with yourself)
2. Conflict between people and the natural world
3. Conflict between ideas
4. Conflict between inertia and progress

In company pitch best practice, founders are taught to begin with a tight explanation of the "problem" they are going to solve. So for example, the first minute and slide of a talk might set up this problem:

People want to buy electric cars but are worried about their ability to recharge, so they keep buying gas cars.

When coaching entrepreneurs and executives on making pitches, we often spend a great deal of time right on this point, working furiously to get it as concise and relevant as possible. Because everything flows from this problem definition, it's critical to get it right (and then to resolve it). Though in pitches we're trying to be as explicit, clear, and jargon-free as possible, this may not exactly apply to other kinds of presentations you may be working on.

For example, if you're giving a talk to your local church group about how to attract new followers to your ministry, saying something like "we don't have enough followers and need to attract more," is less a statement of the conflict, and more the title of your talk. The conflict needs to be expressed in a way that sets up the potential for resolution. So, in the church example, some better conflict definitions might be:

- People say they want meaning in their lives, but don't seem interested in our church's teachings, despite our focus on meaning. What are we doing wrong?
- A large share of our new parishioners only come to a single event before deciding not to return. What can we do to change this and keep them for longer?

You'll notice in both cases that I made a statement of fact followed by a question. This is a very common convention for problem/conflict statements, especially if the cause (perhaps not the solution) to the issue is already understood. Commonly, this means that problems centered around access, pricing, usability, and so on. will require a follow-up question to clearly elucidate what you're focused on for the purposes of this talk.

If the problem is more around mindset or organizational readiness, as in "what do we need to do in our company to adapt to the AI-centric future of work?" it can also be beneficial to elaborate on some of the mental blocks that prevent the answers from being obvious—though these may not fit in the terse problem definition. And if the conflict you're trying to raise is somewhere far in the future—or about a culture your audience may not understand well— you may need to relate the conflict to something happening now/more urgent. In every case, personalizing the conflict in your terms will help the audience understand it.

Let's continue with Johann Hari's example for establishing the conflict. After having set the scene and provided some context for why this was important, at 40 seconds into the talk, Hari says this:

> And I realized there were loads of incredibly basic questions I just didn't know the answer to, like, what really causes addiction? Why do we carry on with this approach that doesn't seem to be working, and is there a better way out there that we could try instead?

Here he asks three very provocative questions, each of which are obviously important and not easily answerable by the audience immediately after hearing them. They setup the conflict of the entire talk, and he spends the rest of his time answering these questions.

Not What They Already Know

As early as high school presentations, most of us are taught to lay out some of the assumptions or biases whenever pursuing a hypothesis. These form a framework for the listener to consider the validity of what you're about to say next. Unfortunately, in most forms of persuasive professional communication, these biases can lead to a kind of audience boredom.

That is, if there's something the audience is already likely to know, it's critical that you not repeat it, or spend too much time elaborating on the importance/factuality of the point itself. For example, if you're giving the aforementioned presentation about EVs (electric vehicles) to a room full of auto sales people, it will not serve you well to present them with a litany of "this is what the buyer is thinking" statements to support the problem definition. If you have some survey data that is different from their lived experience, you might be able to bring this to bear in order to frame the conversation using the same data set.

If you are trying to persuade, you'd be well advised to steer away from any statement that can be prefaced with: "You probably already know this, but . . ." The reasons for this are obvious, and in the statement itself. If I already know it, why are you wasting my time with it? It also can leave audiences feeling like you are a newcomer to the topic or don't really understand the nuance, since you're having to restate things that are as obvious to them as the fact that the sun will rise tomorrow in the East. A good rule of thumb is that if you think this is something the audience has heard before, they probably have.

Before you go off on a mental tangent about the stupidity of the general population, it bears pointing out that when it comes to professional communications, it's usually a good idea to play to the top of your intelligence. As we'll explore later in this book, this is also a core tenet of improvisational theater—and reflects an understanding that, despite what Fox News might have you believe—smart is persuasive. People want credible expertise when navigating a tough or important topic.

Knowing as much as you can about the audience can only help you here. However, if you think there might be an asymmetry in the viewer's understanding of facts, you may want to consider putting a couple of them in the problem definition. I'd suggest framing them as "did you know?" or "most people believe, but . . ." statements to help create and maintain interest—even among the experts in the room.

What-If versus Why Questions

In Hari's example, the conflict hinges on a series of questions that really boil down to "why are things this way?" This is arguably the best kind of high-level or strategic way of presenting ideas. Why questions often elicit deeper thought processes among audiences, and can be a useful way to address a big, broad topic. Hari doesn't tell us up front what the answer is, but we can glean from the title and opening questions that the answer is going to surprise us.

But sometimes you can't use a why question—and instead have to go with a "what if" question as the heart of your conflict. In fact, most talks have a clear-cut choice of which way to go that is entirely up to the speaker to decide. So decide we shall.

What-if conflict statements are best if you want to provoke the audience into thinking about how the future world can be different from the one they inhabit today. It invites a broader thought process and allows the listener to open their own "world" and occupy it without needing to be exclusively constrained to the reality of the present day.

When to use each is up to you, but invariably your conflict—and the impact of your first Act, hinge largely on how well this statement is set up, the emotional impact of said conflict, and the audience's interest in accompanying the hero (you) on your journey of discovery.

THE INFLECTION POINT

After setting up the conflict, it is imperative that you also elaborate on the inflection point that prompted you to pursue an answer to the challenge you just proposed. That is to say, the audience likely wants to know why you care so much to pursue it, and how you approached that pursuit.

Common conventions include:

- So I decided to do some research.
- So I decided to devote my life to finding out this answer.
- So I decided to create an experiment.

This inflection point is the moment in the story where the hero decides to set off down the road to find the answers they seek. In the *Wizard of Oz*, it's when Dorothy decides to follow the yellow brick road that Act II begins. Before this moment, we need to know what her conflict is and why, but the inflection point tells us that a journey is about to begin.

And the journey is often as important as the destination—especially if you're covering topics that require a great deal of inquiry or are highly subjective/confrontational. The audience wants to understand how you arrived at the conclusions you are invariably going to offer, and they will rate the quality of the results at least partially on how much they respect your approach to the process you took.

So they need to be let into how you approached the problem and why. The inflection point marks the end of Act I and the beginning of Act II in most stories. It is generally the transition statement between the problem and the solution.

7

The Journey and Battle

Acts II and III

ACT II—THE JOURNEY

Once the hero (you) sets off on the journey of discovery in Act II, the action in the presentation shifts from problem-solution setup to the meat of the piece: What do you know that others don't, how can you prove it, what do you want us to learn?

It's now that the old-school conception of how to make an argument comes into play. At the close of the first act, we ended with a hypothesis—whether framed as a question or a statement. Now we need to validate or disprove the hypothesis with the facts and the best arguments you have. These can be summarized as points and counterpoints.

Structuring the Journey with A-Ha!

Before we begin, one quick note about structuring Act II/The Journey using the A-Ha! Method. It's important to remember that the goal is not to overload the audience with facts and arguments. They will not be able to process, remember, or even pay attention to all the reasons why you are right (or the right person to lead this charge). After setting up the problem in a tense way in Act I, you need Act II to be economical, and to not beat the audience over the head with your knowledge.

Also remember your timing—if you only have 15 minutes overall to deliver the presentation, it's important to leave enough time for the emotional peaks and valleys of Act II to generate those A-Ha! Moments in the viewer. Though

I argue for the rule of three below, it may be true that in shorter presentations you'll need to consign yourself to a maximum of two A-Ha! Moments in this section to avoid overwhelming the viewer. If you have more time, you can probably get away with structuring each of the points as an A-Ha! Moment.

The Rule of Three

In the most common types of presentations, this means no more than three arguments should be made with supporting points. In comedy or script writing, creators often refer to the "rule of three" for something to be maximally impactful and funny. This means the character, situations or plot points come in sets of three. Though not based on any science that I know of, the received wisdom of this approach should not be taken lightly, and does comport with our understanding of the human capacity for knowledge acquisition and synthesis. Try to keep your arguments to three, wherever possible.

I would go so far as to say that if you only have two good arguments, stretch your understanding and push for a third to include in the presentation, even if the third is something of a throwaway or a counterpoint.

In company and product pitches as well, Act II is usually comprised of three overarching points:

1. This is the right market.
2. This is the right product.
3. This is the right team.

Though there may (and usually are) several slides explaining these points, they form the foundation of the argument you're making that your audience should believe or invest in you. Think of them as subheadings that may be supported by several smaller points below, but roll up ultimately to the audience saying, "yes, I believe in them," or, "yes, I feel this way."

Making Points

As with everything else in great professional communication, you need to ensure your language is as economical as possible when making points. This does not mean that you can't embellish or consider the visualization of the arguments you're making. Rather, this means that you should generally not spend more time or words on a point than what is absolutely necessary for emotional clarity and connection with the audience.

Let's look again at Johann Hari's talk referenced in the previous chapter. Act I ends around 1 minute in, when Hari indicates that he is going to go on a journey to discover the truth about addiction. The points he makes in Act II can be distilled as follows:

1. We believe that just by using drugs you are likely to become an addict. But there are several examples that disprove that idea, including accident victims and their addiction rates post-morphine.
2. The original drug studies were flawed, perhaps because they ignored social context or connection. The Rat Park example shows different behavior if addicts have social outlets and opportunities.
3. Can this be implemented in a way to help addicts re-establish connection rather than punish them? Portugal provides an example.

Hari has the benefit of being an author and a journalist when he sets out to make his arguments, knowing what he does about story structure. But you will also notice if you watch the talk that he includes several audience-participation "thought experiments" to help the viewer personalize the information he's providing. He asks people to imagine getting into an accident, filling water bottles with vodka, and the implications of not having their smartphones. For each point, he connects it to the audience with an example to ensure that even people with low levels of empathy will be able to understand the material.

In a strict understanding of the economy of language, these extra layers of meaning-making wouldn't be necessary. He could make his points as dryly and impassively as he wanted to, delivering the material in a straightforward way.

But—and this is critical to understand here—his entire speech is about fostering more empathy, love, and understanding for addicts to bring them back into the fold of a society and social structures that are supportive and caring. He'll get to more of that in the final act, but in this moment it's critical for him to develop as much empathy as possible to make his final point work.

The Dangers of Prescriptive Statements or Questions

As you can probably tell from my use of Hari's talk throughout these chapters, I think this is an excellent presentation. Perhaps one of my favorites of all time because of its clarity, structure, and impeccably authentic delivery. But I don't agree with everything Hari does in the speech, and his crowd work is probably our greatest divergence.

As a general rule, it's a bad idea in my experience to ask the audience to imagine something through the prism of "you do this" or "you feel this way"—that is, prescriptive rather than proscriptive. As I've learned from many years in the startup pitch world, it's often true that the people in the audience don't have a shared experience, or come to a particular topic with a strong, preexisting bias.

For example, asking a room full of venture capitalists (or VCs for short) questions like:

"Have you ever had trouble making your mortgage payments?"
"Imagine you've just been released from prison after serving twenty years."
"Is capitalism working well?"

Each one of those questions will provoke a vastly different answer depending on who's in the audience. VCs, in particular, are unlikely to have trouble making mortgage payments, to have been imprisoned for a long time, or to disagree with the efficacy of capitalism. By setting up these questions/ statements to have yes or no answers, you are creating the space for "no" to emerge in the audience's mind. And as a general rule, getting noes in a persuasive presentation or pitch is a bad idea. The more hostile feelings and emotions your audience has, the less likely they are to agree with you, rate you highly, or give you what you want. You want to court controversy but approach it from a different angle.

So let's take one of Hari's audience empathy arguments as an example. In this paragraph he's talking about the need for connection to combat addiction, and attempting to make the audience really feel their privilege as compared to the as-yet-undefined addict:

And at first, I found this quite a difficult thing to get my head around, but one way that helped me to think about it is, I can see, I've got over by my seat a bottle of water, right? I'm looking at lots of you, and lots of you have bottles of water with you. Forget the drugs. Forget the drug war. Totally legally, all of those bottles of water could be bottles of vodka, right? We could all be getting drunk—I might after this—[laughter]—but we're not. Now, because you've been able to afford the approximately gazillion pounds that it costs to get into a TED Talk, I'm guessing you guys could afford to be drinking vodka for the next six months. You wouldn't end up homeless. You're not going to do that, and the reason you're not going to do that is not because anyone's stopping you. It's because you've got bonds and connections that you want to be present for. You've got work you love. You've got people you love. You've got healthy relationships. And a core part of addiction, I came to think, and I believe the evidence suggests, is about not being able to bear to be present in your life.[1]

In this paragraph he makes several assumptions about the audience and puts them out there. Let's take a closer look:

- We could all be getting drunk now, but we're not.
- You can afford an expensive TED ticket, so you can afford lots of vodka.
- You won't end up homeless.
- No one is stopping you from this alcoholic—homeless slide.
- You aren't an addict because you have bonds, work, and people you love.
- Your relationships are healthy.
- You can be present in your life, whereas others can't.

Now those are quite a few assumptions. Without knowing precisely who's in the audience, it's hard to estimate how many of the several hundred people in the room, or the more than fifteen million video viewers might have disagreed with one or more of his points. Perhaps they are, in fact, drinking right at that very moment—or they have a problem with alcohol already. Maybe they are not, in fact, well integrated into their social lives, or don't feel especially loved. Perhaps they are under another's care (e.g., a teenager) or have trouble being present due to various factors.

Now there's nothing wrong with making assumptions or even courting controversy with your audience. I've advocated for that sporadically throughout this book. But I want to caution you against using confrontational devices with the audience's sense of self unless they are really useful. More often than not, these same assumptive "pokes" can be reframed in a more universal way without reducing any of their heft.

For example, instead of making the point that "you can afford a TED ticket so you can afford lots of vodka," it might be better to say something like "vodka is not especially expensive, and throughout the world, even people of few means—who could not afford a TED ticket—would be able to afford enough vodka to get plastered daily. In fact, in places like Russia, vodka is often cheaper than clean water."

Obviously, my restating has a certain florid quality—I added several context points (Russia, the TED ticket's cost) that are not explicitly necessary, but this is how I might have made the point of talking about the same topic to this audience at that time. I'm saying the same thing as Hari without poking the audience with a stick that invites them to question whether or not they fit the assumptions made by the speaker.

Particularly in talks that are more pitch or fundraising in nature, it's critical to avoid these kinds of confrontations with the audience, but comedians will tell you the same thing when asked. If they want to poke the audience, they'll soften the statements with modifiers like, "I know some of you . . ," or "I'm sure many of you have experienced . . ." or "you know that thing when?" Each of these accomplishes the same purpose as the accusatory form without risking the audience's disconnection from you. Wherever possible, try to heed this subtle but important difference.

Interestingness

In almost any presentation you're going to give, it's likely that you'll have many more possible points of supporting evidence than you'll be able to cram into the time allotted. One easy way to decide which points are worth sharing and which aren't is by using the interestingness of each point as a factor.

Ask yourself the simple question: Is this point super interesting? Is this something people already know or is it novel? Even better—is it counterfactual? That is, something people believe to be true but can be empirically disproven? Will the audience leave your talk remembering these points for use in a water cooler or Thanksgiving dinner argument with colleagues or friends? If so, you will have accomplished a critical point of success in your journey to persuade.

Order of Arguments

Once you've ranked all your possible points by interestingness, it's time to consider how they should be placed into the presentation—and in what order. If you're delivering a pitch, there are some generally accepted structures for how to organize your material—and those are discussed in the resources section and throughout this book. But even then, there is quite a bit of leeway to decide how you might organize your thoughts.

Let's consider the second act of a company fundraising pitch as a good example. Generally speaking, you'll be expected to cover key points on the following topics:

- market
- marketing/go-to-market strategy
- traction
- competition
- team
- unit economics

I put these arguments/concepts in the order that most companies I've worked with are likely to present. But there are various scenarios where I might want to rejigger the order specifically to highlight some of the company's strengths in a more compact fashion.

As a general rule, you want to organize your arguments into one of two formats:

A. Strong—weak—strong—weak—strong
B. Weakest, medium, stronger, strongest

There are no absolute right or wrong answers here, but it very much depends on what you have to work with and what impact you're trying to have. Hari's talk uses the B format above—going from weakest (how come grandma's not an addict?) to the strongest (Portugal has cut addiction substantially in the real world) quite well.

But if you're in a situation where you might have to cover a wider range of material, such as a pitch or management presentation, you might not be able to neatly structure in order of impact. Maybe your company's market argument, traction argument, and team argument are strong, but you're in a space with a lot of competition, your unit economics are a bit weak, and your go-to-market strategies have hit some snags.

The instinct would be to bury those counter arguments, but I would be wary of doing this. First off, any savvy viewer/investor/executive will know to ask about those topics, and then you will just look like you were trying to avoid them. Another approach would be to make your strongest points first, and then put all the stuff you don't like at the end, perhaps in an effort to create cosmic balance. Unfortunately, this approach will only result in the audience's disposition to shift to "no" as you approach the final act—or your ask.

In these circumstances, it might be best to structure your arguments so they start strong, end strong, and weave the weaker points throughout the rest. Where you can take liberties in structure, do so—never let an expected outline dictate the right way to make an argument if your content leads you in a different direction.

Don't Spoil the Punchline

One other terrible hangover from the bad old days of persuasive presentation teaching is the idea of putting the hypothesis at the front of an argument. This would often take the form of "I think we should build a rocketship, and here's why." But while it may be tempting to lead with the point, and then go back and argue it, this breaks the best practice convention for how to tell a story and to persuade.

It is better for you to build toward the conclusion rather than spoiling it up front. Make the arguments first about why your company is well positioned to go to Mars, then tie it together with something like "and that's why I think we should launch a Mars mission today." This allows the audience to develop more connection to your argument, and also for the emotional energy to build in the room in the direction of your true point.

I was guilty of doing this often in my presentations, I'll admit. I think a combination of my tendency to speak in refrains—moving back and forth in time—combined with a desire to confront the audience's preconceived assumptions, led me to a pattern of spoiling the punchline—or telling them the point up front.

I call it spoiling the punchline because it's probably easiest to understand the problem through the lens of comedy. If you'll permit me, I'll use a guffaw-worthy dad joke to illustrate the point.

Times New Roman and Helvetica walk into a Bar. "Get out of here," shouts the bartender, "we don't serve your type."

Go ahead and groan now. Get it out of your system. When you're ready to proceed . . .

Imagine if we reversed the order of this joke, in the style of most professional presentations: The bartender yelled, "Get out of here, we don't serve your type," and I looked around the room until I saw who he was screaming at: Helvetica and Times New Roman.

It's technically the same ideas, just presented in a different order. So why doesn't it work as well? The reason is the element of surprise. In the first version, I don't know where you're going with the joke, and find the premise— that two typefaces are in a bar in the first place—fantastical enough that I want to learn more. "This isn't real," I'm thinking, "but something interesting is going to happen." And then the punchline hits, and the whole thing makes sense. Surprise is a core element of both comedy and persuasion, and you could do well to learn from this example when making your points.

Build the world, take the audience on a journey, and then hit them with the point. It will leave a stronger impression for sure.

The Elephant in the Room Is Dumbo

In the Disney movie *Dumbo*, a circus elephant who is the subject of ridicule for his large ears, eventually learns how to turn them into an advantage when he discovers he can fly. Not dissimilar to the story of Rudolph (make fun of that nose until you need it), this allegory helps kids and adults alike understand the importance of finding the power in difference and making it count for something.

Often, when you're giving a presentation or pitch, there will be a clear elephant in the room (EITR). For example, if you're pitching a startup that promises to let people rent out spare rooms in their home to travelers, your EITR is—of course—Airbnb. Once the premise of your pitch is understood, it's going to be impossible for the audience to suspend disbelief and take that journey with you until you clearly state that you know Airbnb exists, and that you contextualize what you're about to say relative to Airbnb's strengths and weaknesses. The audience might assume you're naive or trying to avoid a challenge to your idea or authority otherwise.

The same is true in a business presentation where you're going to propose doing something that's already been tried in the past (a given for most companies), a TED Talk on a subject already covered by a popular video (hard to avoid at this point), or even a wedding toast where many of the attendees have been to each other's nuptials.

Like the proverbial elephant, you need to address this issue head on, make it clear that you know the contextual challenge, and that you're going to address it. You need not answer it up front, but you need to let the audience know that you know the key detail as soon as possible, perhaps with the caveat that you'll get into the weeds a bit later on.

But also like Rudolph, you're going to need to explain why your unique talents/ideas are necessary, important, and vital to persuade people that your differentiation can be used to improve the entire enterprise or to usurp a market leader. Don't hide your differences, embrace them—but make them count.

Counter Points and Counterfactuals

Sometimes, the best way to explain something to an audience is to frame it as a counterfactual (if circumstances were different, then . . .) or a counterpoint (circumstances are different, therefore). That is to say, use the negative frame of reference to get the audience to embrace your hypothesis or point.

In her excellent—and guffaw inducing—talk "What We Didn't Know About Penis Anatomy" (see the resources guide for a link to the talk) the scientist Diane Kelly does a masterful job of taking us down this path. In explaining the story of her discovery on how mammalian members are structured, she clearly explained the school of thought that led to the design being a foregone conclusion, and the negative reinforcement she had received from advisors as she began to pursue this endeavor.

The idea was that everyone thought they already knew how a penis worked, and that it was a hydrostatic skeleton. But this didn't make sense to Kelly, so she pursued the question in more detail and—despite the disbelief and odds—figured it out. Throughout the talk, as she reveals more and more of her process, we see that she's moving from one negative idea to another—questioning and debunking things that are believed to be true but might not be.

She even uses counterfactuals to great effect when discussing, for example, the characteristics of the mammalian penis, saying effectively, "if the penis was a hydrostatic skeleton, it would wiggle while erect." I'll suggest you watch the talk in order to grasp the full impact of the science behind this work, but the behavioral science inherent in her approach is faultless.

She could have framed it more like, "hydrostatic skeletons wiggle when inflated. Penises don't." This conveys the same information, but in a drier and less thought-provoking way. Just as with the talk as a whole, sometimes opening the world to a different frame helps people really connect with the material and understand that their perspective needs to be challenged.

One suggestion is to avoid using this technique for each of your points, as it can feel high-pressure and raises the computational intensity for viewers, as they hold open various scenarios that are not true.

Once you've successfully structured and made all the points you want to make, the time has come to shift gears and open Act III—The Final Battle and Conclusion.

ACT III

Act III generally begins at the point in the story when the protagonist has identified the challenge, gone on their journey to figure it out, and is ready to do battle with the final boss before arriving at the end of the narrative.

In the case of most professional presentations and pitches, however, this final act tends to focus less on an explicit battle between good and evil, and more on the protagonist wrapping up all they have learned into a cohesive, understandable, and often actionable worldview or unifying theory.

The Unifying Theory

People love unifying theories of behavior—a simple explanation or set of explanations that provides clarity about a range of observable things in the world. Though often reductionist and simplistic, unifying theories can help the audience understand what they've just heard and turn it into action (especially important in pitches and corporate presentations, where action is often the desired outcome).

Of course, these can also be humorously stupid, as with most acronyms that organizations use to convey otherwise straightforward ideas. For example:

- DARE: Drug Abuse Resistance Education
- START: Strategic Arms Reduction Treaty
- USA PATRIOT Act: Uniting and Strengthening America by Providing Appropriate Tools Required to Intercept and Obstruct Terrorism

I'm sure your organization also does its fair share of pointless acronymization, and often in a backward looking way (as with the ones above, which were undoubtedly led by the acronym and not the substance of their underlying ideas).

Okay, so these acronyms are silly, and everyone agrees that they are not strictly necessary to convey information, so why are we discussing them in the context of your closing arguments? It is because of the underlying reason people are attracted to ideas like acronyms in the first place: the desire to make order out of chaos in a neat and concise package.

Though your points may not lend themselves to a specific acronym, almost every persuasive presentation tends to bring together the points made before into some kind of unifying theory that helps the audience understand what's been discussed in totality—and makes it easier to take action thereto.

This can take the form of something as simple as a bulleted list, an acronym (though I'd reconsider if possible), or even just a statement.

Let's go back to Hari's TED Talk for a moment. Right at the end, he drops his unifying theory for addiction:

I think all along we should have been singing love songs to them [addicts], because the opposite of addiction is not sobriety. The opposite of addiction is connection.

Now, in absolutely scientific terms, this is BS. Addiction is a complex psychological state that cannot be boiled down into a single, simple statement. But don't we just love it when someone does that for us? And this closing explains some of the power of Hari's talk, even after all these years: a simple, easy to understand, alternative telling of the universe as it exists. A unifying theory, in other words.

In my TEDx Talk about failure, called "Failosophy," I shared a slide in the last section of the presentation that highlighted the unifying theory.

Failosophy

1. Understand & Unlearn attitudes about failure

2. Model people's failures, not successes

3. Celebrate (don't punish) failure to drive innovation

4. See your life as a portfolio of failures & successes

Closing slide from the author's TEDxFRA speech about Failure, titled "Failosophy"

The slide shows a skater who's fallen on the ice, and attempts to bring together all the different perspectives on failure I'd been sharing into four key points:

1. Understand and unlearn attitudes about failure.
2. Model people's failures, not successes.
3. Celebrate (don't punish) failure to drive innovation.
4. See your life as a portfolio of failures and successes.

The concept being that if we embody these characteristics, we'll be better able to leverage our failures to create success. Each one of the bullets was made as a point in the presentation, and then brought together here at the end for clarity and distillation. It's a way of restating what you've said, but showing it in the context of something that is more actionable.

The Closer

As much effort as you put into the first sentence of your talk has to be spent on the last sentences. As a general rule, I recommend that you write these last lines first, so that you can have a destination to aim for—a common strategy among many fiction and TV writers. Visualize where the characters and story end up, and work toward the goal.

There are some crucial differences and similarities between the closing of a presentation and the final episode of your favorite serialized program. First and foremost, any drama that was generated during Acts I and II needs to be fully resolved in Act III, and before the closing. You cannot leave important ideas dangling, because viewers will spiral on why you didn't answer those questions and be forced to reconsider what you were actually trying to say.

If you ask a provocative question up front, you need to have answered it by the end. If you introduce a character on their journey, the journey must resolve, and so on.

These points of resolution can happen in different places in Act III. Sometimes it's appropriate to set up the final resolution in the last sentence—as with Hari's talk. Other times, the punchline of the talk happens a few statements earlier, and this is followed by a denouement or action items/next steps phases.

For example, in a business presentation, it is often customary to end the conversation with a proposed set of next steps as a point for discussion. If Hari had wanted to make his TED Talk more actionable, he could have added a sentence or two after the love songs part referenced just above about how the people in the room could make a difference in the lives of addicts around them. Something more prescriptive and "to-do-list-y."

When you do a business presentation with next steps, I want to encourage you to nonetheless craft an ending that is impactful, connected to the beginning, and lands with maximum A-Ha!—even if there is a boring/procedural step afterward. In fact, in a large-scale presentation setting or company pitch, I'd suggest bringing your talk to a close, waiting for applause, and then moving to the "next steps" phase.

The Ask / *Shark Tank*

One of the most interesting things about *Shark Tank* is how it gets company pitches into a format that can be easily repeated and compared. The beginning of each pitch starts with name and financial ask, and the end always takes the form of something like "who's ready to invest?"

As a general rule, this kind of final statement weakens the speaker's position. Rather than being seen as smartly "asking for the sale"—more on that later—it makes you seem focused on a singular, win-lose goal (funding, green light, etc.) rather than on the more win-win, collaborative side, where you're both educating and open to feedback.

Good sales people know to stay in "collaboration" mode for as long as possible in any pitch, and to switch to active sales mode (e.g., "what color car can we get you into today") once it's clear that the prospect is ready to buy. Failing to understand that inflection point in the audience's mind will destroy any chance for a collaborative sale—or shifted, shared understanding.

That's why ending with an ask before seeing how the audience responds is generally not the best strategy. You may be getting out ahead of yourself, and if the question is direct—for example, "How much would you like to invest?"—you may find yourself getting an immediate no, before the audience has a chance to ask their questions and express their interest—however mild it may be.

The best advice is always to end your presentation on the strongest note possible. Stay in character and in the story, and create a situation where you're inviting applause or the excitement of the crowd. You don't need to ask them a question to get them there, you need only present an idea or a call to action that is both supported by the journey you just took and intriguing enough to imagine a better future. End your talk, listen to the audience, then proceed to ask is the best way to approach this challenge.

The Circle Back

One of the most exciting things in any presentation or story is when something from the very beginning gets brought back at the end and explained / tied together uniquely. TV writers are masterful at this, often weaving in long jokes across many seasons (see Garol in *Broad City*) that are resolved only truly by the end of the series. But even in persuasive presentations, it's possible to use this convention to elicit strong audience enthusiasm of the form "hey I remember that . . ."

One of the easiest ways to approach this is to make reference to the first character or scene you set in the ending. If you are the protagonist or focus, bring it back to you. In my failosophy talk, I presented myself as the centerpiece of the journey and circled back to frame the ending as a statement to myself. In another one of my TED Talks, this time about gamification, I began the conversation with the fear that parents have about their kids' overuse of videogames and ended on the note: "the kids are gonna be alright."

Circling back is not essential, but you definitely score bonus points with the audience for doing it, and it's something relatively straightforward in most persuasive presentations I've seen. You can do it too.

The Closing Emotions

In constructing your talk using the A-Ha! Method, and in the exercises in this book, you can see a common thread around identifying the emotional energy we want to see from our audience and then crafting the story, narrative, pacing, tone, etc., around those goals. This is no more true than when considering the closing emotions of a talk.

As a rule, North American audiences want to leave a talk feeling inspired, hopeful, future-oriented, and with a belief that things will get better. I have noticed, however, that many people seem uncomfortable with the idea of integrating inspiration into talks that might deal with more mundane, analytical, or business-minded concepts. But this couldn't be further from the right approach.

Every company pitch, business presentation, or persuasive talk has—in your mind—a goal or objective. There's something we want the audience to feel, be, or do after listening to the talk, and that is a goal of the entire endeavor. The best way to get people to take the action you want, or to engage in the way you propose, is to get them excited, motivated, worked up, and so on.

The most skillful presenters don't need to lean on rah-rah tactics to get their audiences excited. If done well, the end of a presentation can prompt a standing ovation, an extra loud hoot and holler, or even a shout out of affirmation from the crowd. If you've tapped into their optimistic emotional energy, they may have an involuntary response and feel the need to let it out. This is a good thing.

Don't shy away from crafting that emotional journey, even if your talk is more business-like. I've never seen someone lose by evoking strong, positive emotions in people—and you are likely to succeed by trying.

8

Slides and Other Speaking Aids

PowerPoint, which we know (and loathe) as the "standard" of presentation software, was invented in 1984 by Robert Gaskins. A computer scientist from Berkeley, Gaskins wanted an easier way to make transparencies and handouts. Overhead projectors had eclipsed the slide carousel as the primary way of providing visual reference for lectures and academia. This had the benefit of lowering the cost and creation time of the material because film slides had to be composed and developed by professionals. But transparencies also allowed lecturers to make on-the-fly notes or changes by simply writing on the clear plastic with the light blaring through it.

If you have never experienced a lecture with slides on transparency (and usually a blackboard for additional material), well—you're probably young enough to not know who A-Ha! (no relation) the rock band is, but that's beside the point. Transparencies were awful, cumbersome, complex, and expensive, and it made sense that someone who worked with them every day would want to find a way to make them easier.

Thus PowerPoint was born. Even before its sale to Microsoft and subsequent rise to global domination, PowerPoint was already changing the world. In fact, its impact is so great, that we now use the term "powerpoint" to refer to a slide deck file. We also see many breathless headlines describing how "PowerPoint Is Killing Critical Thought,"[1] or that famous business leaders, like Steve Jobs, banned slide deck presentations entirely.[2]

The critical consensus boils down to three major complaints about PowerPoint:

1. Slide decks reduce people's critical thinking about problems.
2. Slide decks are an unnecessary crutch that pulls focus from the talk itself.
3. Most PowerPoints are neither aesthetically pleasing nor concise.

All of these criticisms have some basis in fact and are valid. But they throw the baby out with the bathwater when they insist PowerPoint or its main competitors—Keynote, Google Slides, and Prezi—be banned from school or work. A well-crafted, A-Ha! Method slide deck can actually improve your presentation because:

A. It uses visuals to support the talk, never to pull focus from it.
B. It helps visual learners understand your material better.
C. It provides a content framework and structure for you to develop against.
D. It is optional—never a crutch. You can and will give your presentation without slides.
E. It is made in Keynote with arresting, simple visuals, so it will be guaranteed to look good.

In my view, creating slides is an indispensable and essential part of preparing a presentation, and you must do it yourself. Every presentation I've ever given begins with a Keynote document—even if I never intend to show any supporting visuals. The synthesis of the ideas, visuals, words, and structure allows me to create better, faster, and more precise presentations. Moreover, the editing and content hierarchy approach of slides is second-to-none. I do all my best thinking in slides.

In this chapter, rather than dwell on the negatives about slides, I want to walk you through my process in the A-Ha! Method for creating killer slides every time. But more importantly, you'll be left with an understanding about why using the slides as the framework for content creation is such a powerful approach—and why you should never skip the Keynote step or outsource it.

POWERPOINT VERSUS KEYNOTE VERSUS PREZI VERSUS SLIDES

I make all my slide decks in Keynote for Mac because I believe it is the superior option for anyone who is serious about creating a great presentation. I believe in this strongly enough that I would encourage you to switch your computing stack to Mac if you haven't already (and why haven't you?) if you want to take presentations and professional communication seriously.

I don't get compensated by Apple for saying this, but Keynote really is better. It combines the simplicity of the PowerPoint framework (slide deck) with advanced aesthetic tools that can make anyone look like a professional presentation designer. I routinely get comments on how gorgeous my presentations look, but let me let you in on a secret: I couldn't draw a straight line with a ruler if I had to. My secret weapon is Keynote, and it should be yours too.

Wherever I use Keynote in this book, you can substitute PowerPoint or Google Slides if you want. Ultimately, they can produce most of the same output, even if less well—and each have their own advantages (ubiquity and collaboration, respectively). Prezi is not my favorite tool. I think the animation between slides is cute but distracting—and as you'll see, my framework is always simple, arresting, and visual—not gimmicky. I haven't used a slide transition in years, I have no plans to do so now, and I'll explain why.

In any event, use the tool that makes you the happiest, but if you want to take this really seriously, it's time to switch to Keynote.

MASTER SLIDES YOURSELF

Sometimes when I peruse job boards—such as Upwork or Indeed—to understand market demands for presentation skills, I am disheartened. While most corporate jobs require some level of proficiency with PowerPoint, in many cases, I'll see jobs that seek "presentation designers"—often taking the form:

> We have a PowerPoint presentation for our fundraising cycle already done. We need a professional designer to come in, make it look good and consistent with our branding, and to help us consolidate/edit the content.

This sounds perfectly reasonable on the surface. But to the skilled presentation guru's eye, I see an organization that isn't taking presentations seriously. The slides and the spoken presentation go hand in hand, and unless they are developed together—by the same person/people—they will be disjointed, inauthentic, and very likely too long. I'm not just talking about the slide deck with this criticism—I'm describing the entire presentation's quality and it bears repeating:

The slides you create for your presentation are not ancillary, and should not be outsourced to anyone but you. If you are working in a close team on the presentation and slides, it is acceptable for the team to work on it together, but unless you have iterated the deck and presentation in unison, I guarantee you will not get the best of your tools or your team.

That is to say, there is a place for visual designers in slide decks, but that role is before and during the creation of the presentation—not after. Master slides should be completed before you get to the first serious editing iteration of your presentation, and visual designs on individual slides should be built in concert with the slide content itself. And one note: if you absolutely need a designer to build a slide that you think won't make sense without complex design, my suggestion is: rethink the entire point you're trying to make.

As I'll illustrate in the next section, simplicity of ideas is a necessary precursor to simplicity of visual design, and if your thoughts are too complex to be elucidated orally—with few exceptions—it is the thoughts you need to invest in fixing, not the visuals.

THE 1 + 1 + 1 APPROACH

Hopefully by now you're scared straight about the right way to approach slide deck making—or at least curious about why I take this idea so seriously. To put it bluntly: the slide decks I create are essential tools in my overall storytelling arsenal, and I make the most of the power they offer to create a talk—and visuals—that always impress. You can too, and it starts here and now.

The first step in creating a presentation is to open a new Keynote project. You'll have a blank slide on the left. In this phase, we will do absolutely no visual thinking—we're just going to use the slide deck the way we might use a set of flash cards or Post-it notes: as a container for content that we can organize as we see fit.

The framework I use is pretty simple, and I call it 1 + 1 + 1:

1 slide
1 idea
1 minute

That is, in a normal presentation, each slide should represent a single idea, with approximately a minute for delivery. So in a 10-minute presentation, you'll ultimately have approximately 12 standard slides: a title slide, a closing slide, and 10 informational slides, advancing approximately every 60 seconds.

In the finished product, it may not be possible to hew to this (admittedly) strict rule. Sometimes, we'll want to move faster through a slide than 1 minute, and other times we may need longer than that to truly explain the idea we have to deliver. That is perfectly fine—I won't hold you to 1 + 1 + 1 in the *finished* product, but when we're creating the initial slide deck and presentation, it's essential that you use a rigorous approach to telling your story. The stricter you are up front, the more flexibility and ease you'll have later in the process.

Now there are some implications for 1 + 1 + 1 that aren't immediately obvious but emerge from the process of using it during this creation phase:

- If an idea takes longer than 60 seconds to explain, you need to break your ideas down into smaller parts so they can be covered in 1 minute.
- If an idea needs more than 1 slide to explain it, you need to break your ideas down into smaller parts so they can be covered in 1 slide.

Bring this structure and rigor to the process now and it will free you later.

AGILE SLIDE DEVELOPMENT

Throughout this book—and in the A-Ha! Method courses and coaching, I advocate for the same agile method to develop content that I use in my own practice. Each step of the way, the goal is to create an iteration of the content that improves on the previous one, incorporating the new ideas, structures, or learning that have now been acquired.

The reason for taking a fast, agile approach is that the details can actually be very stress-inducing and deeply distracting. For example, when pitching an idea to your executive management team, a 90-day, $2 million project may be viewed very differently from a 180-day, $10 million project. If you sweat those details in the first go around, you'll have a lot of difficulty cutting through the noise to get to the meat of what you need to say.

The downside to the Agile approach is that your presentation will appear extremely unfinished until the late-middle of the process. But this is OK. The work that you put in at each phase won't be lost, and you'll be able to see how it evolves over time for your own—and your team's—edification.

Where to Begin

Start by creating a new slide for each idea you want to express. Don't worry about visuals or anything other than the statement you're going to write on the slides. Keeping in mind the approximate length of the presentation, start by writing one idea on each slide. Grammar and spelling don't matter. The point is to get all the ideas out into the deck as quickly as possible.

n.b. You can find slide outlines in this book's resource guide.

When you're done, you should have a set of slides that are white with black text on them, comprising one idea per slide, approximately as many as the length of the presentation you're planning to give.

What If You Don't Know the Talk Timing?

If you don't know the length of time of the talk you're going to be working on yet, you can use various times as rough guideposts to help you get into the zone. Here are some standard timings to consider:

- short pitch: 3 to 5 minutes
- standard pitch: 15 minutes
- short talk: 5 to 10 minutes (6 and 9 seem very common)
- TED Talk: 18 minutes
- standard conference talk: 30 minutes
- conference keynote: 45 minutes
- academic lecture: 60 minutes

As a general rule, given the audience's shortened attention span, I think anything much over 30 minutes is too long. However, some content types and presentations nonetheless call for longer and more in-depth material. As a general rule, I suggest forcing yourself to design for the shortest content type you need to master first. It is generally much harder to edit key ideas down for brevity than it is to fill time. Just consider the difference between pitching your company within 15 minutes or 3 minutes. Both of those timings are standard for company pitches—and founders raising money must be able to master both. Which one do you think will be harder?

Presentations with Existing Structures

Sometimes presentations you give will have existing structures you need to adhere to. The most classic example is the company pitch. If you're part of an accelerator, they'll likely give you their preferred pitch outline, and if you're doing it on your own there are several pitch deck frameworks that are commonly used, including 10/20/30 by Guy Kawasaki, and Y Combinator. Links to these frameworks can be found in the resource guide.

If you know you have to follow a slide structure, begin the process by importing that outline to your Keynote and using each of those ideas as a slide framework. You can always add more slides if needed, but don't take any away.

How to Structure the Discussion

As you're going through getting slide outlines down in rapid succession, be sure to consider the content creation frameworks we've already covered in the book—including the placement of A-Ha! and the act-based story structure to develop the narrative. But don't worry too much about the specifics, just use your knowledge to synthesize what you're thinking about.

CHOOSING THE RIGHT VISUALS

As you're iterating through the presentation development phase, you will eventually want to start thinking about images. This should generally be done after you've gone through a few iterative cycles of content *creation, consolidation, summarization*, and *reorganization*—which you will pair with the *memorization* phase in the next chapter for maximum confidence. But once you've done a few versions of that deck, and you think you have the content structure and pacing correct, it's a good time to start thinking about visuals. Say it five times fast:

- creation
- consolidation
- summarization
- reorganization
- memorization

A Visual Framework

I think presentation visuals generally should come in one of these formats:

- opening and closing (title) slides
- simple visual and text slides—the most common form
- table, chart, or other data slides—used sparingly and appropriately
- video, demo, or audio slides—used to take the audience on a different journey

Let's take a quick look at each of the formats to understand their purpose and structure.

Opening/Closing Slides

Your opening and closing slides should be almost identical, containing the title of your presentation, your name, and your contact info if appropriate. In most cases, opening and closing slides don't need a visual, though it is common to put a company logo or brand mark, and/or the branding of a conference or event if you've been invited.

Some people like to weave in the brand mark or contact info onto every slide of the presentation, but this has never made a lot of sense to me. Once the conversation is underway—and in the middle of your talk—if the audience is furiously writing down your contact information or trying to remember what company you're representing, you've probably already lost their attention. You're in control of shaping what you say from the stage and, by extension, are the primary influencer of where the audience is focused. Use this power wisely.

If your contact information is on the opener and closer, I suggest using a QR code and writing out your email or social media handle. Then, when you get to the end of the presentation, instead of saying your final words on the last content slide, you can switch to the ending slide and finish your talk such that the audience gets an extra 15 to 20 seconds to write down your info or snap the QR. After you've impressed and taken the audience on an A-Ha!-based journey, it is then the best time to share contact info.

Simple Visual and Text Slides

This is the workhorse of your slide library. Comprising a large, high-resolution image paired with no more than a single statement, these slides can be designed to perfectly reinforce the material being presented verbally from the stage. Images used need not be literal, and the statement need not be a copy of the slide's "title." Sometimes, the image and text are used to reinforce a conceptual—rather than headline—idea from the presentation.

For example, in my failosophy TEDx presentation, the section called "swing and miss" refers to the idea that society has swung the pendulum of failure opprobrium too far—from a strict definition of success to a world in which everyone is a winner.

An example slide from the author's TEDxFRA talk entitled "Failosophy", showing a conceptual pendulum: https://qrco.de/bczBoH

I never use the phrase "swing and miss" in the verbal presentation. But it encapsulates the point I'm trying to make in that moment about society's overreaction. And the visual, which shows a kid swinging on a tire, illustrates the fact that our culture doesn't really let kids hurt themselves too much any-more—the tire swing is too dangerous for many of today's parents. Again, I don't reference this idea directly, but the visuals reinforce the concept rather than the literal words.

If used correctly, these slides can also help you with your memorization, and their creation will go hand in hand with your learning process. The visual and simple set of words can act as a mental trigger to help you remember the material you're supposed to cover in that section of the presentation. Of course, you may not be able to see your slides during your presentation, so you can't *depend* on this as a crutch, but it is nonetheless effective when available.

Table, Chart, or Data Slides

Most technical and company presentations today have some amount of data in them, typically in the form of a chart or table. As a general rule, I want to encourage you to not include them in any presentation that is intended to be given from a stage.

The reason I want you to resist this temptation is manifold: first and foremost, if you're presenting to a large room with the visuals on a screen behind you, it can be exceedingly difficult even for people in the middle of the room to read the details contained in the table or chart. Second, whenever you put a chart or table up on the screen, some percentage of the viewers will tune you out while they try to parse the material you're presenting. After all, you've given them a five-column by five-row table, and we're keyed to think that the details must be super important, so we'll narrow our focus and start reading. Even if you still think this is a must-have, consider what happens when you invariably have to advance the slides before some percentage of people in the room have finished parsing the data you put up on the screen. It's bad enough that the audience tuned you out when the chart came up, now they are going to be disappointed when they can't finish.

Does this mean you shouldn't put data or chart slides up? Of course not—sometimes they are unavoidable or—at least—very important to your storytelling. So here's the best practice for using data/chart slides:

1. *Use them sparingly.* Really consider whether or not they are absolutely essential, or if there's a way you can convey the same concept or information without them.
2. *Simplify.* Charts and graphs should be presented in the most expected format. Don't make people read the legend in order to understand what you're trying to really convey. Make it understandable in a way that the audience says, "Oh I get it, revenues are going up," and that's really all they need to know. You can always share the underlying data table later.
3. *Alternative forms.* One of the slides in a company or project pitch that always creates some angst is the competition slide. You often need to represent your competition in a way that provides some more information than just their name—for example, how they are different, or what

their advantages might be. If you're in a crowded market, this can get unwieldy, fast. So in competitive slides, consensus has developed around two different approaches: the check box chart and the x and y axis map, which you can download in the resource guide. Each one of these is designed to convey key information, but really to make a broader point. In the case of the checkmarks—it's that our product/company has more checkmarks than the competition. In the x and y axis chart, it's that we're in the upper right quadrant. In both cases, the audience will assume that the criteria and the axes are relevant by default and, therefore, that you're highly differentiated, which is probably your objective. Again, you can always fill in the blanks for folks later.

4. *Presentation context.* If you're in a big room, you might need to make the charts and graphs really, really, really big to make them understandable. If you're presenting virtually (e.g., on Zoom) the slide will blow up to take over the whole screen (probably), making it much easier for people to read the content.

5. *Consider leave-behinds and handouts instead.* If you have a big room presentation to give, but also need to share some really detailed chart/graph data, consider presenting a simplified version to the room and following that up with a detailed handout or leave-behind. In particular when I'm developing a pitch deck, I will create two different versions—one for sending via email and one for presenting in a room. The first has more detail and is self-contained. This means it makes sense even if I'm not there to present it. The second only really works when I'm presenting. Because the latter version is so much harder to make, I always start with that.

In summary, you can use charts, tables, and graphs—but use them smartly, explore alternatives, and make sure you're prioritizing the attendee's understanding above all else.

Video, Audio, Demo Slides

If a picture is worth a thousand words, a well-thought-out video, audio, or demo slide can easily be worth ten thousand. But when to use them isn't always immediately obvious.

The first rule of thumb is to avoid shifting the audience's attention and energy to a clip or demo unless absolutely necessary. That is, does such a distraction produce better results than you could have otherwise given? In the case of a product demo, there's probably no way to easily do a purely audible walkthrough that will have anywhere the impact of an actual demo. As a general rule, in this case you should choose the demo. The same is true of a video or audio snippet that helps explain a core concept in the pitch.

But often, presentations include audio and video as a crutch rather than a core part of the presentation. Consider why you're including it. If it is just a flashier way of conveying some other information, is it really going to deliver the right punch?

It's also important to remember that audio or video embeds and demo sequences raise the technical complexity of your presentation by an order of magnitude. The vast majority of technical faults I've observed in presentations are related to one of these three content types—and that includes over Zoom. Failing to check a single box (or leveling the audio) might make it impossible for people to hear the content, and often the demo software fails.

As with everything in the high-wire world of presentations, it's a tradeoff and risk you must mitigate. But you must also be fully prepared to deal with the situation if it goes awry. Therefore, even if you include a video, audio, or demo segment to go more in depth on a key topic, you must also have a completely "flat" version of that material to deliver on a moment's notice. If you can't talk through the content of your video, you don't know your material well enough.

A Note on Infographics

As the popularity of infographics has risen, so too has their use in presentation formats. Infographics are powerful and generally simplified ways of conveying numerical data that leverage graphical design techniques to make content more understandable and approachable.

As a general rule, they are great for use in presentations, but apply the same criteria as you might to any table or chart or graph. Is it legible at a distance? Am I focused on the right content? Will the audience be able to quickly know what I want them to know? You may find that an infographic created for a document will need to be simplified for a presentation setting.

How to Find Visuals, Licensing

If you follow the outline presented here, you'll most likely need arresting images more so than all other kinds of visuals. But how do we find the right photos/illustrations?

Once you're in the phase of the A-Ha! Method where you're building your visual presentation, you'll want to start searching for appropriate content. Using the keywords and concepts we defined in the previous section, you can search some key repositories.

- *Stock photo/video sites, such as iStock.* Anything you license from these sites—and there are several affordable credit/subscription plans if you are going to be making a lot of presentations—can be used in your decks without any licensing issue. They are usually available without any citations needed and in large resolution. Plus you can download a sample version with watermarks to temporarily place in your deck before you need to commit financially. If you work for a large company or are in school, your institution may already have a license for one of these platforms. Be sure to ask.
- *Free stock/video sites, such as Pexels.* There are several stock photo/video/ illustration sites that are completely free—though they typically request or require a citation/link. These services can be very useful—especially if you're on a budget—though as you might suspect, their selection can be more limited. I remember searching for an image to describe the inner critic (a self-critical voice in one's head) and couldn't find anything that even remotely worked in the free stock world. While it's good to try free first, don't hesitate to pay if it makes a difference.
- *Google—Creative Commons searches.* Google has a very powerful image search tool, but as a general rule will return initial results that are copyrighted. This is not good for you, as copyrighted images generally require you to get permission from the holder—and/or pay them money—to use. However, if you click on the tools button under the image search bar, you'll see "Creative Commons only" as a licensing option. This will constrain the search to images that most likely will be available without payment, but subject to the citation/link rules of their creative commons license. This is a wordy way of saying that you can probably use any of the images if you follow the attribution rules the creator has requested.
- *Create your own.* Sometimes there really isn't a substitute for creating your own content. Perhaps it is so unusual that only you can make it. For example, one of my coaching clients needed to describe the super strength of vaginal muscles that can be fostered using Kegel exercises. She had a designer make a "super Kegel" illustration. For obvious reasons this was not available as a stock photo, and I encouraged her to spend

the money to get the visual just right. Other times—as with a demo or product shots—stock images literally don't exist. Use platforms like Fiverr and others to help you create the content and invest where you think it will have the most impact—a mockup of a future product, for example, is always money well spent.

Technical Criteria

Always search for and download the largest image format that is available. Keynote will automatically resize the image to best fit the slide format you're using, but bear in mind that your presentation is likely to get really big, really fast. This isn't a huge problem, but just something to consider. However, if your slides end up running in a really big room—for example, on a projector or giant screen—you'll be glad that you used images/video that can be scaled to 1,080 or 4,000 resolution or higher.

Organization

For each presentation, I recommend creating a document in which you include the link to the image, any attribution necessary, and even a thumbnail. This will allow you to quickly find the image again later if needed, and to include the correct citation if required. I know it will slow you down as you create, but take it from me—this will come in handy.

Also be sure to store all your images in a common folder for easier retrieval later, and rename them so they fit the concept of the image you used, rather than just sticking with their file name.

Citations

The easiest way to include image citations in a presentation is to add a URL in a lightly contrasting (white or black) typeface somewhere at the bottom of the slide in ten-point font or even smaller. The link should generally be clickable if possible, but in most cases, this will meet the citation criteria without overwhelming the slide with visual clutter. People who view your slides up close will be able to see the citation, and those with the file will be able to click on it.

For a full reference guide to creative commons attribution rules, be sure to check out the Creative Commons attribution page. And if this all feels like a huge hassle, don't be a cheapskate (or copyright scofflaw): just pay for the images directly.

Transitions and Animations

Much like videos in a presentation, transitions and animations come with significant technical hurdles and issues. Unlike videos, demos, and audio, however, animations and transitions are almost never truly necessary, and are bound to distract from your presentation overall. Though there is a sliver of utility, it's best to start with the reasons you should eschew these ideas.

First and foremost, transitions and animations are usually gimmicky. Slides shifting and objects moving create visual "interest," but because the slides are intended to be subservient to the spoken word, they pull focus instead of intensify it. Plus, while it may seem cool and cutting edge to you to show a push animation, it's probably (guaranteed) that everyone in the room has already seen it before. And once you do a slide transition or animation, do you need to continue using the same one for the balance of the presentation, or are you now expected to choose a different one for each slide to keep it even more visually interesting? Frankly, it's a bottomless pit of unanswerable questions, and I'd just skip them entirely.

Probably the biggest reason to avoid these is the incompatibility issue. Sometimes, your slides will not render properly on a target machine (e.g., the A/V crew), because of a mess up with fonts or other technical elements. If you follow my advice and produce in Keynote, sometimes your target machine will only have PowerPoint, making various elements of your deck incompatible without adjustment—including typefaces and animations. In those cases, you'll always want to have a flat (PDF) version of your presentation available so that you can still present. Other times, you won't have a deck at all, so the fancy animations won't justify their effort and expense. A flat slide deck with absolutely no bells and whistles should more than suffice, if your content is worth listening to.

Now there is a small sliver of utility for animations—even if never for slide transitions. Animating objects on the screen can sometimes be useful if it helps create clarity about some data or other crucial point. For example, if you're slowly walking through growth statistics for three years in sequence, you might want to animate the build of those bars so that the audience can't jump ahead of where you're going with the story line. In those cases where you feel strongly that animation is useful, be sure to use it sparingly and with the most compatible (build, appear, slide, push) animations rather than complex or otherwise gimmicky ones, like fireball. Who needs a fireball animation?

One other advantage of avoiding animations and transitions is not having to memorize a click sequence in addition to the content itself. Animations often require build clicks—meaning that you have to press the slide advance button to bring the next frame or build in, in addition to the standard "next slide" press. It's bad enough when you have to remember the sequence ("does this video play automatically or only when I click?") and ten times worse when the A/V folks—or a third party—are advancing the slides on your command. And if you're trying timed advance, you'll only bring yourself a world of hurt trying to remember the specifics of each transition statement and timing. Don't get involved in this morass if you can avoid it.

Easy, compatible, and flat—but beautiful—always wins the day. Stick to the simple stuff and your slides will sing . . . backup.

9

Confidence = Timing, Rehearsal, Memorization

Possibly the greatest scam in all of public speaking education are programs that claim to give you tactics/techniques to improve your confidence. Because a lack of confidence seems to be the way most people describe their issue with public speaking and professional communication in front of crowds, it stands to reason that enterprising schools and teachers would focus on this specific data point.

Here's the thing though: there are absolutely no shortcuts to improving your public speaking confidence. None. There is only work. At its core, public speaking confidence is about *knowing your material* well enough that you can deliver it regardless of the obstacles you might face. And there will be many.

I've seen plenty of my clients start off hoping for quick fixes to their confidence, believing that if they just memorize or follow some tricks (picture everyone naked?) they will magically become competent—if not great—presenters. But why settle for "mistake free" when what you really want is to close that deal, get that promotion, change those minds, improve the world? If you want to be able to do this well, you need to develop your self-assuredness by working on the underlying structures that build confidence and knowledge of the material:

- timing
- rehearsal
- memorization

Of course, it helps if you start from a place of deep knowledge about your subject, rather than just knowing what you read on Wikipedia. Think of the topic you know the most about in the world—everyone's a geek about something—what's yours? Now imagine you're in a conversation with someone who is a neophyte on that topic, and is asking you questions, to try to get you to explain this topic to them. Do you feel confident that you can have that Q&A with this individual without messing up, forgetting important details, or missing the point? Or do you think you could confidently and effectively explain everything they needed to know about original Beanie Babies without missing a crucial beat?

Odds are you've got at least one topic on which this would be true, and—because I believe in you—I'm sure you could hold forth on a couple of others as well. How did you get to this level of knowledge about the Marvel Cinematic Universe? Did it just come to you magically? Did you read a single blog post and suddenly became an expert on the topic? Or did you painstakingly watch movie after movie, read book after book, and slavishly consume all the stellar think pieces you could find? Clearly it was the latter and I'm sure if you had to get up to give a presentation about the MCU, after a few tries, you'd be as amazing at it as you are in casual conversation.

This is both the secret and the rub. No one can make you more confident at a task but you. The best we can do—and what I'm hoping this book is delivering to you now—is to provide a framework and approach that can help improve your confidence. But you're going to have to do the work. And here's where we start.

AN OVERVIEW OF THE PROCESS OF GETTING CONFIDENT

Rather than work on overall, generic confidence, we're going to build it through a specific talk. I can't promise that your overall confidence for all talks will improve right off the bat, but I am very sure that by following this process we can make you a compelling, competent, and confident presenter for this talk. Repeat the process for future presentations, and—with enough time—you'll develop a mastery of general presentational confidence.

At this point in this book, if you've been doing the work in the accompanying exercises and/or workbook, you've accomplished several of the items below. The remainder represent a simplified timeline and process map that I use in the creation of every one of my talks—and that I teach to my students.

Even if you aren't doing the exercises (and why aren't you?) you can follow this process to create a talk and learn it. If you haven't, why not come up with a talk idea for a 10- to 15-minute presentation and catch up by completing the first set of steps below?

1. Write the last statement of the presentation.
2. Write the first statement of the presentation.
3. Write the title and description.
4. Create an outline slide deck using 1 + 1 + 1.
5. Note which ideas are the A-Ha! Moments.
6. Note where the various acts begin.
7. For each slide's idea, write a paragraph or two.

Begin Iterative Test and Development
8. Present the paragraph version out loud.
9. Edit and adjust as needed to improve the talk.
10. Present out loud.
11. Acquire first pass images for slides (if using).
12. Present out loud, advancing slides (if using).
13. Edit and adjust as needed to improve the talk.

Repeat at Least 3 Times
14. Present out loud, timed—recording yourself, if possible.
15. Watch recording, evaluate timing, and adjust talk and slides for clarity.

Optional
16. Present to others, requesting feedback on live or video presentation.
17. Adjust as needed, based on feedback.

Final Sprint
18. Give the presentation to yourself without slides at least once a day for a minimum of seven days (or compress to multiple times/day if you have a deadline).
19. Practice the dead eye stare presentation method at least three times.

Day Before Presentation
20. Practice on the stage or staging environment if possible, advancing slides.
21. Make any necessary adjustments with A/V crew.

Day Of Presentation
22. Run the presentation at least once—preferably twice. First thing in the morning and within the hour prior to your talk if possible.

An Agile Approach

As you can see from the above steps, the process of getting confident in a talk takes a lot of iteration. I've cribbed this philosophical approach from a software development strategy called *Agile development*. Though you could get an entire degree in Agile, it can be best summarized as having an emphasis on regular deliveries of product, even if not complete. The idea is that each time you're getting external feedback and using that to iteratively improve your product. This is contrasted with *waterfall* development, where software is built and tested in private until the developer thinks it's ready—and then it's dropped on the world for the first time.

The problem with waterfall will be immediately obvious to anyone who's used experimental software that clearly hasn't been tested in real world scenarios. The same is true of developing a great talk and the confidence to deliver it. The first time you give the talk, it—and you—are not going to be stage-worthy. You might be cringe-worthy, however. But that's okay. We're going to present over and over again, out loud. We're going to deliver this to ourselves, to the camera, to our friends/family, and to peer support groups until the talk is good, tight and easy to deliver.

The key is to not get discouraged as you go.

Ruthless Editing

Whenever I create a talk, invariably I end up with a couple of slides and ideas that won't fit into the time allotted. I generally don't spend a lot of energy getting the timing right until after I've turned a corner on the overall quality of the talk. This means I believe that if I had to present it right now, it would be OK. Then I start focusing on timing, and this is where things can get a little emotional.

I think of every idea, and every slide I create as one of my children. A lot of thought, care, and effort goes into each one, and by the time I've practiced the presentation a dozen times, I am generally very wedded to each idea. It is precisely this feeling you must combat to create a great talk.

As you go through and work on ensuring the timing and messaging are correct, look for things you can cut. Less is generally more, and giving yourself some extra time/breathing room by removing one or two slides/ideas is likely to make the presentation flow more smoothly. Moreover, this will make you less stressed, and therefore likely to speak slower. If you're aiming for 15 minutes and your timed presentations end at 14:59, you probably have too much material.

For a 15-plus-minute presentation, aim for 1 full minute less than the allocated time for your talk. If it's a 3- to 4-minute pitch—then you need to use every second you've got. But in either case you have to be willing to edit ruthlessly. Take out anything that doesn't materially advance the point you're trying to make. If it's not absolutely essential, remove it.

And therein lies another gotcha of presentation development. If you feel like you need to stretch your words to fill the allotted time, you are either talking too quickly, or haven't fully nailed the right presentation content. Most speakers find it challenging to get to all their material in the time they have—and this holds equally true for a 15 minute and 60-minute presentation. If you feel like you're padding the content, use that as a signal that you might not be fully engaged with the material and that it's not quite ready yet.

Editing makes the finished presentation sing. Don't skimp on this step.

Timing

The average person speaks in a range of approximately 100 to 150 words per minute (WPM), depending on their region, culture, dialect, language, and age—among other factors. Comfortable speaking speed in your part of the world—and for you specifically—may vary, but this is the range of normal.

Professional presenters—like TV hosts—tend to speak a bit faster; 150 to 200 WPM are super common for these folks. Though you probably haven't noticed a chipmunking effect (where voices tend to get higher when sped up), that is likely because these professionals practice and study their craft for years to deliver that perfect talking head approach. They make it seem normal, even though it probably isn't.

So what pace to use when giving a presentation? I think aiming for one of two targets is ideal:

1. For an audience mostly composed of native or fluent English speakers, 170 to 175 WPM makes the most sense.
2. If your audience includes large numbers of non-native / second language speakers, I recommend slowing down to approximately 150 to improve their comprehension.

Translated Talks—100 WPM

There is also a corner case that most aspiring public speakers won't need to deal with right away but is important to be aware of: the simultaneous translation. Sometimes, when you're presenting in a foreign country, to a foreign audience or where sign language for the deaf is warranted, the event organizer will make a real time translator available to provide simultaneous translation for your talk.

I remember being in Tokyo giving an early talk on gamification at the invitation of a publisher and expert there. They assigned three simultaneous translators to my talk, because of how computationally intensive it was for them—they could only work 15 minutes at a time. Prior to the talk, they asked me to explain several technical terms they had seen in my work, and confirmed the correct pronunciation and use in English. They sat in the very front so they could watch my mouth closely, and as I spoke, they translated my words to the audience, who listened through their headsets.

It was truly magnificent to watch, especially because Japanese has a very different sentence structure. As a general rule, they have to wait until halfway through an English sentence before beginning their translation, so they can ensure all meanings are correct. And when it came time for the Q&A, they translated back and forth—between the audience (from Japanese to English) and my response (from English to Japanese). Despite speaking several languages, I found it astonishing, and I thanked them profusely at the end.

Translated talks are challenging in many ways, not the least of which is that you can hear the translation as the speaker and you have to be able to tune it out. But the reason for bringing up this story here is not to frighten (or excite?) you about international speaking work. Rather it is to highlight that in this scenario I had to slow waaaaaay down, to almost 100 WPM, so the translators could do their job. The obvious implication of this was that my talk went long. The lesson: if you have to give this talk with translation, slow down even further and be prepared to cut at least a third of your material.

How to Figure Out Timing

Until now, we've been talking about words per minute. But what if you don't instinctively know your words per minute speaking cadence? Never fear—no one really does. We generally tend to know that someone speaks fast or slow, and we know when we're rushing or moving at a normal pace. But you can become more familiar—and therefore more fluid—with what seems natural to you. As part of the practice, you'll develop a subconscious awareness of whether you're speaking too quickly, and this will help you stay on pace.

Listening for Timing

Laura Bergells has an excellent YouTube video that provides a clean understanding of speech pacing in English. You can watch it by snapping the QR code below, and use it to help understand a baseline speed for yourself and others.

Laura Bergells Youtube https://qrco.de/bczBoV

Tracking Your Own Speed

With inspiration from Bergells, I've created an exercise designed to help you pace yourself. We're going to use the following paragraph for you to say out loud, while you track with the stopwatch feature of your smartphone.

Most people have no idea how to speak at the right pace—it's something that just comes naturally. But there is an average pace of speech for people depending on their industry and job. For example, the average person speaks at somewhere between 100 and 150 words per minute. But a newscaster or podcast host probably never uses less than 150 words per minute, and might end up closer to 200 words per minute. Is it really possible that you might speak at twice the pace of the average person? With some modulation and variation in your pace for emphasis, and consideration for your accent and language comprehension of those in the room, you may need to fine-tune your pace. For translations or foreign audiences, 130 may be perfect. For native speakers, this might be too slow. Aim for 175, and eventually you'll have this down, instinctively. Practice makes perfect but remember to stay between sleep-inducing and cocaine-fueled where possible.

The process is quite straightforward: reset the stopwatch to zero—hit start and then begin reading the above paragraph. If you complete it exactly within sixty seconds, you've read at 172 WPM—my proposed ideal for most kinds of talks. If you complete it in forty-eight seconds, you're speaking at 200 WPM—newscaster speed.

Now try a slower cadence. Here's the same concept in a paragraph tuned to 130 WPM:

> Most people have no idea how to speak at the right pace—it's something that just comes naturally. But there is an average pace of speech for people depending on their industry and job. For example, the average person speaks at somewhere between 100 and 150 words per minute. But a newscaster or podcast host probably never uses less than 150 per minute, and might end up closer to 200 words per minute. Is it really possible that you might speak at twice the pace of the average person? With some modulation and variation in your pace for emphasis, and consideration for your accent and language comprehension of those in the room, you may need to fine-tune your pace.

As you're speaking it out loud, do you notice the difference? If you do the exercise a couple of times, you'll probably start to *feel* the speed of the words in your mouth muscles, even more so than in your brain. This is good—we want the pacing to be something you come to as naturally as possible. The pace you use in your finished presentation will not be precisely any of the ones listed above—and I definitely do not expect you to retool your presentation to conform to these pacings. The idea, however, is to ensure that you have a muscle memory for different speeds, so practice this exercise a few times until you can feel yourself bringing the paragraph to a close right on the button.

Varying Pacing

One of the biggest mistakes you can make as a speaker working on your craft is to try to adhere to a single pace throughout the entire talk. Even if it's super fast, nothing will bring your audience to the edge of distraction faster than an unvarying pace.

As we discussed in the A-Ha! Moments chapter, one of the subconscious ways that audiences know what information is important is based on tone and volume. Good speakers will increase their pitch and volume as they approach the summit of the content while simultaneously *decreasing* their speed. The combination of these elements says to the limbic brain "Hey, listen to me!" and makes it easier to hit the high notes of your most critical points.

If you think about preachers and newscasters, you'll immediately see this pattern. A newscaster may be talking about a cat stuck in a tree at a fierce clip, but when they are wrapping up the item, they'll slow down, raise their tone (often cocking their heads), while they deliver the closing punchline or sign off. It's very specific. Preachers—especially in the African American tradition—also have a telltale cadence that lets you know with tone, volume, and pace that they are about to make a critical point. You probably shouldn't sound like either a newscaster or preacher (unless this is, indeed, what you're doing), but you can learn tricks from them to improve your presentation skills.

Therefore, you need to leave yourself an extra buffer (not less), once you feel you've nailed the timing of your talk. You are going to need to slow down as you approach the A-Ha! Moments and that is going to take more time. This is why I recommend the easiest strategy for most beginning speakers is to aim for 1 minute less than the timer in long form speeches. This is so you don't feel rushed.

The Stress of the Timer—On Stage and Off

When you're first working on developing a talk and the skills of public speaking, the timer may seem intimidating. My coaching clients usually start off very stressed out about the timing—paying attention to it in a *Squid Game*-ish way that suggests they will die if they get it wrong. But the timer isn't absolute—no hole in the floor is going to open up and swallow you.

You can go over or under the timer, and that decision is up to you. Just remember: in a public or recorded event, going too far over time is considered rude and inappropriate, and will make it harder for you to get asked back. If you know most TED Talks are approximately 18 minutes in length, you can start to pay closer attention to the recorded length of the videos presented online. You'll see that most of them aren't 18:00 on the dot—with some going slightly over and some going slightly under.

If you're on stage at a major conference—or indeed if you are recording or giving your presentation over Zoom, you will probably be face to face with a countdown timer. In the Zoom version, the timer is the clock, usually on the same screen that you're staring at. If you're on a stage, they will often have a countdown clock that starts out green, shifts to yellow as you get to the last few mins, and then turns red—while it starts counting up—once you hit your max time.

Any timer that's shoved in your face is liable to make you stressed out, and our natural reaction in those kinds of situations is to speed up. This is—for all the reasons we've already discussed—a bad idea.

As you give the presentation over and over again with a timer, and you practice your pacing as above, I promise you'll start developing an intuitive sense of where you are and how you're tracking against the timer goal. You'll know more or less what time count a specific point is at, and as you deliver the presentation in flow, you'll intuitively know whether or not you need to speed up or slow down. I know this sounds crazy—especially if you've never really been conscious of your own timing or pacing before—but it is the result of practice, and you will get there.

The key thing is to think of the timer as your friend, not your boss. It's helping you keep track of the audience's expectations and energy level by proxy. Use the power of this tool.

A Note on Accents and Second Languages

As we discussed above, when giving a presentation to folks in a foreign language, it's imperative that you slow your pace down (sometimes waaaaay down) to ensure they can understand and/or receive translation. But what if the audience are native speakers but you—the presenter—have an accent or are presenting in a second language?

Never fear. This situation is exceedingly common, though it does tend to flummox accented speakers. I know there is tremendous societal pressure and often racism associated with people whose accents do not sound like the majority's. My mom is a smart refugee with a very thick accent, and in her chosen profession, she always said she felt that people discriminated against her because of it. Perhaps, if you're one of the millions of people reading this book who have an accent or learned English as a second language, you're feeling the same way about your presentation skills.

I always start off by pointing out that your accent is real, that the audience will hear it, and that you cannot control their judgment or opinion. You can shape it and guide it, but whatever prejudice or issues they have are their own. Some percentage of the people in the room will simply not grok you, and that's OK.

But this doesn't mean you don't need to put some specific effort into being as understandable as possible, and as compelling as possible. I don't mean doing accent coaching (though I wouldn't stop you if you wanted to), but rather to *slow down* and make sure that you are being very conscious of words that are hard for majority-accented people to hear clearly. If you have an especially thick accent, you may need to cap your pace at 125 WPM, and that's OK. Better to deliver less material well, than more material poorly.

Perhaps these are consonant sounds that your native language transposes differently than English. For example, in Hungarian (my family's primary language), the letter "S" is pronounced "SH" like Shalimar. The letter combination "SZ" makes the sound soft, as in "Superstar." For many Hungarians, training themselves to pronounce the S correctly is a life-long affair in English. For other people it's L and R, or the overuse of guttural sounds for CH and G. Whatever it is, by now you probably know that you have this issue, so why not work on it? First off, remove those troubling words as much as you can from your discussions. Second, make a list of words that are being mispronounced (someone watching you present a couple of times can be really helpful here) and practice saying them over and over again.

Some of the most successful entrepreneurs, politicians, physicians, experts, and academics spent their whole lives speaking with a thick accent. You can too. The key is to use the techniques described here to improve your chances of getting where you want to go.

Timing and the Fourth Wall

One of the most common ways that speakers break the fourth wall is by calling attention to the timer. I can't count the number of times I've heard a speaker say something like this, typically toward the end of their talk (obviously):

"Oh gosh, it seems like I'm out of time . . ."
"I had a few more things to say, but I'm out of time so . . ."
"Let me just move through these a bit quicker because I'm running out of time . . ."
Or the weirdest—when people just stop talking when the timer hits zero, even if the sentence they were saying isn't anywhere near complete.

Don't do any of these things.

Breaking the fourth wall is a bad strategy in general, and while you think you may need to explain to the audience what's gone wrong, in most cases, the audience won't really know what you were planning to say or in what order. So you're really in charge of the ending of your talk—it ends when you say it ends.

It is an important skill to be able to land the plane softly, even if you find yourself in an emergency timing situation. My general rule of thumb is this: whatever point you're currently elaborating on when the timer runs out, you should finish. Wrap it up there, perhaps delivering your very last line, say thank you, and go off the stage on that specific slide (don't try to advance to the end). If this takes an extra minute, so be it.

It does take some finesse to do this and make it look easy. But even if you do it in the most abrupt way possible, as long as it feels like "hey that could have been the ending," you'll be fine. Okay, so you didn't get to make all your points—but you got most of them in. That's a good start. In subsequent tellings, you'll be sure to cut a slide or two and give yourself the buffer we described.

MEMORIZATION

The fear of public speaking is well understood and widely held. But what, specifically, are most people afraid of? In talking with lots of speakers at all different skill levels, the answer seems to be embarrassment. And if you ask them what they're most concerned about causing embarrassment—it's forgetting their material.

You Can't Forget Something You Know

If there's one central theme or thesis in this book that I'll keep harping on, it's that all power and confidence comes from knowing yourself and your material. If you do not have a serious memory disorder it is likely that you have normal memory function, and can remember important things as well as the next person. Yes, people with exceptionally good memories have a built-in advantage when trying to learn new material—but even average memorizers can get there with some effort.

This does not mean you'll perfectly remember and recite every single word, phrase, or concept that you intended to convey at the outset of your talk. But what it does mean is that you can get across the major points—a couple of A-Ha! Moments and why you're the right person for this topic—even if you stumble, make mistakes, or forget key things.

But therein lies the rub—if you are focused on precise memorization as a priority over knowing the material, you're likely to get so wrapped up in getting your words right, you'll miss the point of the talk—which is to connect and persuade. Therefore, focusing on a script like an actor might is probably not the best strategy.

You're Not a Playwright or an Actor, Probably

It takes a lifetime of skill to write dialogue for people that sounds natural. Only the best writers are able to convey that kind of effortless reality, and it's what separates the best writers from mediocre ones.

Similarly, it takes a lifetime of skill and practice to read someone else's words on a page and deliver them with gusto, meaning, emotion, and unerring consistency. Only the best actors can give life to words with that degree of aplomb.

So, let me ask you this: Are you a phenomenal playwright or actor? If not, you'll want to abandon the idea right here—right now—of you scripting your talk, word for word, and memorizing the same. While I have no doubt that you'd be able to successfully accomplish this task and be off book, I also know from experience that this will produce a wooden, unrealistic, and poor overall talk.

What you need to do is make your presentation sound natural, effortless, like the only thing in the world the audience can imagine you talking about. Think about other times in your life when you might meet those criteria. Talking at a cocktail party. Arguing with your spouse or parents. Politely discussing politics or sports. Ha.

The goal is to take that same effortlessness, apply some rigor to it, ensure it's professional and on point, and make it possible for you to deliver it time and again. In order to accomplish this, we need an entirely different approach to scripting and memorization. And that's just what the doctor ordered.

Iterative-Decline Memorization: The A-Ha! Way

Memorizing has never been my strong suit. I was always a great extemporaneous speaker, meaning I could BS my way through a teacher asking me to talk about homework I never did, or a topic I wasn't prepared for. But that kind of spontaneous hand-waving rarely achieves greatness, and certainly isn't the right way to approach remembering things when they're important.

Over my lifetime, I developed a method for memorizing things that has served me super well as a public speaker. I do not claim to have invented this approach, and indeed—I know it's an amalgam of lots of trial and error and learning from others. But it is the way I do it, and it works for me and my coaching clients. It can work for you too.

Here's how.

Filler Words Don't Matter

Generally, speakers refer to words like "umm," "ah," "well," and the like as filler words. These are phrases people often use to fill the time when their brain is working to catch up to where their words ought to be. Many public speaking programs spend an inordinate amount of time on filler words—Toastmasters are even encouraged to use a clicker to count how many filler words there are in a given talk.

But I think the best strategy is to do nothing. Yes, you heard that right. Don't spend any time worrying about your filler words. As you go through the process of creation, memorization, and practice, you'll find the number of filler words you use will naturally decline. And even if you use some—and who doesn't— unless it's egregious, the audience will never remember you did that. If they do, that means the point (and delivery) of your talk was severely lacking.

Therefore, excessive filler words are a symptom of the underlying issue— where people over-invest in memorization instead of naturally understanding their material.

Precision Is Irrelevant—Only Points

It bears repeating: the goal of your presentation is not to say the precise and exact words you set out to say. Unless you are reading someone else's text, it is expected that you will bring yourself to bear, and no two discussions or presentations are precisely alike. Missing a word, phrase, or even a supporting point is not important. What matters is the overarching impact. Move beyond your self-critical need for perfection and start from the place where you are the expert, and your audience is happy to pick up whatever you have to put down.

Managing Your Internal Critic

In my experience, this internal critic (that self-critical voice you might hear from time to time) is the toughest thing for aspiring speakers to overcome. If you have a particularly strong internal critic, you might hear from them regularly. But even people without a great deal of self-criticism often hear their critic when trying something new, and especially something as high stakes as public speaking.

Contending with your internal critic takes a lifetime of learning, and major coping skills. So I won't pretend to provide a shortcut for this, especially if you're someone with a serious case (like me). But what I have learned is that you need to start by naming the inner critic as just that—a voice that isn't real, telling you that you're messing up. When you hear it, approach it with com- passion—it is usually a voice from our childhoods trying to protect us from harm, embarrassment, and mistake-making. It is, in effect, a frozen childhood defense mechanism. The best approach I've learned is to acknowledge it for what it is, and to respond to it with a relatively simple statement:

"That was true once. But is it still true? I'm older now and I'm going to take care of this by defending and protecting us."

Sounds hokey—but even someone like me feels this when I go to speak, and I'm sure you've had some of this too. You can't smash it down; you can only calm it with compassion.

Now I will let you in on something amazing and beautiful about the inner critic, if it's helpful for you at all. Over time, its power and voice will grow quieter around your public speaking. The more you do it, and the more you find yourself enjoying it, the less self-critical you will become. I believe part of this is the experience of *flow*—the state where you lose track of time or space and become one with the experience you're having. For some people this happens when they garden, run, play music, or even speak publicly. The beautiful thing about flow is that it puts you in the moment, and the more relaxed—even excited—you are about the activity, the more likely you are to go into flow. Repeated exposure to a flow state will make you happier and calmer overall, further improving your performance. The key is to create a positive feedback loop—and part of the goal here is to give you the tools and techniques to break the fear-criticism cycle and replace it with something wholly positive.

If you're interested in reading more about the inner critic—and it's worthwhile if you think this sounds at all like you—you might like *Taming Your Gremlin*, by Rick Carson. And for those of you interested in flow—one of the concepts that most informs my perspective on success in professional communications—you'd do no better than to read *Flow: The Psychology of Optimal Experience*, by Csikszentmihalyi. Both books are linked in the resource guide.

Specific—General

The core of the memorization method advocated here is switching your rehearsal process from specific to general and back again. Each time you change the frame for trying to remember something, you'll acquire just a little more information or confidence, and this will translate into faster and faster memorization.

In essence, the approach looks something like this:

1. Write down each idea on a slide in sentence form.
2. Practice #1 out loud a few times, knowing you'll likely deliver it a different way each time.
3. Convert each slide/idea into a full paragraph in the speaker notes.

4. Practice #3 out loud a few times, noticing how you're converging on a specific way of referring to the material.
5. Convert each slide/idea into a single phrase (less than a sentence) and use that phrase as a prompt for each slide/transition.
6. Practice #5 out loud several times, noticing how it's getting easier and easier to remember the core points, even without the text crutch.
7. Add visuals to each slide/idea and a couple of title words that define that slide/idea (see previous chapter on slide design).
8. Practice #7 out loud several times, noticing the image and short word prompt are sufficient to get you to remember what you meant to say.
9. In a separate document write down a TERSE bulleted list of ideas—one for each slide. Do not write more than a single statement, which need not be grammatically correct.
10. Practice your presentation out loud using just the list in #9 to prompt you to say the next thing.

I've included a full set of examples in the book's resource and study guides that allow you to visualize my process with an actual talk that I've created and given. To further help illustrate the point, I created a deck using a fictional presentation about non-fungible tokens, more commonly knowns as NFTs, as an example.

A. **Slide Idea Form**

People don't want to believe NFTs have value, but there is a market for them just like art in the real world, and if enough people believe, they will be real.

B. **Slide Paragraph Form**

NFT's get a bad rap, and are often the butt of jokes from commentators and the chattering classes. At their core, the argument they make Is that NFTs are ludicrously easy to copy, and what kind of value can bits have anyway? Even the counterargument that IRL art too doesn't have much inherent value, is usually batted away by skeptics saying, "but at least it is physical, has craftsmanship, and is difficult to copy." But the truth is that any student of markets and their history—both good and bad—knows that the value of an asset, any asset, is entirely based on what market makers and traders believe it is. That is to say, if enough people believe, anything can fly.

C. **Slide Phrase Form**

NFT's rap, jokes, easy to copy, bits no value, but art? real world crafts-manship. Markets made by belief, can fly.

D. **Slide Visual Word Form**

A slide of a Dutch master's rendition of a tulip with the phrase: Markets are Beliefs (n.b. the image reference is of the Dutch Tulip Frenzy which, if you don't know about it, is an instructive lesson on all things human behavior).

E. **Terse Bullet Point Note Form**

NFT joke, craftsman, market belief, fly

PUTTING IT TOGETHER

As you can infer from the above example, each time I create a new mnemonic to remember the material, the fidelity of my memory improves. By varying the types of prompts, I'm also forcing my brain to think about the issue from many different angles and remember based on several inputs. And through practicing and repetition, I am able to further reinforce and commit the ideas to memory.

To be sure, this takes quite a bit of practice. And an allergy to effort will not serve you well here. People are often shocked at how much practice we speakers put in for our one, 15-minute TED Talk. The truth is that practice combined with an effective memorization schema—rather than rote text repetition—provides the optimal balance of efficacy and accuracy.

Rehearsals

As you've seen throughout this book, I have a strong belief that practice is critical to success in this field. While you probably know how to practice something you want to learn, it seems important to highlight some of my best practices for . . . well . . . practice.

Focus Mode On

It goes without saying that you need to be completely free of any distractions during your rehearsal times. This means ensuring that all your devices are set to "stun" (e.g., focus mode on the iPhone) and that you avoid responding to any interruptions during that time. If you benefit from it, I suggest blocking time on your calendar to rehearse, and letting your significant other or colleagues know not to bother you during those times.

Rehearsal Time Required

You can safely budget twice as much time as the length of your talk for rehearsal blocks at the beginning of your process. So, if your talk is 15 minutes in length, assume you'll need at least 30 minutes in that moment to practice. If you can afford to go three times, I'd recommend blocking that much time in your calendar so you can also re-watch or re-listen to yourself and take notes thereafter.

Rehearse Often

The amount of lead time you have before your presentation determines how loose or tight your rehearsal schedule needs to be. With months, you can pace your initial rehearsals out perhaps by a week at a time. With days, you'll need to devote a substantial number of hours to repeat rehearsals.

In any event, developing a new talk for an experienced speaker tends to require at least 15 to 20 complete run-throughs of the material. If you are following the process in this book for the first time, you may need even more leeway to do this.

As the talk gets closer, I tend to rehearse more often, culminating in two complete run throughs on the day of presentation. One in the morning when I first wake up, and one right before I go into the final stretch. As you move through the rehearsals and get more confident in the material and your delivery, you'll find that subsequent run-throughs take less and less time. That is, the final couple of talk practices I do are not done at 1x speed, but rather at 5x speed. I know the material and am just making sure my muscles and memory are limber.

But at the beginning, your run throughs need to be minute-for-minute, because pacing and timing are a big part of the experience. So leave enough time for this but don't allow so much time to elapse between rehearsals that you can't remember your last practice session.

To Record or Not to Record

Some people love having recordings of their talks, and others simply get more frightened by watching themselves flub the material at the beginning. I often recommend for more anxious speakers to wait for recordings until you've at least reached the second slide phase (paragraph) so that you can start somewhere that isn't a total gong show. I would suggest recording yourself at least once per phase, and leaving enough time to review it.

Speak, Speak Out Loud

Even more important than recording yourself however is listening to yourself speaking out loud. I know many people wonder why I admonish them to give the presentation out loud every time, even if people aren't listening or recording. It can obviously make others give you a wide berth, concerned as they might be for your mental wellbeing. But despite the embarrassing nature of being a self-talker, speaking out loud is critical.

As you practice using this approach more and more often, you'll begin to find that you have been listening to yourself and that is informing your approach and decisions going forward. Even though you don't need to apply any conscious energy to it yourself, the reality is that if the words are said out loud, you will perceive them differently—and this will increase the fidelity of your rehearsals relative to the live talk.

I am someone who writes and thinks in full words and sentences, so for me, the verbosity helps me refine and improve my work. It is the only way I know how to do things. For many of you, thoughts and ideas live in your head in non-word forms, and translating them to language is itself a process. I understand and respect your learning differences but—and this is critical—the finished product of your work is inherently bound up in spoken language. Therefore, everything you do, from the content creation to the practice, needs to consider that your audience is going to be receiving your wisdom primarily through their ears.

An Audience of Your Own

Another tactic that I find very useful for most speakers is to have people listen to or watch your presentation as you're going through each development phase to provide feedback. This may also help you train your eyes if you're uncomfortable in front of a crowd, as you'll have someone to look at while speaking (more on that in the next chapter).

But if you're going to get a live listener, it's important that you follow some best practices to ensure you're getting the most out of it that you can.

First, the person listening needs to know that you want specific, not general feedback. That is, you want to hear which words, ideas, slides didn't make sense, which transitions were too bumpy, where they got lost, where you mispronounced, etc. It means being brutally honest and hyper critical, and the listener should be encouraged to take specific notes. Now, this remit generally excludes asking your mom or partner to provide the feedback, but if you think they have a "negative Nancy" inside them, perhaps giving them ground rules will help unleash the monster. And make no mistake, that's what you want. The least useful feedback is "that was good." You want to know what you can make better.

To view a checklist, you can use with reviewers, visit the resource guide.

Crucially, you must also be open to hearing their feedback. Ask for a copy of their notes if helpful, but listen closely as they share their thoughts. Sometimes their substantive feedback may not be super helpful (you are the expert in the topic after all, not them), but you should listen to it anyway. Many people in the audience will be at your proctor's level of understanding, and you'll have a sense of how they might react—especially to more complex technical concepts.

Even better is if you can have a dispassionate third party provide feedback. This is especially important if you are giving a fundraising or other sales pitch for the first time and need to know what kinds of objections might be raised. For my last startup, when we were out raising money, our lead VC organized a coaching session with one of his colleagues before we pitched the big boss. His colleague was—to put it mildly—an asshole during the pitch. But after I took a couple of deep breaths and calmed my ego, I realized why our investor had gone this route. Sharply critical feedback need not change how you present, but it does prepare you for the worst-case scenario, and that is very valuable.

Check this book's resource guide for more information about sessions you can join for feedback from the author and community.

The Dead-Eye Stare

One of the strategies I use to help practice a presentation is to do it in a "dead eyed stare" manner. That is, I stand about eight inches from a wall, soften my focus, and give the presentation in real time like that. I'd recommend you do at least a couple of presentations using this approach.

But why rehearse in this fashion? The reason is simple: most speakers need some amount of eye contact with their audience to be comfortable. We look for the listener's feedback in the form of nodding, staring, and note taking. Subconsciously we parse that information to determine whether or not we're doing a good job.

But often you can't see the audience. This may be because you're doing a recorded talk directly to camera, you're on a Zoom without being able to see others, or simply because the lighting on the stage is designed to prevent you from really seeing the crowd. TED Talks famously are lit in this way, but plenty of other talks I've given have had the same issues. If you are too wedded to the idea of needing nonverbal audience cues, you may find the absence of them to be disconcerting and it may keep you out of effective flow.

Practicing in this way can help you minimize the need for that feedback when it comes time to give the presentation. Give it a shot.

Notes and Slides Are Crutches

It's undoubtedly true that we want you to be able to give your presentation without notes or slides as a crutch. This helps ensure that if you face a major issue—technical or otherwise—you'll still be able to deliver your presentation. The memorization and practice techniques outlined above will undoubtedly help you reach that goal.

But if you do have slides to look at, or are able to take notes up on stage with you, is it bad to use them?

The short answer is of course not. Whatever it takes to help you deliver the best experience is fair game, and I have relied on my slides and notes often. There's no shame in it. But if you practice with that as the memory crutch you need, and something takes a turn for the worst, you will regret it. So think of them as nice to have rather than a must have, and you'll be perfectly set up for the future.

Now, let's make sure you've got the right strategies going into your speaking day by following some best practices.

10

You Are a Rockstar
(And So Is Your Hygiene)

If you've ever worked for a rockstar, or had more than a passing interest in their work, you've probably heard of their green room, and many of the rules they make promoters follow before and after their performance. These "riders" are usually explained with the following story, variously attributed to the Rolling Stones and several other major bands:

> [They] requested that there be M&Ms in a large bowl before every performance, but the green M&Ms have to be removed.

Apocryphally, the point of this story is that the band's management used this as a "test" to make sure that the promoters were following all of the requirements—from production to safety and comfort. But sorting out green M&Ms is just one of the outlandish rider items that various celebrities have been tied to at one time or another.

It may sound like a joke, but the green room for a major rockstar is deadly serious. This space—meant to be their oasis before the performance—is often occupied by the star/entourage for hours leading up to the show, and it's incredibly important that the energy be exactly as they require it. Mellow for some, amped for others—as comfortable, relaxing, and inviting as possible.

Even before getting on site to the venue, major performers have been engaged in a pre-show ritual that is out of sight. A good night's sleep at a luxury hotel, massage, work out, strictly controlled food regimen, highly scripted time to transfer to the venue, and an established post-event schedule are all common. The bigger the star—contrary to popular belief about hard partying—the more regimented their routine is. Once they learn the optimal combination of psychological and hygiene factors to produce the perfect show, their management tends to wash, rinse, and repeat to ensure the most return on the hefty investment associated with the tour. After all the hard work, in other words, it's a small price to pay to make sure that the audience gets the full experience they were promised.

You may be asking yourself why this allegory is relevant—however interesting it might be. The reason is simple:

> When you agree to give a speech at an event—big or small, live or virtual—you are agreeing to give a *performance* and you need to treat yourself like the *rockstar* that you are to get the most out of the effort you've invested.

So many speakers I've coached fail to see that their work is a type of performance, though the signs are pretty obvious. There is a stage, microphones and lights, an A/V team, a script, some visuals/scenes—heck there's even a space called the "green room" at most major events. It's no coincidence that we spent so much time in this book going over story frameworks and presentational tips. You are a performer, like a stand-up comedian, stage actor, or musician . . . but different.

After all the weeks or months of preparation, the investments you've made in creating content, perfecting your delivery, travel, and even clothes, are you sure you want to risk it all because you didn't sleep well enough, or spent the day doing high-impact tasks that left you feeling depleted? The answer is, of course, no.

Everything that happens in the 24 to 36 hours before (and the few hours after) a speech, needs to be carefully planned, considered, and executed. We call this "speaker hygiene," and it's the subject of this chapter.

A Note About Privilege—Resources

Warning: the advice in this chapter is going to seem very bougie. I know that many of you reading this don't have the luxury of avoiding work the day of a performance, or traveling a day early, or any of the other expensive and privileged things I'm going to suggest below. Obviously, there's nothing wrong with you, and there's nothing wrong with picking and choosing the things from the chapter that you *can* implement in your life. I don't want it to sound like an all-or-nothing prescription, nor do I want you to do things that will ultimately leave you worse off.

All that having been said however, the framework presented here is the one that a professional speaker would and should use. The more money you make or are trying to make from public speaking, the more these strategies become accessible and necessary parts of your process. But even for the casual or neophyte presenter, there are lessons here to implement in your practice.

MANAGING YOUR SCHEDULE

Once I know the timing for my talks, I create a little timeline/worksheet to map out my agenda for the day of and prior to the event. I've included a chart below that shows some of my proposed timings. Your mileage may vary, but this is as good a starting point as any.

Presentation:
T-minus 1 hour: green room, final practice, A/V prep, solitary
T-minus 2 hours: practice, shower/dress, head to venue
T-minus 3 hours: minimum wake up time
T-minus 5 to 2 hours: eat, exercise, sleep/nap, relax, practice if possible
Night before: sleep 8 hours
Day before (if possible) stage and A/V check, A/V materials in

Speaking Info Sheet

If you are booked to speak by an event organizer or speakers' bureau, they will generally produce an info sheet for everyone involved. This sheet will include all the particulars of your talk, including the title, length, A/V requirements, travel, addresses, and contact information of key stakeholders. It is important that you have this speaking info sheet with you. If you're organizing your own speaking program, I recommend creating an info sheet for each talk you give, so that you have a standardized form of key required information.

To view a copy of this info sheet template, visit this book's resource guide.

Traveling In

If you have to travel to an event—even if it's from your bedroom to your living room—you need to build in some buffer for delays and rest/reset prior to your talk. I've seen countless speakers—in an effort to maximize their time in the office or with their families—schedule themselves to fly on the day of a talk, and fly home at the end of the day. If they were trying to represent how little they cared about the speech, this would be a perfect way to do it.

But actually, the problems with this strategy go well beyond the perception it may create. Travel can be unpredictable, delays are common, and in light of pandemics, border restrictions, and other fast-moving societal changes, travel isn't as reliable as it seems. You need to leave a buffer for delays.

But you also need to build in a buffer for sleep, rest, and reset. I love to travel and am very good at it, but the last thing I want to do is roll from a taxi-flight-taxi-hotel sequence directly to my talk. There's no possible way I can give my best performance.

So I recommend for all talks that require significant travel (e.g., by plane, or a drive longer than 2 to 3 hours), that you plan to arrive the *day before* your talk. It can be the night before, to minimize your time away, but ideally there should be a night's sleep between your travel plans and your talk. If your talk is in a very different time zone, and/or you are very impacted by jet lag / time changes, I highly recommend coming even earlier to allow yourself to adjust. For example, if you're going to Asia from the United States, I would arrive a minimum of two nights prior to any talk I'm doing.

Generally, conference organizers (or your company) will pick up the cost of travel for invited speakers—though it is often not a lucrative line item until you're at the top of the field. But hotel rooms are usually fairly easy for organizers (or corporations) to come by, and I recommend asking for the time you need to adjust and be your freshest. Plus, don't you want to take advantage of this business trip and see/do something? More experience will only make you a better speaker, so do it (and write it off).

Getting to the Venue

Though it may seem like you know the relationship between your hotel room/ home and the venue where you'll be presenting, I can tell you from experience—this isn't always true. I have had situations where I didn't look closely enough at the event outline, assuming my talk was in the same hotel where I was staying—only to find out at the last minute (!!) that I needed to take a shuttle. Or perhaps I'm in the right building overall, but finding the specific room where I'm presenting may be a little more challenging than expected.

I can't say I've ever been late to a talk because of this kind of last-minute venue confusion, but I have come close by my standards, for example, I arrived with less than an hour to go. And I don't want you to make the same mistake.

The solution is simple: the day before (or as far in advance as possible given the schedule), you should travel the route from your hotel room or home to the presentation venue. If you're attending a conference, this will give you a chance to get registered and meet some of the key people. And, as we'll discuss below, you almost certainly will want to get a feel for the stage and do a quick A/V walkthrough for a major presentation. It's a good idea to combine all of those activities so you can be ready and familiar on the day of. The key is to always keep your stress in the optimal range, and knowing your way helps manage it.

GETTING INTO THE ZONE

The 30 to 60 minutes right before your talk are crucial to your success. You need to be in the best possible headspace prior to going out on stage (or launching on Zoom) and the way you do that is to carefully manage your time immediately prior to the talk.

My preferred approach is to arrive at the green room super early—at least an hour before my talk. This allows my arrival to be calm and relaxed. I'll check in with the team and let them know I'm there for them to mic at any time. And then, I find a quiet corner and run my slides—preferably staring into a wall.

At this point, I've already seen the room and know what to expect, so the only thing I need to do here is to expect the unexpected. I want to run the talk one last time to ensure that I have as much confidence as possible in my ability to deliver no matter what. I'll typically give the talk in double time at this point—I shouldn't need to work on my timing quite as much anymore.

Once I've run the talk, my practice time is over. And now it's time to get psyched up. I'll always have some music or meditation on my phone ready to go (see below) and I'll run this on my headphones until just before I need to make the final prep to go onstage. I generally do not speak to other speakers and keep to myself here. There can be a lot of temptation to chat with others, and you may find this relaxing, but I think it's a waste of energy. There'll be plenty of time after.

Another way you can sap your energy before your talk is to spend too much time listening to the person who comes on before you. If they are really great, you might want to do it, but there's not much value in most presentation settings (as discussed) for you to be intimately familiar with the preceding talk, nor for you to make reference to it in any way. This is an area where public speaking is very much not like stand-up comedy—we usually don't do call backs. You might, however, want to have a working understanding of the audience's energy levels, and so paying attention to the final few minutes of the preceding talk can be instructive.

And be sure to use the restroom at least 10 minutes before your talk. More on that below.

In those final few moments, where you're standing (or sitting) in the wings, knowing you're about to walk out on stage, take several deep breaths. Make sure your phone is off, everything looks OK, and that you can clearly see and understand the technical process (how you get the clicker, where you step, etc.). The more you can anticipate and know the process, the calmer you'll feel as you take the stage and get underway.

Pre-Talk Nerves

The generally accepted best practice for calming yourself down and getting into the zone before any challenging activity is to practice some mindfulness meditation. Grab your smartphone and look for a short (5 minutes maximum) guided meditation on apps like Calm, Headspace, or even YouTube. Do this prior to your talk and pick out the one that you think might be best for your mental frame. Then bookmark that and come back to it 30 minutes before you're slated to go on.

If you're like me, music might be just what you need instead. Sometimes I want to get pumped, and love playing bands like Arcade Fire. Other times I want mellow, and so I'll play music that calms and enervates, like Tycho. I know you're deeply curious about my musical tastes, so if you want to crib my Spotify pre-talk playlist, snap the QR code below. Don't judge.

My pre-talk Spotify Playlist: https://qrco.de/bczBoW

If you're decidedly not like me, you might want to do some physical exercise—take a walk, stretch, jump up and down a bit—prior to your talk. I've heard that a bit of exertion can help calm/engage the mind, and it sounds oh-so-wonderful. I really love this journey for you.

Conserving Energy

Probably the biggest mistake that I've seen speakers make is to fill their day with events, meetings, talks, lectures, socializing, and the like before their talk. For example, if you're scheduled to go on at 4 p.m. at a conference, a speaker will feel compelled to spend the entire day doing conference activities. Or if the event is not interesting, you might feel compelled to put in a full day's work on your office tasks while waiting for your presentation to start.

This is a terrible idea. The concept of decision fatigue has been well documented, and arises from a depletion of carbohydrates in your brain. Basically, the longer you've been awake and the more demanding tasks you've performed in the time leading up to the "decision" the worse you can be expected to perform. It's not just sleep habits that need to be managed, it's also mental depletion habits—and industries from aviation to criminal justice are all adapting to this new reality.[1]

If you spend the day before your talk doing other activities, by the time you get up on stage, you will be hard pressed to give your best performance. Think about how you feel after a normal workday—are you enthusiastic about going and doing another mentally taxing activity? Can you hype yourself up (perhaps with caffeine or Adderall) and perform energetically and adequately? For sure. But will it be your best? Absolutely not.

No matter how much you feel like spending the day schmoozing or doing work, don't. As a general rule, when I'm presenting at a conference, I do not do any conference activities before my talk—and I even avoid the attendees seeing me. I want the first impression to be me up on stage, and I want to save all my energy for that. *After* my talk is over—everything is fair game, and I can often be found on a boat party, at a talk/seminar of interest, at a meal, etc. But before—I try to do as little as possible.

And in keeping with brain glucose findings of decision fatigue, I tend to make sure I have something sweet—chocolate or a piece of fruit—to eat right after I'm finished with my talk. It helps replenish my energy and be my best, bubbly self when attendees want to corner me to talk about what I had to say.

If it's an option for you, and you absolutely have to get some work done the day of your talk, consider taking a little power nap a few hours before you're scheduled to go on. Closing your eyes for even 20 minutes (providing you have enough time afterward to get motivated) can be a very powerful way to do a bit of an energy reset.

EVENT TIMINGS

Part of the process of becoming a great communicator with the A-Ha! Method is knowing yourself. This bleeds over from what you say to how you say it, and even to when you perform.

Most people don't realize that it is possible to ask event organizers for a particular time of day or day of the event if you like. There's no guarantee they can accommodate, but usually they will try to take this into consideration when finalizing the program. They have to consider the content's flow, the attendee's mental states, and the speaker's travel schedules when laying out the agenda, so there's no harm in throwing in your request.

But what is better? A morning talk or an afternoon one?

Well, a lot of that depends on you, your energy, whether you're a morning person or not, and when you think you will be your best. Keeping in mind that you have to be up 3 hours prior to your talk, for some speakers an 8 a.m. breakfast speech is perfect; they're up at 5 a.m. anyway, so everything is peachy. Other people tend to be at their most fluid and intelligent later in the day, and so a late talk might be ideal.

Various slots at a conference are also typically reserved for certain "kinds" of speakers. I've organized dozens of major conferences and minor events, and this is the rubric I generally use:

- The opening and closing keynotes: high-status speakers, greatest impact
- The session before and after lunch: speakers who can command the audience and get them motivated (pre-lunch audiences are anxious; post-lunch, lethargic)
- The closing talks of the day or event: speakers that are able to draw attendees so attrition can be minimized

If you fall into one of these categories, or would like to, you can make a pitch to occupy one of those slots. Just tell the organizer you think you'd make a great after-lunch speaker because you have a rousing subject, and they'll probably jump at the chance to put you in the toughest slot in the house. Just make sure you can deliver.

Sleep Habits

The night before your talk, you need to get a good night's sleep. You may be the kind of person who feels perfectly refreshed with 5 hours, or—like me— you might need 8 or 9 to really be at your best. In any event, ensure that you've left yourself that much for cold, dark, quiet sleep. It is essential.

Now especially if you're traveling, sleeping in an unfamiliar bed, or just nervous about your talk the next day, it's going to be tough to get a full night's restful sleep. You may find your mind racing or just that sleep stays fitful. Many performers report having a great deal of difficulty sleeping before major events, but I promise you this will improve over time, as you get better and better at building confidence in your speaking.

To minimize the chances of having a bad night, however, I recommend a few key steps.

First, make sure you have earplugs and eyeshades with you. This is critical if you're staying in a hotel as the noise and light may be different from what you're used to at home. Even if you don't like sleeping with them in your day-to-day life, this is a great time to take advantage of their benefits.

Second, meditate or perform some calming exercises before you settle down for bed. Leave the final 30 minutes of your pre-sleep ritual to non-screen-based activities, like reading, meditation, or stretching. It is good advice to practice this every day, but I know how hard this can be. Just this once you can do it.

Third, I'm not going to advocate that you take sleeping pills—natural or otherwise, but I do find it helpful to have some at the ready in case you really cannot get yourself down that night. I'm a champion sleeper in general, but taking a bit of melatonin the night before a big talk just helps get and keep me asleep that much better. Of course, do not try a new medical regimen on your sleep habits the night before you give a talk. You should have already experimented before and understand the impacts any pharmaceuticals may have. And yes, I do know this is the slippery slope that has imperiled many talented young artists over the years, and I certainly don't want the same fate for you. Nonetheless, sleep is so important that I highly recommend talking to your doctor and making sure you have what you need in your arsenal.

Lastly, if you're like me and find that you can fall asleep easily but often wake up in the middle of the night, mind racing, I suggest you have some tools at the ready to deal with this. One is to have something to read. Another might be to practice meditation. You may also even be able to calm your mind by repeating from memory a few parts of your upcoming speech, just to prove that you can do it.

Whatever steps you take, ensure that you're aggressively preserving the sanctity of your night's sleep. Don't take a redeye, don't go out partying hard the night before, and certainly don't leave yourself groggy when you need to be awake and alert. It's just that important in your journey to becoming a great speaker.

DIET

Almost as much as sleep, the food you eat the day of your presentation can have a big impact on your success. Now, everyone's diet and metabolism are different, so I won't try to give you a specific prescription for how to approach this planning. Rather, it's to raise your awareness of some considerations you ought to make for your diet.

Critically, you don't want to be up on stage at a moment where your energy is crashing after a meal, or where you're so jittery (see caffeine in the next section) that you have trouble being in flow. Both of these scenarios are problematic, and you should avoid either of them.

So, knowing what time your presentation is and how your digestion/metabolism works, you should plan your eating in accordance with whatever will give you the greatest chance of a level, calm energy at presentation time. Generally speaking, I avoid eating anything in the couple of hours before a talk (unless it's early, early morning) to try to control my energy level. It can be especially tempting if you are the breakfast speaker, and the organizers have put out a tasty spread of pastries and fruits. If you must eat something really close to your talk, I suggest minimizing your carb intake (neither pastry nor fruit really work for this) to avoid a potential crash.

The balancing factor with food—and indeed most things in this chapter—is that you want to learn better habits for presentation days, but you also don't want to be experimenting on yourself when the impact/cost of such an experiment may be your talk's overall quality. Critically, you need to balance these things out and consider what's best for you.

And again, after your talk, I recommend having some carbohydrates at the ready to replenish your depleted mental energy.

Caffeine

Caffeine and other stimulants are commonly used to raise our energy levels, and it can be very tempting to slam some back right before a presentation.

This is especially true if we're feeling a lot of aversive anxiety toward the talk, which can often manifest as tiredness. But of all the options at your disposal to manage your mood and energy on the day of your presentation, caffeine presents the biggest risk for most people.

I have definitely been there: unusually tired, grabbing an extra cup of coffee in the green room while waiting to go on, only to find myself jittery and speaking a mile a minute just a few moments later. Don't be like me—factor caffeine into your plans and you'll be able to maximize its value.

The first thing to know is that oral caffeine has a delayed effect, typically taking around 20 to 30 minutes for most people to become active. So, in a standard TED Talk, if you slammed a cup of coffee right before walking out on stage, you wouldn't expect to feel the effects until after you came off the stage. So why bother?

If you drink a cup of coffee 30 minutes before your talk, you're liable to start your talk at the peak of your stimulated self. Given our tendency to talk fast at the beginning when we're most nervous, this can have major deleterious effects on our performance.

The key is to ensure that your energy level and (by proxy, if you're into measuring such things) your resting heart rate are on the high side of calm. What you might call alert or "ready to play" state. If you put it in an athletics context, you are warmed and limbered up—so you're not starting from a true calm state—but you're not so keyed up that you perceive everything as a threat. The way you felt before that perfect tennis or golf match? Like that.

For me, this means I'll allow myself a half cup of coffee around 40 minutes prior to going up on stage. This will ensure I have that little extra oomph, but that I will have passed the peak of the caffeine's kick when the talk begins. Having that peak arousal occur 10 minutes before going on stage is optimal. If you can't time your metabolism that closely, it's fine—just consider the constraints I listed above, and act accordingly.

n.b. For coffee and tea lovers who usually take cream: don't. I'm #team-dairy, but it does tend to make people a bit more phlegmy and dry-mouthed, and those are two qualities you want to avoid.

And a note on other stimulants, like Adderall or cocaine. I know lots of people who use one or both to get themselves hyped up before a talk. I can't and won't lecture you on how to live your life, but I will gently remind you: the goal is not to seem like a hype monster when you walk out. For an example of what it looks like to have energy but not seem crazy—watch Tony Robbins when he comes on stage. He is clearly pumped and energetic, but he doesn't have that bonkers bouncing-off-the-wall energy that we tend to associate with most motivational speakers. That is the kind of energy you want to emulate—alert, in the zone, but not crazy.

EXERCISE

Don't take exercise advice from me.

Now that we've got that out of the way, despite being a bad exerciser, I've actually found that speech days give me the perfect motivation, time, and excuse to work out. I like to use my time before my talk (remember: I'm not sapping my energy) to do something enervating, like an elliptical. Of course, I need to make sure the workout doesn't leave me tired and less energetic than I would have without it. If that's how my energy works, I would leave working out until after my talk.

But if you can work in a good bit of cardio or a light weights workout before your talk and get pumped up, all the better. Just don't do anything like "leg day," as you almost certainly will need to be able to stand for a couple of hours. Same with shoulders, as you'll need to be able to maintain your arms in a lifted position for some time. Again, the key is to do what makes you the happiest and healthiest without overdoing it.

RESTROOM USAGE

There's no polite way to put this: the anxiety associated with speaking can make you want to go to the bathroom.

The worst possible thing for your confidence is to feel like you desperately need to use the restroom in the few moments before going on stage, or—worse yet—while you're up there speaking, suddenly having the realization that you have to pee. It is going to break your concentration, leave you stressed, and has the potential to ruin your talk.

Now you probably have your bathroom needs under control in your regular life, but let me reiterate—speaking days are not exactly like regular life. In particular, you won't have the luxury of a break in the middle of your talk or, indeed, in the few minutes or so beforehand. So be sure to time your bathroom breaks accordingly.

I will use the restroom—whether I feel like it or not—around 15 minutes before I go up on stage. It's part of my pre-presentation routine, and it does wonders. It's a kind of insurance policy. And similarly, to the sections on diet and caffeine, consider your beverage intake as it relates to your bathroom needs around speaking.

You may want to arrive on the dais super hydrated, but if you don't have much of a bladder and drank a liter of water right before, I promise things are going to get awkward part way through your talk. Make sure you're well hydrated earlier in the day. As a general rule, I'll deprive myself of a bit of water right before the talk. That is, I'll take a sip or two just to make sure my mouth isn't dry, but I'll avoid drinking an entire bottle right before taking the stage.

Depending on the setup of the event, there may also be some water on the dais or table for you, and you can feel free to grab a sip in the middle of your presentation if your mouth gets dry. Of course, having a dry mouth will make your speech more difficult to give and understand, so you want to make sure you're lubricated well enough to deliver without going over.

I highly recommend drinking a big glass of water right after your talk though. It really dehydrates you more than you think (see sweat) and you'll want to come back into balance as quickly as possible.

SWEAT

There is nothing that is more disturbing to public speakers than sweat—and nothing more unavoidable. If you are one of those people that congenitally do not sweat—I applaud you—and you can skip this section. But if, like me, you're a sweat-er, read on.

Sweat is a natural reaction to both being warm and being aroused. It is also, however, something that can make you appear unprofessional or worse—undermine your presentational confidence. Trust me, the first time you watch a video of yourself with dark pit stains, you'll know what I'm talking about. So I think it's worth spending a little bit of time on the issue.

Knowing that sweat is natural doesn't make it any less likely to happen. And because anything that can shake your confidence is really bad in this context, we want to prioritize feeling confident about your sweat over any other kind of remedy.

Start by getting some prescription strength antiperspirant. You may be able to use the store-bought stuff, and if so, great. But having the prescription-strength roll-on will allow you to apply it to critical areas before your talk, and to use it judiciously just for these events.

If you have a great deal of sweat that breaks through antiperspirants, you may also want to consider a "sweat proof" undershirt. Several manufacturers (including Eji's) make a sweat proof undershirt that won't prevent you from sweating, but will keep it from showing under your clothes. We'll discuss clothing choices in greater detail in the next section, but I want to flag that darker colored clothes tend to show sweat more seriously, so making a lighter color choice can be beneficial.

Lastly, try to minimize your body temperature before going up on stage. That is, if you sweat, don't do things that might cause you to sweat before you even start talking. This could include running late to the presentation (because you didn't follow the pre-planning advice above), or a pre-exercise that you do to get your heart rate up. Either way, don't do it. If you've ever been in a TV studio, you'll notice that it's usually incredibly cold there. That is both to protect the equipment from overheating, but also to ensure that the presenters don't sweat on camera.

If you have control over the temperature in the room where you're presenting (e.g., at home), I recommend turning the air conditioning way up in the hour before you're scheduled to go live, so that the room starts as cold as you can tolerate. You'll probably need to dial back the A/C to avoid a whooshing noise in the video, so starting colder allows you to stay cooler, longer. If you're presenting in someone else's room, part of the benefit of checking the space out in advance is to give you the opportunity to adjust your clothing to the temps in the room. If it's running super hot (as it typically does in Europe, for example), you may want to dress differently than if it's Thailand-level air conditioned (really cold).

Clothes and Personal Branding

The clothes you wear for your presentations serve several purposes. First and foremost, they brand you—it is often the first thing people really take in about your presentation, and so what you wear matters for making a good first impression. But your clothes also need to be functional—giving you the kind of confidence (I look good, I won't look sweaty, etc.) and protection from the elements necessary to do your best.

Let's begin at the most important part of this equation: how your clothes make you feel. Above all else, I would consider choosing your clothes based on the feeling they give you. Do they make you feel powerful? Comfortable? What is the emotion that would best give you the confidence you need while up on stage? Wear that.

With some exceptions, I also think your clothes should fit your personal brand rather than the event's dress expectations. Most dress codes for events have gone out the window, but sometimes you might feel pressured to wear a suit or dress because the other speakers are natty. That is perfectly fine, and you should do whatever makes you feel like you fit in, but remember your brand must come first.

When I was touring the world speaking about gamification, I would initially eschew wearing anything super formal. In fact, for my first TED Talk I think I arrived wearing flip flops. I did this to make sure I felt comfortable in the heat of the Belgian summer, but also because my topic was games related—and I was playing the part of "gamer telling everyone else what's going to happen." Thus, I had a part to play, and that part was—by definition—more casual than the people in the audience I was speaking to. It helped convey my ideas, and you can consider both the positive and negative sides of dressing up for yourself.

Another common allegory is about the technical founder that wears a suit to pitch American VCs. As a general rule, you're told, don't do that. The VC wants to see a real nerdy person, and the suit sends the wrong message. Conversely, if you're pitching investors in the Middle East, you may want to wear a suit regardless.

And that does bring us to the dress code issue by region. Wherever possible, it's valuable to know the expectations of dress in the place you're speaking. This will often be listed on your speaker information sheet, and if you're traveling somewhere with expectations of modesty, you may want to ask more pointed questions about what you can and cannot wear.

Another consideration for your clothes is how well they travel. If you are going to give lots of live presentations, you may want to have a set of presentation clothes that you can easily travel with. And if you intend to do a lot of talks, I'd also recommend getting a rotating set of tops that you can comfortably wear once and never again. Early on in my speaking career, I'd wear the same thing regularly, and sometimes people would make a comment like "you must really love green—you're always wearing it." Needless to say, that is embarrassing and a pretty cheap problem to solve. It doesn't mean you can't re-wear these clothes, but just pay attention to the context and try not to repeat yourself too often. The one exception is if you're going for a Steve Jobs–esque standard look, but you'd better be sure you can pull off a turtleneck like the pros.

The last thing to think about is color and pattern. In almost every case, you're going to be recorded—and this is especially true if you're giving remote presentations. Generally speaking, you should avoid green just in case a virtual background is being used—either by you or in post-production (a mistake I made often, because I love green). And also, you should avoid wearing any tightly checked patterns (like houndstooth) or with a lot of detail. This can appear strangely to the viewer in recorded content. Simpler, solid colors are best. Also, if your oeuvre is more casual, you may be tempted to wear logo'd clothing. Don't do this, as any broadcast of said logo may require clearance, and your talk recording could end up on the cutting room floor.

For home Zoom presentations also, be sure not to wear a color that blends with the colors in the background. If you follow the advice in this book, you'll set up a real (e.g., not virtual) backing screen for your at-home speeches. But even still, if you're sitting in front of a super white wall, don't wear white. And if you are using a virtual backdrop, avoid matching that color. You may blend into the background—and if there's one thing we don't want you to do, it's that.

TECH SETUP

Whether you're doing a real world or virtual talk, you'll undoubtedly need to do some technical setup to make your presentations happen. Let's take a look at the best practices for both scenarios.

LIVE SETUP

Typically, if you're giving a live presentation, there will be some kind of audio/ visual support. At a major conference or event, this will include a large-ish team of experts who are responsible for audio, presentation decks, and so forth.

The most important thing is for you to go to the tech rehearsal (if offered) and make a point of checking in with the tech team well in advance of your talk. I suggest the day before if possible. Go up to the tech desk, introduce yourself, and ask for an opportunity to walk through your slides and/or to practice slide management and speaking from the actual stage.

The slide step-through is especially important, because often things can get lost in translation—even if you're not translating from Keynote to PowerPoint. Fonts and slides can get messed up, and I can't count the number of times I've sent my slides in advance to the production coordinator, only to find that the wrong version (or no version at all) is available to the A/V crew. Having some time to go over this well in advance will make it possible to make any necessary changes.

Backup to the Backup

And speaking of changes, it's likely you may want to be able to tweak your slides or presentation in the day prior to the event. I highly recommend against making changes the day of the event if you can. To ensure that the A/V team has the right current content, you must do a walkthrough—and you should have:

1. A slide deck in all formats (KEY, PPT, PDF) on a USB stick
2. The slide deck in all formats uploaded to a cloud service (e.g., iDrive, Google, Dropbox)
3. The fonts and underlying audio/video files in the presentation saved separately from the deck itself
4. A clearly articulated versioning system

You need these backups-to-the-backup just in case there's a last-minute problem—and they happen more often than you think. You should also include the PDF version because in some situations, this is an essential fall back to ensure that at least your basic slides can get shown.

Embedded Audio and Video Considerations

Be sure to tell the A/V crew directly if there is audio or video in the file, and how it's going to play. Don't assume that they've paid close enough attention to your deck to know this. They need to level the audio and may need to change the lighting scheme when a video plays, so it's essential they have clarity about this.

Who's Advancing

In most cases, when you receive the "clicker" for slides as you walk on stage (or control of the Zoom feed), you will control the actual slides that show up. The A/V team should explain the functions of the clicker to you and how it works. Pay attention even if you think you know how it should work—events may implement the same tech, differently.

For example, at some events with bigger broadcast budgets, your action on the clicker won't actually advance the slides. It will instead present a big arrow to an A/V team member who is responsible for advancing the slides. They prefer this kind of setup if they need to master the audio and video in real time, as it gives the producer control about which input to call for. But by definition, this means that the person working may miss your press, and it's almost always true that they will ignore it if you accidentally press back on the handheld. You may need to tell them to reverse out loud if this happens, but as a general rule I'd suggest never trying to go backward in your deck.

Just remember to ask who's really in charge of the slides before you make assumptions.

Tech Setup at Home/Virtual

All the same rules apply as described in the preceding sections for remote/virtual presentations, such as those you might give via Zoom. Whether you are presenting from home or the office, there are a few technical things you need to master well before the talk.

Physical Setup

To setup correctly for remote presentations, you need to have a few things:

1. Camera
2. Microphone
3. Lighting
4. Background

Camera

For a camera, your laptop or desktop's webcam will probably do fine—and by now you've probably upgraded your camera if you have an older machine. In any event, make sure your camera is relatively high resolution and that the lens is cleaned properly before your event.

Microphone

If you have a reasonably new computer (especially a mac) you probably have an excellent, built-in microphone. However, you will need an earpiece to go along with that mic to ensure that there is no echo created while presenting. Even if your echo cancellation works super well in general, make sure you're listening to the event on an earpiece. AirPods became popular during the COVID-19 pandemic, but lower-end versions may not always have the best actual microphone for picking up your voice. If you're going to give a number of remote presentations, I recommend picking up a standalone, high-quality microphone like a Blue Yeti. Use this in conjunction with your earpiece to maximize the quality of the overall recording.

Lighting

You want to make sure that you're nicely lighted for any virtual presentations. Lighting kits for Zoom talks have become cheap, powerful, and widely available. Just make sure that the light source is set up correctly to shine on your face at a distance that prevents unsightly shininess. It's also important to manage the windows in the room you're presenting in. If the windows are behind you or to your side, your webcam may pick up incorrect lighting cues and you'll find yourself washed out—or with the lighting getting darker and brighter. We don't want this. If you have natural light in your room, congrats—but this is not a good time to depend on it. If you can't block it out entirely, make sure the light is shining on your face and not on the side or behind.

Background

Many online presentation apps like Zoom have powerful virtual backgrounding capability. This uses your computer's graphics processor to figure out what's your face, and then replaces everything that's *not* your face with an image you choose. This has been used successfully by many people during the COVID pandemic, and it works fine for casual meetings that aren't being recorded for posterity.

If you are planning to deliver quality presentations from your home or office, I suggest setting up a live background behind you that works to create some visual interest and depth, and to position you appropriately in it. During the remotes-from-home that became so popular during the pandemic, you saw many people setting up almost comically fake backgrounds so they could sit in front of them. A well-placed book, some fake flowers, and an object against a non-solidly colored wall (e.g., with shelves or wallpaper) is a great go-to solution.

The reason that these folks don't use an actual green screen (and why I'm going to caution most of you against depending on one), is that even though the special virtual backgrounding tech works better with a green screen, it still tends to look fake. A green screen is a powerful tool if you're going to be recording long form video content (e.g., a course or lecture) because it can give you the power to place things in the field of vision in post-production. But for the standard streaming presentation, a physical background—no matter how comically fake—is better than virtual.

Some presenters who do this a lot construct a little corner in their home or office that is specially designed for delivering streamed presentations. This can include—as I've seen some do—an actual monitor that can be used to deliver your slides instead of using the slide sharing features of Zoom. You may not always be able to use this on-camera screen, however, as organizers may want you to use the classic screen sharing approach for their video recording purposes. But if you're going to do it a lot, and have the resources, this might be a good investment for you to make.

Computer Hygiene

Another area that many speakers neglect is ensuring their computers are configured optimally to give virtual presentations. As you might have noticed, sometimes apps like Zoom cause your computer to slow down a great deal, and if that happens in the middle of a live broadcast—or one that's being recorded, you may come to regret it. So make sure you have a device that is current and powerful enough to do the basics of this function.

Even if you have a super new computer, you should follow certain steps to ensure that you get the best performance each time.

I create a separate user on my machines called "presentation." When I have a presentation to give, I'll reboot into this user before beginning. This user's workspace only contains the tech necessary to give presentations, and nothing else. There are no extraneous background processes running, so I can be sure that the maximal CPU power is being allocated to the stream. If you can't or won't create a new user, I nonetheless want to strongly recommend that you reboot your machine 15 minutes before your call time for any virtual presentation. This will help your machine run faster and more efficiently.

You may not have much control over your internet speed, and it's entirely possible that you may become glitchy during a presentation, but never fear—just keep moving forward and trust that the recorded version will not contain this error. Obviously, if you get completely cut off, you will need to come back online to continue.

Presenter Configuration

There are many configuration options for most online presentation software, like Zoom. Rather than go into the specifics, it seemed prudent to cover a couple of the most important basic concepts.

First and foremost, every presentation app will let you control the camera and audio inputs (separately for audio in and out). Sometimes, this will not be in the app, but rather at the system level. So one of the main reasons for doing a run through is to figure out where this is. Before you go on, step through all these settings and make sure you're configured the way you want, for example: (cam) built in HD webcam, (audio in) Yeti Nano, and (audio out) AirPods. If you have multiple options for each, be sure to choose the right set.

Additionally, if your presentation contains video or audio, you may need to make several configuration choices before sharing your screen. On Zoom, there are two awkwardly placed checkboxes on the share screen interim page, where you have to remember to check "optimize video" and "share audio" so that your audience can see decent video and hear the audio output. Unfortunately, if you forget to check these, your screen share will work but embedded media will not.

And speaking of screen share, at this point in the historical arc of COVID-19, I'm sure everyone has experienced the fear that they would accidentally screen share the wrong app, or that a notification might appear on your machine that would be, delicately, private.

The best way to mitigate this is to use the "presentation user" configuration I mentioned above. Then you can globally disable all notifications, and you shouldn't have extraneous screens to accidentally share. But in any event, when you're sharing a screen with an audience, don't share your entire desktop—as tempting as it may be. Those are the scenarios that are most likely to cause your computer/app to crash, for inadvertent notifications, and also to create that inception-like endless window effect. Not cute. Always share just a specific screen from an app unless there's a good reason to share the desktop. If you have to do this, that's even more reason to use a specific user for presentations—so that you can keep the desktop clean.

And when it comes to the slides themselves, be sure that you have the apps set to play in "window" mode—a relatively new feature that was added to Keynote and PowerPoint in the past years. This will allow you to run the slideshow without it also taking over your entire screen, but rather just in a window (that will nonetheless appear full screen to your audience). If you have a second monitor, you can also configure your computer to show the slide show on one screen while you keep the other free to manage and navigate the Zoom meeting.

Most importantly, you should not lose sight of your screen. Prompts and such from online presentation apps are essential—they may include comments or chats that you need to respond to (like, we can't hear you). So screen real estate management is critical.

Run Throughs and Tests

If you're speaking at an organized online event, you will likely also get a chance to do a run through of your talk, including any screen sharing that needs to happen. This will be to ensure you're familiar with the controls of the event, and also for the organizer to check for inconsistencies in their process or your performance.

Never miss a walk-through opportunity. As annoying as it may be to rehearse using Zoom or another app you've used a hundred times, it gives you a chance to learn the specific processes of the day, meet the people involved (good networking), and for you to make any last-minute changes to your material based on some real-world interaction.

In addition to the event run-through that will happen a few days before, and especially if you are a main organizer, you should create your own walk through. This can happen 1 hour before the event itself, but do all the steps: get ready, reboot the machine, launch the program, run the slides, and talk. Obviously don't join the actual program's "room" if you choose this approach, but make sure that you go through all the steps and have everything set up right. I can't tell you how often—even with my pro setup—I end up having to do a last-minute zig or zag. You'll be glad you avoided it.

Quiet on the Set

During the pandemic, we saw lots of people's pets and significant others interrupt their Zoom calls. While that is cute on TikTok, it's not a good look for a professional presentation that—hopefully—you're even getting paid for. For this reason, about an hour before your talk, make sure that everyone in your household or office knows that you are not to be disturbed. Block your calendar and set your phone to silent. Put a note on your office door that you're recording and not to bother you. Disable your doorbell and other noise making appliances. Get the room as quiet and calm as possible.

Checklists

As we've seen in this chapter, both online and live presentation pre-planning can follow a set of guidelines or steps that, if practiced regularly, can help bring some order and predictability to your presentation day. To make this process even easier, I've created a series of checklists for each kind of presentation you can download and use to manage your pre-event hygiene. Visit the resource guide to find out more.

A FINAL NOTE ABOUT VIRTUAL TALK HYGIENE FOR SPEAKERS

Almost every piece of advice I've given in this chapter applies equally to virtual talks. That includes your sleep, eating, caffeine, etc. But most importantly— it's essential that you leave enough time for everything before your talk so that you're not stressed out. This means ensuring that you have showered and dressed well before, that the temperature in the room is set, that you create a quiet space as much as possible, and that you reboot your computer and ensure your tech is working in plenty of time. Be sure to practice just as you would in a regular environment, and be doubly sure you aren't raising your heart rate in a negative way.

When we present at home, we have a tendency to take things more casually, and to have less energy in our presentation. If possible, I highly recommend that you stand up while delivering, as this has been shown to increase the energy of most speakers. But also, be as mindful of your time and headspace as you would otherwise. The presentation is no less fraught just because you're virtual—and as we'll see in the next chapter, there are elements of Zoom that are actually much harder than a live presentation.

11

During Your Presentation

Reading the Room

In the previous chapter, we took a look at speaking hygiene—the things you need to do before your talk to ensure you're successful. The basic phases of presenting are:

1. Preparation and creative
2. Hygiene (the 24 hours before)
3. Presenting
4. Post-event (1–2 hours after)

As you can see, there are four phases, of which three take place within a 24-hour period—the presentation day and its aftermath. The first, preparatory phase takes a long time, and can often be spread out over weeks. The last few elements are—by definition—tied to a specific time point that will come and go whether or not you're ready. If you're supposed to present at 10:15 a.m. on Tuesday, that's when you'll be going on. If you've ever been a performer of any kind, you'll understand the need to respect the event time. But even if you're not, I think visualizing it as a hard deadline helps make our emphasis on this phase make a lot more sense.

Now, during the actual presentation, different rules are in effect. The 5, 10, 15, or 45 minutes that you're on the stage are a time when I want you to feel as free and connected to your material as possible. Removal of the extraneous mental processing ("Am I on time?"; "How was I going to reference this point?") by knowing your material will reduce your mental burden. But there are still some specific considerations and things you can focus on to ensure maximum effect and impact during this phase.

The Show Must Go On

In the most basic way, once your presentation has started, it is entirely up to you to keep the show (your talk) moving along. You may have A/V or other supporting characters to help make it a success, but because all eyes are on you, whatever you do will give the audience a cue as to how they should feel. If you are anxious, they will be anxious. If you are hostile, they will be hostile. They can read you better than you can read them, but—as we'll discuss below—you can learn the skills necessary to level the playing field.

First, you have to be fully committed to the idea that you're going to do your talk. Come hell or high water—and there probably will be some of both—once you start talking, you're going to finish. In the most basic of senses, this means that you need to plow through your own insecurity and get 'er done. But it also means that you need to take whatever obstacles or impediments that come your way, and run right through them as though (mostly) nothing is happening.

You've probably been a part of a play or other performance by now, and if not, you've seen films and TV about live performance. One of the adages you'll hear theater people say the most often is "the show must go on." And it must. So in the spirit of "preparation is power," I give you this chapter.

Whatever Can Go Wrong, Will

Sometimes called Murphy's Law, the idea that things that can go wrong, will, has a longstanding basis in both neurosis and fact. The more often you present, the more likely it is that disruptive things will happen. Whenever these circumstances arise, how you handle them is entirely up to you. You have both the control and the knowledge necessary to pivot and bend in all the right ways.

In a previous chapter, I made reference to a mariachi band that started playing—at full volume and in the same room as me—in the middle of a keynote I was giving in Mexico City. This is not something you can specifically prepare for, nor would I want to scenario plan all the different kinds of interruptions that might happen. The critical thing is for you to know that interruptions will likely happen, and to have trained yourself on what to do when they do.

In pilot training, instructors attempt to reshape the "top response" from pilots as they learn to fly planes. The top response is the body/mind's first reaction to stimuli—and in some cases, it's necessary to retrain someone to a different response. For example, in flying, your plane may begin to give you a stick shaker warning, letting you know that it's stalling, and you will soon lose the lift of your wings, and plummet to the earth.

A layperson would probably pull back on the airplane's yoke at that exact moment, in an effort to pull the airplane away from the ground. While a perfectly logical instinctive reaction to this threat, it is precisely the opposite of what a pilot needs to do in that situation. Pulling up in response to a stall warning is going to end up as a disaster. What you must do, against all instinct, is to push *down*. The physics of this are not important, but as an Av geek I still feel compelled to explain.[1] By increasing the downward angle and velocity, you improve the wings' ability to provide lift. But even more important than knowing how it works, is knowing that your commercial airline pilot is probably going to be OK in a stall situation. And this is the lesson for budding speakers: How do I change my top response?

Fight or Flight / Feed or Breed

The sympathetic nervous system controls our fight/flight instinct, and the parasympathetic controls our feed/breed instinct.[2] Public speaking has a tendency to invoke the sympathetic system aggressively. First, there's the fear of failure and embarrassment, which can raise combat tension, but also just the energy of the stage—with its loud noises, bright lights, and big crowds. A really overactive fight/flight response might produce a panic, when the person loses the ability to think clearly and just tries to get away from the provocation at all costs.

One of the tricks of being a good communicator is making sure that you have control over this fight or flight response. First and foremost, you'll use the techniques of this book to give yourself more confidence and knowledge, and that will help quiet down the most pernicious parts of the instinct.

When we talk about the calming influence of meditation or deep breathing, we're really talking about activating the parasympathetic nervous system (PNS) to bring us into controlled alignment. Remembering that anxiety (sympathetic response) is *totally normal* in a public speaking context, may help you contextualize the need to invoke the PNS. The reason we spend so much time on creating the context for PNS activation (sleep, eating, breathing, etc.) is that this kind of anxiety is present even in super experienced speakers, like myself.

But what if there's a new stimulus, like an interruption? While we'll look at different kinds of challenges below, it bears mentioning that the best way to stay calm in the face of unexpected adversity is to not pretend you can stay calm! In fact, you are going to feel nervous and startled no matter what. The critical thing is to immediately switch into your new top response, and remind yourself that you got this. Because you do. So, don't fight the nerves—this will only make it worse—acknowledge them and move on to the important stuff.

Interruptions

External interruptions, like the mariachi example, are more common than you might imagine. They can happen in many less dramatic ways than being played off by a band, but generally center around a disruptive noise or other event (e.g., all the power goes out). I often think about this axiom anytime there's a power failure: someone, somewhere, was giving a speech right as the lights went out. I'm glad I'm not them.

If you become aware of some noise or other external interruption, the absolute best thing for you to do is to proceed as though it's not happening. Just keep talking. Yes, your mind will be filled with anxiety as a result of the interruption, wondering how long it will continue, how many people noticed, is it ruining your talk, and the like. But most interruptions are transient and will pass fairly quickly (even if it feels like a lifetime). Thereafter, your audience won't remember the interruption as much as your stoic ability to keep going, and the brilliance of your material.

Heckling

Though exceedingly rare in common public speaking, sometimes you do get heckled. At his 2009 State of the Union speech, President Barack Obama was heckled by a congressman who shouted "you lie!" at him mid-speech.[3] I've chosen to omit the lout's name here because—whatever you think of the various political factions—we offer no harbor to hecklers in this house.

Obama's reaction was that of the consummate professional speaker—someone who's a true master of the craft. He briefly paused, but just long enough for the room to explode in rebuke to the congressman. He then follows this up with a "you're wrong," and moves on to the rest of his presentation. It was a stunning breach of decorum, but more importantly—the speaker knew exactly what to do—and that is to let the audience react and defend you, and not to give the heckler more energy or power.

Now, you've probably seen hecklers in comedy situations be dealt with entirely differently. In my recollection—albeit perhaps a bit hazy—queens at this famous drag bar in Orlando that I used to frequent during grad school were notorious for how they dealt with hecklers. In one particularly salty exchange, a favorite drag performer of mine shut down a drunk man in the audience who kept heckling them with the phrase—and I quote: "Don't try to come for the bitch with the microphone. I own this room and can spend the rest of the night making fun of you and your ugly friends if that's what you want."

It was—as is often the case with drag—a great lesson about how to handle the most aggressive kind of heckler. You start from Obama's place: quiet, ignoring, leaving it in the audience's hands—but fundamentally committed to continuing, no matter what. And if the person continues to be disruptive, you have to remember that *you* have the mic and the audience is mostly focused on you. But if it doesn't stop—and this will almost never happen—you can bring the interrupter to a close. Simply tell him (and it's probably going to be a him) that you'll be happy to discuss the matter after the presentation, but that you're going to continue.

Or you could call him a bitch. That is, as ever, your choice.

Disruptive/Distracted/Distracting Audience

On a Zoom call, they're the people who forget to turn off their microphones while you're speaking. In the real world, they're the people who think nothing of picking up a phone call while you're speaking, or talking to their neighbor in full voice. They are the incidental disruptors—impolite people misunderstanding the protocol.

Often, these folks flummox novice speakers. First and foremost, you can see people being distracted as a reflection of the fact that you're not maintaining their attention. Thinking this can allow self-doubt and panic to creep into your otherwise calm and collected mental process. In fact, it does practically mean that you're not maintaining their attention, but it is impossible to expect perfect attentiveness from all audiences all the time.

You must, must, must, learn to override this panicked instinct when you see this happen. Keep calm and carry on, focusing instead on the material—or someone else in the room if you can see a face that is focused on you. You can be sure that if the person is being super disruptive, other audience members will let them know as well, and in a virtual presentation the moderator should take responsibility for controlling the situation.

People Leaving

People are going to walk out of your talks all the time. In real life, they'll literally pack up their stuff and walk out the door—often letting it slam behind them. In streamed events, they'll do it by leaving the room or closing the window, resulting in a minus-one on the attendee counter.

No matter how good you are, or how amazing your material is, some people are going to walk out. They won't like you or what you have to say, or—as is often the case at major conferences—they weren't paying attention to the session subject and realize that they don't care about the topic after you've already started.

This is perfectly normal. It still unnerves me when it happens, but I just remind myself that it isn't a reflection of my skill or topic but, rather, just something going on in the person's life. I don't mean to sound flippant about people "voting with their feet," and am clear that it is mentally disruptive for many speakers. But I think it's a good time to practice the mantra that you can't control others' choices, no matter how persuasive you are.

You will probably get feedback on your presentation after the fact. If you're a startup raising money, you'll get a check. If you're a speaker at a conference, you'll probably get scores in a couple of weeks and some quick "awesome job!" shout outs after your talk. But the key thing is to not let what's happening during the talk be seen as a reflection of the quality of what you're doing. It isn't—that feedback will come after.

If it helps and you can see the crowd, it may be useful to zero in on someone who is really living for what you have to say—preferably in one of the first few rows. You're looking for the person who is nodding along, paying close attention, excited enough about what you have to say to sit in the front. Bring your attention back to this person periodically (while still scanning the room) to help you get recentered.

In virtual event settings, one of the ways I tell my coaching clients to deal with this, is to put an object with a face (it can be a doll, cutout of your best friend's picture, etc.) in line with the camera on the computer. Don't block the lens, but imagine you're positioning this person as a sympathetic viewer right in your sightline. Feel free to focus on them instead of the black, unfeeling gaze of the camera.

Technical Faults

Technical difficulties are probably the most frequent kind of disruption in a presentation, and I have lost count of all the times it's happened to me. The key thing with technical faults is to remember that your voice is the priority above all others.

Some basic advice:

If your slides are wrong, keep talking.
If the presentation equipment dies, keep talking.
If your mic goes out, switch into theater voice and *keep talking!*
If the stream gets wonky, keep talking—the recording will probably be fine.

Knowing your material and knowing that the audience is on your side and wants to hear you is probably the best insurance here. I remember one speech I gave at a small O'Reilly conference in Seattle, held at Microsoft's offices. It was in the evening, and each of us was asked to create a PechaKucha talk—a deck of 20 slides that would advance automatically every 20 seconds without our involvement. The total length of each talk was 400 seconds, and it was something us speakers were taking seriously.

I went up to the front of the room at around 7:58 p.m. Unbeknownst to all of us, at 8:00 p.m. sharp, Microsoft's automatic power-saving routine started, and all the presentation equipment turned itself off. The projector went dark, and the screen behind me started rising up into the ceiling. To my left, I could see the A/V guy start to panic, and it was impossible not to see the anxiety on the faces of the folks in the audience.

But (and you're probably sensing a theme here), I knew my material. And with minimal disruption, I just kept talking. I knew it was what I had to do. The A/V tech eventually figured out the problem and restarted the projector. The audience started clapping, and only later I found out that the slides had continued to advance (the computer stayed on) and when the projector came back online a minute or two later, I was at exactly the right spot in the presentation.

Now, I would have been justified—especially in that intimate setting—to have stopped and waited for them to restart in order for me to continue. I don't think anyone in the audience would have objected. However, I knew this wasn't the optimal way to approach the problem, and I knew my material, so why not just continue. Was I panicked? For the first 20 seconds, absolutely— and then I settled back into my talk. Remembering that my voice—and not the slides or any other content—was the key offer to the audience, made it easier to just ignore the lack of visuals and move forward.

If I can survive a complete projector failure and a live Mexican band mid-talk—so can you. I don't possess any superhuman powers. I just know what the brief is, and I know what the value I'm delivering needs to be, and I just keep going no matter what.

Dangerous Interruptions

There are, however, some interruptions that can be dangerous, and you should treat those slightly differently. Though it's never happened to me, it makes sense that some presenters have been interrupted by earthquakes, tornadoes, structural failures, or violence in the crowd. If anything happens that you think threatens your safety, you should definitely stop presenting and seek shelter. It is not your responsibility—despite being up on stage—to save the folks in the room. This is the organizer's duty, and you should not take it on.

A good rule of thumb is to use Obama's strategy from the heckler. When something disruptive happens, give yourself a quick pause—just a few seconds to figure out what's going on, and then act accordingly.

I have had a presentation where the room's whole power went out and I just kept talking, in raised volume, until I came to another logical stopping point in my presentation (approximately 20 seconds later). This "pause" allowed me to see if the room's lights would come back up, knowing, as I did, that the audience would be lost if the lights stayed off for too long. When they didn't immediately come back up, I simply stood on the stage, saying nothing, and gave the A/V team time to make an announcement. In this case "please hold tight for a moment" gave me the cue that I needed to know that I should not continue or leave the stage. I waited, and the lights were soon restored. Once everyone had settled down, I continued.

These are just a few examples of the worst things that have happened to me in a presentation context. Do this for long enough and eventually they'll probably happen to you too. Just remember—the show must go on and you know your material—the right path should be readily illuminated.

Reading the Room

One of the sixth senses that makes speakers (and stand-up comedians) really shine is their ability to read a room. This is the skill—often viewed as unconscious or innate—to understand what the audience is feeling or thinking, without having to think about it. Reading a room successfully can help speakers adjust their material if needed to keep the audience engaged. Though it's not absolutely required, it is a nice-to-have skill—and the secret is that you can learn it.

The cues that tell you what an audience is feeling are not extra-sensory—they are right there in front of you. However, when you're presenting, it is the worst time to spend mental energy listening to the audience's subtle changes in behavior. You need to devote your entire strength to being calm and staying in the zone during your presentation.

The best way to develop this skill is to borrow a tactic from stand-up. Go and spend time in another person's presentation (not before your talk), and just listen to the room. Don't pay attention to the speaker or even keep your eyes open, just listen. You'll hear the subtle audio cues of people opening and closing laptops, shifting in their seats, unwrapping food, etc.—and this will give you an auditory landscape to analyze. Try to tap into your understanding of the audience's mood, and compare what you thought was happening to how they respond after the event is over.

There are a few reasons I suggest focusing on the audio cues, as opposed to the visual ones. First off, it's not always possible for you to see your audience, either because of lighting IRL or webinar mode online. If you're too dependent on the nodding of heads or the fixed gaze of the audience, you might be unnerved when you can't see them.

Second—even if you can see the audience, most of what you'll notice will probably be panic-inducing. Because it's hard to know if the audience is really understanding you, you'll be more conscious of the negative feedback (people walking out, distracted, etc.) than you will be toward the positive. Learning to tune this out entirely gives you the most security.

The best way to develop this skill is by doing, and by feeling calm during your presentations. The more you do it, the better you'll get at it.

Empathy

In an earlier chapter, we discussed the issue of vulnerability and empathy as it relates to the content you are transmitting. But how does that translate into the audience's behavior?

The answer is that audiences feed off your energy—anxiety, fear, vulnerability, confidence, and so on. Sometimes the audience will have a momma bear response, and help a really anxious or vulnerable speaker by clapping, cheering, or otherwise encouraging them. You've probably seen viral TikToks of this happening, especially with differently abled adults.

While this is a super nice thing when an audience does it, more often than not a professional speaker's audience starts off from a pre-disposition of trust, belief, and excitement about what you have to say. After all, you are an expert and the conference organizer (who attendees paid to be here, mind you) says you're worthy of some time—so they're probably inclined to hear you out. Folks that aren't interested in you often just skip your session. Even at a conference with a linear program and no breakouts there's always that group of people chatting over coffee in the foyer. If people genuinely don't want to hear you, they'll leave.

If you approach the audience with empathy and vulnerability, they will respect you and give that back to you in turn. Most of the speakers they see throughout their lives are invulnerable—experts with minimal interest in engaging in a dialogue beyond getting them to see they're right. Any speaker who projects an air of approachability—without it being contrived or overly nervous—has a built-in advantage.

This does not mean walking out on stage and breaking the fourth wall with "I'm so nervous," but rather being genuinely approachable, empathetic, and vulnerable—inasmuch as you can be given your personality and the material.

The more you practice empathy for your audience, the easier it will be to develop content and adjust to their energy.

Managing Anxiety

Novice speakers will often say something to me like, "oh you do this so often I bet you don't even get nervous anymore!" Nothing could be further from the truth. In fact, I am always nervous before any speech. This is because I'm not a sociopath—I care about what the audience gets and feels from my presentation. What is different between me and a novice presenter is that while I may be nervous about the presentation's outcome, I'm not nervous about remembering my material or delivering it to the best of my ability.

By knowing my subject and practicing extensively, I'm able to put that anxiety behind me and recognize that the stress I feel before a talk is really about outcomes. It has thus become a bit of good stress (or eustress)[4] that actually helps me focus and get alert/ready for the task at hand

But even for me, in those moments right before I go out on stage, there is heightened anxiety. My heart is racing, my palms are sweaty, and I'm suddenly aware of how loud the room is, how bright the lights are, and so on. Over time, I've come to understand that as a natural part of the experience, and to not feel dissuaded by that final burst of stress. Contextualizing it makes all the difference in my experience, and if you can get to the point where you feel that kind of positive performance stress, you will be in a good position to succeed.

Several performers that I know confess to having the same pre-event stress reaction. Some even more famous ones—like Adele in this *Rolling Stone* interview—have shared their feelings about performance anxiety more publicly:

> I get shitty scared. I've thrown up a couple of times. Once in Brussels, I projectile-vomited on someone. I just gotta bear it. But I don't like touring. I have anxiety attacks a lot.[5]

High anxiety and high performance often go hand in hand. In order to make that stress work for you, you must remember that the anxiety *before* a performance is not indicative of how you will feel *during* a performance. Once you know that things will get better, it's easier than ever to live with that fear.

Walking On and Off

In the moments before your talk, you'll be standing in the "wings"—which is an area of the stage behind a curtain and off to the side—ready to walk on when the time comes. In a virtual presentation, you'll be in a similar "waiting room" where you can typically see the conference as it progresses but are not yet able to command the room or your presentation. Either way, once you're in this zone, it's critical that you bring your focus and energy to the calm but energetic place that will give you the most impact. Your phone is off, there's nothing to distract you. What's next?

The Walk On

One element of the process that usually isn't part of the pre-brief is the last few seconds before you walk out on stage (or get pushed live by the moderator). You know it's going to happen right at the end of your intro music or bio, but the specific logistics can often be a bit of a mystery. If you remember to do so, you can ask questions of the organizer beforehand—or you can just observe how they handle other speakers before you, if IRL.

For example, are they handing you a clicker in the wings or when you walk on? Will someone be prompting you for the precise moment you need to come on, or will you find out that you're on because of a pause in the content? If you're doing a virtual presentation, how long before the actual start are they going to make you live and when can you start the screen share if appropriate?

All of these (and more) questions are super valid and the more you know / can prepare for, the less stressed you'll be in the moment. So I encourage you to ask all your questions and observe.

When you walk on, there is likely to be a bit of "silence." If you're in a virtual talk, the moderator may stop, it may take you a few seconds to get going—and there will be dead air. If you're in a live talk, the MC and music may end during your walk across the stage to the dais (or mark) and you'll find yourself in a room where nothing is happening for a few seconds.

These moments can be incredibly stressful. You're not quite in a position to begin your talk, but the previous activity has ended. Resist the urge to fill the time with something, and instead spend the moments you need to compose yourself and begin your presentation the way you had intended. It may seem awkward, but audiences fully respect a bit of a pause before starting, and you'll find that they respond positively to it if you start speaking within a few seconds.

Remember that the video will probably capture you from the moment you're announced, but that they are unlikely to use the part as you're walking on or getting your screen share setup. So whatever time you need before the actual start is probably going to be edited out in post.

Now that you've reached the dais, the mark, or have the screen share activated, you're ready to begin your presentation.

To Dais or Not to Dais, That Is the Question

At some events, you'll have the choice of having a podium or speaking from the center of a stage or room. Often, these speaker podiums are placed to one side and are made of Lucite or wood, emblazoned with the event's logo. The podium gives you the ability to have notes and a bottle of water stashed away (the organizers should take care of this, but if not—ask).

Many people feel more comfortable behind the podium. It gives you a bit of a "shield" and a spot to lean on, and that can be comforting. I personally like podiums where appropriate, and will generally start my presentations there, if that's an option, and then walk to the center. There's no right or wrong answer here, but you should do whatever makes you feel the most comfortable. Audiences do love to see the whole performer, and the dais definitely cuts you off from that, but overall, it will have minimal impact on your reviews.

A Note on Notes and Prompters

I suggest not taking paper notes with you. First and foremost, if you follow the strategies in this book, you should be able to deliver it without that crutch. Second, they make noise and create additional opportunities for distraction ("the notes are out of order!"). In a weird way, paper notes can actually erode—not support—your confidence.

If you want to have notes with you, and if you have a dais, only bring the notes from our final memorization step (a single phrase)—which should all fit on an index card, sheet of paper, or in your phone's notes app. Ensure your phone is on airplane mode, however.

Teleprompters are not common for most speakers—whether professional or otherwise. They tend to be best used by newscasters, actors, award show presenters, and politicians. This is because word fidelity (hewing precisely to the script) is super important in those settings, and the tradeoff of personableness with accuracy is worth it.

You may be most tempted to use a teleprompter when delivering a presentation from home, and several apps exist on mobile and desktop that do a good job of TV-style scrolling prompting. I would advise you against this however, for all the reasons we've laid out in the book: it's unnecessary, fidelity probably isn't your top priority, it will introduce yet another thing you have to worry about, and technical complexity.

The Confidence Monitor

If you're at a large event, you will likely have a confidence monitor at the front of the stage, just below the audience's eye line. Typically, this is just a giant flat-screen monitor that shows you what slides are currently being projected and what slide comes next. In some cases, the A/V crew can also show your notes.

The purpose of the confidence monitor is right there in its name. It helps increase your confidence by prompting you on what you should be talking about now and what comes next. If you follow my memorization process *and* have a confidence monitor, you will be able to deliver a great talk.

But you can't rely on it, and therefore shouldn't plan your performance around it. It may have a technical problem, it might be too far or too small for your vision, or out of the eyeline you want to keep (e.g., a camera recording). And definitely don't count on being able to legibly read your speaker notes on the confidence monitor. Unless you've got superhuman eyesight, they will probably be a bit too small.

When you present from home or office, the presentation software you're using will likely have a confidence monitor view. This often takes the form of a window that shows the slides and notes, and allows you to move through and/or notate the presentation.

This "virtual confidence monitor" is only useful if you can see it, so in order to take full advantage, you must have two screens, where one is showing you the feed to Zoom, and the other is for your control. If you can't make two screens work, resize all the windows so you can see both apps at the same time.

The Thank You

The best time to thank the audience is after your presentation is completed. It is true that in certain kinds of presentations, the final step doesn't require a signal to the audience that you're done. The crescendo and subsequent denouement will tell the audience it's over and time to clap. But this is reserved mostly for political speeches that have an obvious endpoint.

Even in theater—especially Broadway—the producers will use cues to help people know that this number—last in a series of soaring, emotional appeals—is actually the final one. They will typically do this with lighting. The combination of the song ending and the lights going down gives the audience a never-fail signal that the show is over.

In speaking, however, this is almost never the case. You will decide precisely when your talk is over, typically—and so you are the one who needs to tell the audience you're done. If you've used the A-Ha! Method to its maximum potential, your ending will already be a high point of the talk, and it will be fairly obvious to a close listener that you're done. Ending strong and on a high note—just as in Broadway—is never a bad strategy.

But over the years of doing this, I've come around to the idea of ending with a "thank you." The way I do it is to stick my landing, with all the gravitas and energy it calls for, to take a pause, and then to say "thank you." There are many reasons why I like to do this. First of all, it relieves the pressure on the audience. You're making it super clear that the talk is over, and they can move on to the applause and next phase. Second, I do think it's valuable to thank the audience, and generally believe it's best to do so after the talk (or show) is over—and not before. Maintaining a suspension of disbelief and the sanctity of the fourth wall demands it.

The Walk Off

Once you're done, it's time for the walk off. Typically, there will be some applause, or in the case of a virtual event, the moderator will break in and thank you for your talk. In a virtual environment, you'll generally just get kicked out of the production room unceremoniously, so don't be sad about it. You'll not be expected to make any further remarks at that point unless there's Q&A, so why not move on.

In a real-world event, you'll finish, and then will need to follow the walk-off protocol. First, it's knowing whether or not you're exiting the same way you came. Usually, it's through another set of stairs or curtains. So once your talk is complete, there's no need to bow or stick around if you are expected to just walk off. The digital equivalent of this will be when the organizer removes your feed from what the audience is seeing. That's your cue.

At some events, the MC will come back up on stage (and you may see them start to position themselves at the stairs as your talk is wrapping up), greeting you at the walk off. They may shake your hand or pat you on the back as they get into position to move the show along.

At a small fraction of events, the MC may ask you an extemporaneous question to either clarify or reinforce what you had just said. Usually if this is going to happen, you'll have seen it happen with other speakers and/or they'll tell you about it beforehand, but I have had it sprung on me at the last minute. The next chapter will deal more closely with Q&A and other post-talk logistics, but suffice it to say, a quick answer, quip, or polite acknowledgment will be a powerful thing to have in your pocket for those moments.

The Timer

Most events—whether live or virtual—will have some kind of timer that you can see to help you stick to the schedule. As a general rule, the digital version of this timer will be a countdown clock that will be set to your total talk time and start once you go up on stage. It will count down in green or neutral color until a few minutes beforehand, when it will turn orange or yellow, and then as you get to the last few seconds, it will turn red. In most settings, if you go over time, the counter will shift to a red-colored negative count, showing you the seconds over the allotted space you are consuming.

In events with a lower budget, the timers can be humans—a job often delegated to an intern sitting in the front row with cards that say, "3 minutes left," "1 minute left," and "time's up," or some variation therein. As with the digital timer, they will be in your field of vision, and will probably make themselves known to you at the pre-briefing or right before you go on. The organizer always wants you to keep to time.

In a virtual event, the countdown timer is often actually a count-up timer—and takes the form of your system clock. You will need to check your start time when you begin, and—more than likely—need to keep track of your own timing.

There are also ways that organizers will signal to you that it's time to move on, with or without the timer. At hosted events, the MC may get up and move to the steps of the stage as you near the end of your time, gradually climbing the stairs until they're on stage with you if you've gone too far and they really need you to get off. In a virtual setting, you'll probably get some chat messages from the organizer if you go way over, and may even have the MC break into the voice portion to gently push you off.

No matter how they do it, it's important that you respect the timer. Being slightly over is fine—everyone does it. But more than a minute or two over time is considered rude and a definite no-no. As we've discussed prior, if you see that your timing is off and you're going to run out of time, the best thing you can do is bring the plane down for a soft landing at an airport before your final destination. Better to do that than crash trying to reach the finale.

In any event, remember that the timer is your friend—not your enemy. You know your material and you practiced enough to get the timing mostly right. The timer you see is just there to gently help you land that plane, and as a reminder of your audience's expectations for you. If you can see this positive side of the equation rather than just focusing on the negative, you can learn to use the timer to your advantage.

12

Post Talk

So you've just finished giving an amazing talk, killer pitch, or life-changing meeting, and you've exited the real or virtual stage. Most novice speakers think the talk is over, and this is where speaking prep ends. But this could not be further from the truth. After your talk is over is when the really meaty, good stuff happens: interactions with the audience.

Let's take a look at a few audience interaction scenarios and how to handle them.

TAKING CARE OF YOURSELF

Before going much further in this chapter, I want to stress that the time immediately after a major pitch or talk is critical for your self-care, and for building the muscle necessary to do this over and over again with greater and greater confidence.

The first thing you'll probably notice is something akin to the feeling of a roller coaster coming into the station after doing its run. That last part of the ride, where the cars are forcibly slowed down but don't stop, is often the first moment during the ride that you don't have to contend with your adrenaline amping up your fight or flight response.

For me, these moments are euphoric, something akin to "I survived it," and the sensation in my body is intense relief and satisfaction. All the nervous energy I bundled up is being released almost instantaneously. Then, I've got some physical space to process the fact that I did something big, scary, and exciting—and lived to tell the tale.

Savor this moment as much as you can. Be aware of your body and your mind in those few minutes (and it often takes minutes for the buzz to start wearing off), because that intense pleasure will help fuel you to do this again.

You're also likely to notice other things about yourself that you hopefully didn't pay much attention to while speaking. This may include things like being sweaty, thirsty, hungry, or needing to go to the bathroom. As much as possible, use that time immediately after the talk to get out of whatever gear you had to wear (e.g., a mic) and do a little bit of self-care. I like to have something sweet to eat immediately after getting off stage, and tend to grab a piece of fruit / granola bar (if I'm not doing keto) and a bottle of water as I exit the green room.

I then typically go to the restroom to check out my appearance—making sure I'm not too sweaty and/or to wash my face and take care of business. I do this in a structured fashion because I know how important the next audience interactions are going to be, and despite having just done a herculean task, I want to be at my best for these folks as well.

If you're doing a virtual talk or pitch, and you're doing it from home, unless the moderators have made clear how your further interactions should proceed, you're probably done with your task entirely. This allows you to go reset.

I tend to try to leave myself plenty of space after a talk—real or virtual—to just veg and calm down. It usually takes up to 6 hours for me to return to fully normal after a talk, and during that time I tend to try not to do much other than whatever post-talk activities are warranted and committed to. This means I'll do my best to avoid having major meetings or a big work deadline that same day.

While you savor the incredible feeling of accomplishment and store that sense memory away for another day, you'll also probably notice that you don't really remember the details of your time on stage. You might have a couple of vignettes of things happening (walking up, walking off, a technical fault, etc.) but the majority of the talk should have passed over you in a haze of flow. That's why I suggest paying close attention to the post-talk vibes. These are what you will remember for the future.

Now, if your event warrants it, you may not have the luxury of spending 4 to 6 hours just relaxing. You might have—or want—some post-talk responsibilities. Let's look at those.

Q&A

Probably the most common post-talk activity is Q&A—or a question-and-answer period. Though it is very uncommon at TED-type talks, other events love to include a buffer for Q&A as a way of engaging the audience. In most cases, the Q&A will be moderated by someone else, though at conferences where you are presenting in a breakout (a room that is separate from the keynote track) or at a virtual event that is highly fragmented, you may have to run your own Q&A session.

No matter what kind of talk you're doing and in which session, you should ask the organizer if Q&A will be expected, and record that on the event info sheet. Be sure to ask in detail about the timing requirements. If they say that your session is blocked at 60 minutes, how much of that do they want you to speak for, and how much time are they allocating for Q&A? Also ask how the Q&A will be run and structured, and if there's anything in particular that they expect the audience to hone in on from your topic. This can help you be more prepared.

And prepare you should. I believe that if you're really and truly enmeshed in your material, you should be able to handle Q&A with aplomb. Consider the thought example I've used throughout the book of a casual dinner party conversation with a new acquaintance where the topic shifts to something you're pretty nerdy about. How much prep would you need to talk about that subject? And if they are truly a neophyte—and know little about this topic themselves—how likely will they be to ask you a question that will stump or embarrass you?

The same is true of the conference Q&A, though it may seem higher stakes. The truth is that most audience member questions are pretty similar and relatively easy for you to answer. I remember that at the height of my gamification speaking program, I would travel around the world and do a paid keynote every couple of weeks. Despite speaking to incredibly diverse audiences—teachers in Mexico one minute and nuclear engineers in Miami the next—the things that most audience members wanted to know were pretty much the same all over the world.

My question set would usually consist of one of the following types of general inquiries:

- Can I get another example in category X?
- Can you comment on this other example and what you think of it?
- How will this evolve in the future?

- I have a personal worldview about this topic (usually moralistic), what is yours?
- I disagree with you and here's why.

The last—the open disagreement—is probably the Q&A type that most intimidates first-time speakers, and the one that sparks all the dread. A secret of most audience questions is that they are very rarely (and I mean less than 5 percent) in the form of a direct challenge or confrontation. First and foremost, the audience generally comes from a place of respect for your knowledge, and typically doesn't want to challenge you on an unlevel playing field (you're the expert on stage with the lights on them).

But even when a direct challenge to your auth-or-i-tay is offered, do you really think it's going to be a novel scenario you've never thought of or heard before? Unless you haven't been out talking about your subject (and I hope you have) prior to this presentation or pitch, odds are pretty good you won't be hearing this question for the first time. And—even if you do—there's absolutely no harm in saying:

"I don't know."
"That's an interesting question I hadn't thought of before."
"I'd like to research that and get back to you."
"Why don't we take this offline and chat after the Q&A?"

Any of the above responses is considered appropriate and professional, and even if it gives you some heartburn to admit that you might not know the answer to something, it's best to say so.

Preparation, Though

OK, so you probably don't have to do a ton of prep for Q&A if you know your material, but you may still want to do some. I think the best and most useful kind of preparation you can do is to think of several additional examples that help reinforce core points of your argument.

If you're giving a keynote-type talk, you probably have several additional examples that were suggested but then set aside because they didn't fit or weren't super important. In fact, after doing a presentation variant several times, you'll probably have a "master slide deck" with several examples that you can include—or not—depending on the relevance to the audience in that moment. Each of those examples can be useful in developing good answers for Q&A even if they don't make it into your core presentation, so know them!

Pitch Q&A

If you're giving a pitch—for example, for fundraising—you will almost certainly have a broad swath of questions for which you must have answers but may not be able to include in the core presentation itself. If you've watched Shark Tank or been to any pitch competitions or events, you'll know some of the questions that you can expect. They will most likely be further clarifications or provocations about one of your core slides, for example, competition, go-to-market, financing, and so on.

It is generally believed that the pitch Q&A is where investors tend to actually make up their mind. It's there that they try to pierce the veil of (what they assume is) your carefully researched, rehearsed, and polished presentation. They're using Q&A to get to the meat of who you are and, most importantly, to understand how you think about and approach various problems.

It's not dissimilar to the kinds of questions a detailed job interviewer might ask you, pushing you to think about personal or professional scenarios that help illustrate something about you. But in the financing or sales pitch, the questions tend to be somewhat constrained and to those that will help the "buyer" decide whether or not to buy.

Therefore, even though pitch Q&A is significantly more high-stakes than keynote Q&A, it's actually just as predictable. It should also be something you rehearse with several outsiders who can probe and prompt you to answer tough questions. As you do this probing rehearsal, be sure to take close note of the questions that are being asked, and make some decisions about whether or not you should include them in the core pitch.

The key thing with a pitch deck is that you generally want it to get you the next meeting, not to answer all the key questions that exist. But sometimes questions are so significant or meaningful that they need to be answered before the audience starts wondering whether or not you know your stuff. The pitch Q&A process therefore can be an essential part of the pitch development process itself and should be taken very seriously.

In pitches, just as in regular talks, you're not finished until the Q&A is done. The difference here is that this Q&A might be the difference between success or failure of the pitch.

Good Q&A Hygiene

There are several good rules of thumb for Q&A that I want to strongly encourage you to follow.

Don't Lie

This may seem obvious, but there can be a tendency to make stuff up or to stretch the truth in Q&A to either regain the speaker's dominance or to get the questioner to shut up and stop their line of "attack." But in practice, lying in a response is really terrible. First off, if the audience does their due diligence (especially likely in a pitch setting), they will find out that this wasn't true. Even if they don't, your Q&A may be recorded for posterity, and the last thing you want is someone to think you're making stuff up.

Say I Don't Know

As mentioned in the preceding section, it's perfectly fine to say you don't know or that you'll get back to someone. It's actually more than fine: it demonstrates authenticity, sincerity, and do-gooderness to the audience and they will appreciate you for it.

Parry Interruptions

If you're doing the kind of talk where people are interrupting you to ask questions (either at your invitation or because they feel entitled to), you can and should consider whether answering the question at that juncture is good for the entire room's comprehension. Often, audience questions that interrupt are things which you're going to address a bit later in the presentation. It is perfectly acceptable to say, "I'm going to address that shortly," or some variant of the idea that you're going to get to that question in due time.

You Can Moderate

Sometimes you will be doing Q&A without a moderator, and sometimes a moderated Q&A will get a bit out of hand with questioners that are hogging the mic or pontificating. A good moderator will know how to cut that off and move the discussion along. Whether you are doing your own moderation or not, you can cut off any question anytime you want to, and have complete autonomy to ignore questions you don't want to answer. If the moderator won't step in, you should—it's your time and your reputation at stake.

Don't Attack or Be Defensive

Whatever you do, and especially in a pitch setting, do not attack the audience during Q&A, or retreat into intense defensiveness. People are highly attuned to defensiveness and will generally perceive it as either weakness or—worse yet—obfuscation. The default assumption if you're defensive is that you have something to hide. If you attack, you risk the audience shifting their empathy and alignment to the questioner, and necessarily against you. This is something you definitely want to avoid if possible.

The Twitch Style

In many online pitch and speaking environments, users are invited to enter their questions or comments into the chat as the speaker is holding forth. While most speakers tend to try to ignore this Q&A/chat thread until they're done for fear of losing their focus, I do want to take a moment to pitch you on why you should sometimes consider interrupting your talk to answer a question.

In this new style of interactive live streaming, popularized I believe on Twitch, audiences have come to expect a somewhat disjointed presentation peppered with acknowledgments of their viewers' comments and questions. That is, they want you to multitask but understand that that will produce a more real—if less polished—experience.

In the live streams often done on Instagram or TikTok, you can see a slightly different approach—where the speaker waits through long periods of dead air while they read the comments and respond to certain people. If you just watch the video stream, it will seem incredibly boring and disjointed—it's essential that you split your focus between the audience's comments and the speaker's video.

My advocacy here is not to do your next talks in this format. Rather, it is to consider being able to do a talk where you can accept interruptions. Like all extemporaneous or improvised presentations, it's incredibly hard and—without the right talent or experience—might be fatal to your efforts. So I don't suggest doing this lightly.

I do, however, want you to try your hand at it in a lower-stakes environment or talk. Perhaps if you choose to give your talk to your Facebook friends or affinity group online, you may consider opening yourself up to the tangential style popular in online streaming. Of course, you should have mastery of your material first, and this is even more important if you choose to go this route. But it's a feather in your cap if you can pull it off, and might even set you apart from many of your peers.

Opting Out

You can opt out of doing Q&A, even if event organizers really want you to. I've met many speakers that really don't want to do Q&A or don't have the time for it, and so they say no. And you can too. But I think Q&A is super valuable in short bursts, especially on your journey to perfecting your understanding of your topic and its delivery. You actually learn a lot from the audience's questions and focus, and can—smartly—reincorporate that into your work. I would strongly advise you to embrace Q&A.

Providing Contact Info

As a general rule it's a good idea to put your contact information at least on your opening and closing slides. Both of those slides will likely be up on the display for a while, so it gives people the opportunity to quickly jot down your contact info if they want to stay in touch.

You can also include a QR code if you want to make that even easier for folks. The code has to be super big to work in a projected environment, so be sure to consider its size in practice if you go that route. Such a QR code could easily link the audience to your LinkedIn or optimal social network for the chosen issue.

And therein lies the rub—you can really only offer one communication method to people in this setting. It will take a great deal of energy for them to write down any piece of info, let alone several options. So first and foremost, you need to decide which platform you most want folks to connect with you on. And then you need to spell that out on the opening and closing slides.

Sometimes, if you really want to increase audience interaction, you can verbalize your contact info—though I would suggest against taking that time out of any keynote-type talk you might be doing. And generally, I'd also advise against putting your email address or phone number on your slides unless they are pitch documents or leave behinds. If your presentation is broadcast on YouTube or elsewhere, your contact information will now be scannable by anyone in the world. And conference organizers who are sensitive to this, may simply omit your opening and closing slides as a result. So use a public social media link (e.g., Twitter or LinkedIn) instead to maximize the chances that folks will reach out to you.

The Lobby

After your talk, the place to be is the lobby. If that's a live talk, I'm referring to the literal space right outside the conference room. If it's a virtual talk, it may be the main zoom feed or a "room" that is reserved for general communication. Either way, once you've finished your talk and Q&A, and have had a moment to refresh yourself, I highly recommend you head to the lobby and make yourself available to people who want to chat.

In some conference settings, particularly in breakouts, you may be mobbed by audience members after your speech who want to talk or ask you questions. This is perfectly acceptable, and you should be gracious if possible. But be sure to note whether or not someone is slated to speak right after you. Holding forth in a crowd in their presentation space is generally considered bad form and disruptive, and if you must—take it outside to the lobby (perhaps you see a theme here).

At many TED type events, there are tables setup after talk blocks for speakers to hold forth and answer audience questions. It's a lot of fun if a bit intense. But even if the organizers have not set this up for you, you can emulate the benefits of this "tabletop" approach. When you're done with your post-talk routine, head to the lobby, grab a drink, and park yourself at a table or space, with body language that says I'm open to talking. You'd be surprised how many folks will want to engage with you.

Why you want this engagement may not be immediately obvious, and may be worth repeating. It is in these moments—when the people who were most moved by what you had to say—come up and talk to you that you make the best connections and learn the most about your topic, perception, and audience. Remember: those who come up to talk to you are pretty brave or pretty motivated. It means that they are willing to risk wasting some time or getting ignored/rejected just to interact with you and have a conversation. You want to honor this as much as possible. Even if I don't much feel like chatting with people, I always try to make myself available after a talk, unless I have to immediately catch a flight. Over time this will help you build a community of like-minded people, and may create new and exciting connections for your business or practice.

Book Signings

You've probably been to an event where an author is presenting and then there's an opportunity to get a signed copy of their book afterwards. Well, someday this could be you sitting in the chair, offering signatures. And there's no better time than the present.

If you have a book, you undoubtedly feel the pressure from your publisher to use your talks as a platform for book promotion. They likely even have a partner you can easily use to have books brought in for your signature.

As a general rule, I suggest you always leave time where possible to do a book signing. Much like being available to the audience in the lobby after your talk, the book signing is a moment that can be used to build bigger and better connections with folks. You may not get rich off your author RevShare from the book, but you certainly will meet a few people that you'll be glad you did.

Now, if you're reading this section and thinking, "hold on, I don't have a book," you're not alone. Writing a book is incredibly time consuming and a labor of love, but if your goal is to educate and inform with your public speaking program, you should strongly consider writing one. It will reinforce your talks and help you gain credibility in your chosen topic. It also creates an additional revenue stream for your rhetorical business, and exposes you to people who might otherwise not be your followers yet. In summary, there's little professional downside if you can handle the challenge of creating it.

n.b. It's hard. Really hard.

Panels

Though it is a topic that probably lies somewhere outside the scope of this book, I would feel remiss if we didn't spend at least a few minutes talking about panels.

Whatever you may think of the form, panels—or conference talks where several people and a moderator collectively discuss an issue—are very, very common. Even though they are generally not attendee's favorite sessions and rarely achieve any true impact on the audience's understanding of an issue, they are popular with event organizers for a few reasons:

1. They allow the event to include a lot more "speakers," potentially from different companies and industries, in the same amount of time. This bolsters the program and potential ticket sales, but also expands the organizer's pool of potential sponsors.

2. They are easier on most speakers to handle. Giving a keynote is perhaps the toughest form of public speaking, while panels are often seen as the easiest. The moderator does a lot of heavy lifting, and the panelists are just there to give their opinions. This also means the organizer has to do a lot less pre-event validation of the content because they trust the moderator to ensure they're getting what they need.

3. It makes it easier for event organizers to cover a range of topics on a given subject in a shorter period of time. Panels often have very far-ranging remits and this is done to maximize the potential for audience interest, and also to cover topics that are a bit more multidimensional.

4. Sometimes it's a Q&A optimization. Event organizers may create blocks of speakers who are covering a similar topic and give them each their own speaking slot. But at the end, in an effort to offer Q&A that minimizes impact on the calendar, they'll program a Q&A panel with the people who just spoke.

For a budding or neophyte speaker, the only real advantage of a panel is that it will make it easier for you to get booked to speak at an event, and thus to build a resume of speaking engagements that will help you get more and more attention. The bar is much lower to get on a panel, and even though it can hardly be considered the same as a speech or pitch—it does help move you forward.

Most panels are not taken seriously by the speakers and moderators, and therefore get the same reception from the audience. But you can break the mold, and bring "it" to every panel that you're on. In order to do this, I'd suggest you read Guy Kawasaki's essential blog posts on how to be a great panelist and panel moderator (linked in the resource guide), so that you can understand the options in greater detail.

But to summarize the most important point for our A-Ha! purposes—be controversial! Vehement agreement with other panelists is not interesting for the audience. What they are mostly looking for is the learning that comes from the collision of ideas from one panelist to another. And, just like the audience for cable news, they are transfixed by disagreement or conflict.

So be controversial. Whatever the topic, plan a few argumentative quips and ideas ahead of time, and be sure to work them in. You can respectfully disagree, but disagree you should. Though this may sometimes feel impositional to other panelists who aren't considering these ideas, it is ultimately good for everyone sitting on the dais if you bring the interesting or funny.

The points of conflict in my experience are often similar to the A-Ha! Moments in my talk. That is, they are the counterintuitive or unexpected/unexplained things that drive my thesis from idea to persuasive argument. So it should be relatively easy, if you've followed the teachings of this book to create a compelling keynote, to take that learning and adapt it for panels.

Don't disagree to be disagreeable—spend your energy and words on something where you have a genuine difference of opinion and can move the conversation forward. But being a bit of a catalyst for conflict on a panel never hurt anyone—and it might just help your pursuit of better and better talks.

Feedback from the Organizers

Hopefully, after putting in all this effort, you love giving talks or pitches, and want to do more of them. If you've got a lifelong learning attitude, you will probably want to hear feedback from others about your talk, and to incorporate that feedback into your next iteration for self-improvement.

Most events also have a feedback system. At a pitch competition, this may be summarized by the dollars invested in companies. But at most other kinds of conferences or events, the organizer will invariably ask attendees to rate the event and specific speakers on a scale. These ratings are then tabulated, and—typically several weeks later—shared with each speaker. This will usually include scores and/or some text-based comments from audience members.

Obviously, you should take the feedback seriously, and listen/learn from what people say. But it's important to remember that the scores will likely reflect audience feedback more than the comments because most people don't have the skill to constructively criticize someone else's work in that way. So, while I always pay close attention to the comments, over my career they have been more milquetoast than practical. The scores, however, tell you something about how you're impacting the audience (even if they don't give you enough qualitative data to implement directly in the talk).

One key point that isn't always included by event organizers is the comparative score—that is, the average of all speakers and/or where you fit on the scale of speaker approval for the audience. If you want to know this information (and I'm just competitive enough to consider it essential), you will want to ask the organizer to share it with you. That conversation is also often a great opportunity to get qualitative feedback from the organizer about your talk.

They will rarely criticize you directly, but you should be able to get a general sense of what they think, and use that to probe further—if they actually saw your talk and have feedback.

Of course, if you do a live talk with chat or Q&A on a digital platform, you'll actually see some amount of feedback as your talk or pitch progresses. The overall engagement level is more important than the questions themselves here. You'll want to pay attention to parts of your talk that produced more or less online comments, and consider whether that's because you really captured everyone's attention, or because they were distracted. You can ask for the transcript from most events, but keeping one eye on it (or having someone from your team do that for you) is perfectly reasonable.

Conclusion

Becoming a Professional Speaker

Not every one of you reading this book will have an interest in becoming a professional speaker. Like many of my coaching clients, your focus might be on better presentations at work, or striving toward a company pitch that raises money. Or maybe you just need to give a great wedding toast or TV interview.

Regardless, I hope that the content of this book has been helpful in getting you to think differently (nay, better) about how we communicate in this modern era. Distraction is such a powerful, caustic force in all our lives, but we can harness this reality and learn to break through the noise.

I wrote this book because I genuinely want to see/hear each of you speak more beautifully. And so I sincerely welcome you reaching out—if there's some way I can be helpful or just to see how far you've come. Feel free to use the contact information in the supplemental materials to make contact.

Now, if you've got more than a passing interest in turning your (newfound) passion for public speaking into a career, keep reading. Becoming a professional public speaker is a topic rich enough for its own book, seminars, and course. But here I'll try to do some small justice to the basics of what you need to know to get started. And again, feel free to reach out with questions.

PICKING A TOPIC

By now you've hopefully been working on a specific topic for this next talk. But perhaps you want to take the content from that talk and turn it into more of a speaking program. A franchise, if you will.

In order to do this, you need to decide on a few things about your topic.

First, are you:

1. An inspirational speaker?

or

2. An educational speaker?

The best do both, but in general you need to decide if you're going to mostly motivate or mostly educate. If you choose option two, you will get pigeonholed, but—depending on the topic—that might actually be good. If you're the kind of person that loves to teach, an educational orientation will certainly be useful. Same goes if you're a very specific subject matter expert.

Inspirational speakers, on the other hand, tend to get paid better, even though it's harder for them to get started in the industry. Most aspiring speakers fashion themselves as motivators a la Tony Robbins, bringing all the soaring rhetoric possible to ideas that have been heard a million times before. If you're going to go down path one, you need to have something very original to say, and a great way to say it.

If you've decided to go down the educational path, you won't need to consider the overarching theme of your talk, most likely. People will hire you to speak on your topic, and that's that. You probably won't be giving keynotes—or making that big keynote money—but you will work consistently. However, if you're an inspirational-type person, you'll need to attach your speech to one of the major "themes" that even organizers are generally looking for. These include:

*   the future
*   trends
*   disruption
*   inspiring personal story
*   sales
*   creativity

Again, there's no hard and fast rule, and if you search for many keynote speakers' bureaus, you'll see a range of topics that are tailored to the event organizer's demands. But you should consider picking a lane.

You'll also need a catchy title and tagline, and a few versions of the talk outline for event bookers to take you seriously. This can include a variation set of your "core" talk for specific audiences. Consider that the organizations with the most money to spend on speakers are educational institutions, industry associations, and major corporations—and position accordingly. If you're taking the main stage, you'll need to talk to themes that can work for any of these audiences, and should have a version that can work regardless of where you are.

GETTING BOOKINGS

Getting paid speaking bookings is not easy. There is a plethora of unpaid opportunities at industry conferences however, and I strongly encourage you to start there. Hit up events in your geographic area or topic specialty, such as your alumni groups, industry associations, regional meetups, etc. Bring them your keynote pitch and see if they'll take a chance on bringing you out to speak.

As a rule, these first gigs will be completely unpaid. Sometimes an event will have a small budget for hotels and mileage reimbursement, but you should just assume this is going to be at your expense. If you seriously want to make speaking a major career choice, this is the investment you have to put in. Not unlike actors who start their careers doing regional theater and student films before breaking into the Star Wars franchise, you too need to put in the "grind" to get those big opportunities down the line.

Moreover, you want to do this because it's much easier to practice and test out new material in a smaller, less-fraught environment. That's why stand-up comics often practice their material in small towns or by showing up unannounced at a regular comedy show. Since the audience isn't primed to see them—and hasn't paid the commensurate big bucks—the theory is that they will be more accepting of bad material, and provide guidance on how to navigate it. Same goes for public speakers, you want to "try out" the material and delivery before you charge $20,000 for it.

The more of these small, unpaid talks you do, the better you'll get. But also, you'll start getting folks in the audience that do want to book you for a paid event. Be sure to position that a bit in conversations with folks, along the lines of "oh if you think this talk would be interesting in your organization, let me know—I love speaking to company groups." Create the space for people to bring you business organically.

Now that you are developing a talk and getting opportunities to speak, you should consider some other forms of lead generation. First, start writing (or doing educational videos). You'll need to write extensively about your topic in order to get and keep people's attention, and you should try to position yourself as the expert in their minds in every way. You may also want to write a book—so preparing a book proposal outline that maps to your topic area is a good strategy. Books are pretty good at selling speeches: it wasn't until my first book came out on gamification that I started really getting a lot of bookings.

Moreover, videos of your talk online can be extremely effective at driving booking traffic to your speaking program. Try to get copies of your talks and post them, and consider doing some TEDx Talks or other regional speech cycles to get videos that will be syndicated in a bigger way. Again, exposing everyone to your brilliant delivery and insightful content is the best way to get gigs.

You can also pitch events and speakers' bureaus yourself. Most of the biggest bureaus have a form you can complete to submit yourself for representation—but they'll all want to know your experience and traction as a speaker. High-paying events generally don't advertise for speakers, but you might be able to find some in your company or organizations you belong to.

Your concise speaking pitch should contain information about you, your topic/title, and links to your work. It is a pitch like any other, so be sure to be terse and as exciting as possible. You may also consider hiring some outsourced folks (e.g., on Fiverr) to help you prospect and pitch events—but I'd generally recommend this only for folks with some experience. If you shovel money into your speaking program without having the foundations in place, you will be throwing good money out over bad.

SPEAKERS BUREAUS AND AGENTS

No speaking agents are going to like hearing this, but their business is pretty shady. Conference organizers generally go to speakers' bureaus to help them source and negotiate with speakers. Most paid speakers are represented by someone to whom the bureaus then reach out to determine fees, availability, and so on.

Therefore, unless you are represented by the same agent as the event, you're likely to be paying commission twice: once to the "buyers" agent, and once to yours. A great deal of their work is done based on relationships and databases, so the whole thing is kept relatively opaque, and there are plenty of backchannel conversations that can have a material impact on your prospects as a speaker.

Regardless, you likely need to have a speaking agent to make serious money—and to be taken seriously. I know some speakers that don't want to share the commission (20 to 25 percent typically) and create a fake agent who responds to all inquiries. But I'm not sure that's worth it. Like selling your own home, you *can* do it yourself and save a lot of money. But you'll have a much smaller pool of buyers to choose from, and things will take a lot longer. If you end up breaking into the big time, you can always negotiate a lower fee with your agent.

Once you sign with a bureau—and sometimes even when you don't—they'll list you on their public speakers database, which is good for their SEO. By claiming some of the Google search space for your name, they can take advantage of someone watching your amazing TEDx Talk online, typing in your name to find your contact info, and ending up at their website. Remember: they mostly get paid by event organizers—and only when you get booked—so of course they want to intercede in the workflow as early and as often as possible.

You will, however, want your own SEO power and destination to send folks to. You should definitely setup a simple website, ideally with a URL that matches your name (mine is gabezichermann.com). Focus this site on your speaking program, and include links to your videos, headshot/bio, some talk descriptions and the like. Some speakers like to put their whole calendar up on the website as a form of social proof—but I often question the cheesiness of this. If you have testimonials from others who've booked you and/or have the budget for a sizzle reel, all the better. Check out my website for an example of the latter. It's cringe-inducing for me to watch, but you'd be surprised at how much a good edit and upbeat music can do for one's image.

Be sure to make contacting you easy and straightforward.

WHAT SHOULD YOU CHARGE FOR A TALK

The right answer to the question of what you should charge for a talk is: as much as the organizer is willing to pay. Usually, the bureau representing the event will have a budget in mind, but they will try to get you to give them a number first—just in case they can score a great deal. In many bureau's websites, speakers have an approximate fee range listed, and are often excluded if they are above the target's budget. I always like to create space for events to pitch me at less than my standard quote—sometimes I really want to do them.

But yes, you need a standard rate. Typically, when you're first starting out and are pre-agent, your payments per speech are limited to expenses, or an honorarium that is usually under $1,000/talk.

The amount you can demand is almost entirely dependent on the size of the audience you can command, your track record, and how busy you are. The sky is the limit on how much some speakers charge for a talk.

For example, Hillary Clinton is believed to charge upward of $200,000 for a speech—and so when she's paid, she's mostly only speaking to the biggest (or most important) audiences. Many in-demand speakers who are not quite at Hillary's level nonetheless are able to command $30 or $40,000 for a single talk.

Most professional keynotes are, however, priced in the $10 to $25,000 range in the US today. Typically, online events pay much less, as do most international speaking opportunities. Weirdly, the US is the most lucrative speaking market—though many speakers I know (myself included) have made a lot of money doing talks in the Middle East or Asia.

If you have to travel to your talk, it is customary for the event organizer to also pick up your cost of travel. This typically includes ground transport on both sides, airfare and a night or two in hotels at the venue. Most high-end speakers get first class travel as well, so this part of the expense can be significant for a lot of events, especially if you have to go really far to give the talk.

I remember being booked to give a corporate talk in Europe to an executive management team at one of the world's largest pharmaceutical companies. They paid me super well, but the first class travel I negotiated ended up costing approximately 30 percent of my total fees. Regardless, it's customary and you should ask for expenses. Increasingly, events are offering a fixed amount toward expenses instead of reimbursing the direct cost. This allows everyone's budgets to stay more controlled, and puts some non-commissionable money directly in your pocket.

A common strategy to eke out a bit of additional cash is to negotiate usual and customary travel expenses in first class in a lump sum, and then fly coach. The speaker keeps the difference. It's entirely up to you as to how you want to handle this—but just know it's an option.

And if you're an adherent of the strategy I laid out in this book (especially around speaking hygiene) you probably know what I'm going to say next: always ensure you get two hotel nights if you have to travel far. This will give you enough buffer on the front end to relax, adjust to the time zone, and be at your best.

THE AGONY AND ECSTASY

Public speaking brings me joy. More than any other activity I can think of (maybe except for a great night's sleep or a really tasty sandwich), public speaking fills my emotional cup with happiness. This may not be the case for you—and perhaps at the start of this book you began from a place of reluctance to speak at all. By now—and certainly if you're reading this chapter—I can only hope your perspective has shifted, you're more confident and more curious that ever about where to take your passions.

But you must love the work. Sure, it pays exceptionally well—but it's also grueling and ego destroying. If you don't have a desire to speak and change the world, do yourself a favor and find another place to put your creative/expressive energy.

However, if you feel even the tiniest spark of interest or desire here, *do it.* Take the plunge and put yourself out there right away. Follow the lessons of this book and the abridged advice in this final chapter to turn your skills into capital.

I firmly believe the world needs to hear what you have to say. And with the lessons of the A-Ha! Method in your arsenal, you can successfully cut through the noise and share your vision with the rest of humanity.

I can't wait to hear you speak beautifully.

Gabe Zichermann
Los Angeles, CA
January 2023

Notes

CHAPTER 3

1. "Who We Are," Behavioral Science & Policy Association website https://behavioral policy.org/about/.

2. Matthias Benedek and Christian Kaernbach, "Physiological Correlates and Emotional Specificity of Human Piloerection," *Biological Psychology* 86, no. 3 (2011): 320–29, https://www.ncbi.nlm.nih.gov/pmc/articles/PMC3061318/.

3. Francine Shapiro, "The Role of Eye Movement Desensitization and Reprocessing (EMDR) Therapy in Medicine," *Permanente Journal* 18, no. 1 (2014): 71–77, https:// www.ncbi.nlm.nih.gov/pmc/articles/PMC3951033/.

4. Sylvie Mrug, Anjana Madan, and Michael Windle, "Emotional Desensitiza- tion to Violence Contributes to Adolescents' Violent Behavior," *Journal of Abnormal Child Psychology* 44, no. 1 (2016): 75–86, https://www.ncbi.nlm.nih.gov/pmc/articles /PMC4539292/.

5. Mara Mather and Matthew Sutherland, "The Selective Effects of Emotional Arousal on Memory," *Psychological Science Agenda*, American Psychological Association, February 2012, https://www.apa.org/science/about/psa/2012/02/emotional-arousal.

6. "The AIP Model," EMDR Europe website, https://emdr-europe.org/about/the-aip -model/.

7. Gloria Mark, Shamsi Iqbal, Mary Czerwinski, and Paul Johns, "Focused, Aroused, but so Distractible: A Temporal Perspective on Multitasking and Commu- nications," *Technologies in the Workplace*, CSCW 2015, March 14–18, https://www .microsoft.com/en-us/research/wp-content/uploads/2016/10/p903-mark.pdf.

8. A. J. Cohen, "Music as a Source of Emotion in Film," in *Music and Emotion: Theory and Research*, edited by P. N. Juslin and J. A. Sloboda, 249–72 (Oxford Univer- sity Press, 2001). https://psycnet.apa.org/record/2001-05534-005.

9. Jovan Byford, "I've Been Talking to Conspiracy Theorists for 20 Years—Here Are My Six Rules of Engagement," *The Conversation*, July 22, 2020, https://theconversation .com/ive-been-talking-to-conspiracy-theorists-for-20-years-here-are-my-six-rules-of -engagement-143132.

CHAPTER 5

1. Olivia Fox Cabane, *The Charisma Myth* (Portfolio, 2012).
2. W. Chan Kim and Renée Mauborgne, *Blue Ocean Strategy* (Harvard Business Review, 2015).

CHAPTER 6

1. National Geographic Encyclopedia, s.v. "storytelling," https://www.nationalgeo graphic.org/encyclopedia/storytelling/.

CHAPTER 7

1. Johann Hari, "Everything You Think You Know about Addiction Is Wrong," filmed June 2015 at TEDGlobal, https://www.youtube.com/watch?v=PY9DcIMGxMs.

CHAPTER 8

1. Andrew Smith, "How PowerPoint Is Killing Critical Thought," *The Guardian*, September 23, 2015, https://www.theguardian.com/commentisfree/2015/sep/23 /powerpoint-thought-students-bullet-points-information.
2. Geoffrey James, "The Real Rason Steve Jobs Hated PowerPoint," *Inc*, February 5, 2020, https://www.inc.com/geoffrey-james/steve-jobs-hated-powerpoint-you-should -too-heres-what-to-use-instead.html.

CHAPTER 10

1. John Tierney, "Do You Suffer from Decision Fatigue?" *New York Times*, August 21, 2011, https://www.nytimes.com/2011/08/21/magazine/do-you-suffer-from-decision -fatigue.html.

CHAPTER 11

1. Pilotfriend.com, "stalls," *Fixed Wing Flight Training*, http://www.pilotfriend.com /training/flight_training/fxd_wing/stalls.htm.

2. Roxanna Salim, "An Introduction to the Sympathetic and Parasympathetic Nervous System," *iMotions* (blog), November 12, 2019, https://imotions.com/blog/nervous-system/.

3. Jonah Engel Bromwich, "Congressman Who Shouted 'You Lie' at Obama Hears the Same from Constituents," *New York Times*, April 11, 2017, https://www.nytimes.com/2017/04/11/us/politics/joe-wilson-you-lie-obama-town-hall.html.

4. Sara Lindberg, "Eustress: The Good Stress," *healthline*, January 3, 2019, https://www.healthline.com/health/eustress.

5. Touré, "Adele Opens Up about Her Inspirations, Looks, and Stage Fright," *Rolling Stone*, April 28, 2011, https://www.rollingstone.com/music/music-news/adele-opens-up-about-her-inspirations-looks-and-stage-fright-79626/.

Bibliography

Books

Anderson, Chris. *TED Talks*. Houghton Mifflin Harcourt, 2016.

Carson, Rick. *Taming Your Gremlin*. Quill, 2003.

Csikszentmihaly, Mihaly. *Flow: The Psychology of Optimal Experience*. HarperPerennial, 2008.

Carnegie, Dale. *How to Win Friends and Influence People*. Simon & Schuster, 2010.

Carnegie, Dale. *The Art of Public Speaking*. Clydesdale, 2018.

Fox Cabane, Olivia. *The Charisma Myth*. Gildan Media, 2012

Slutsky, Jeff and Aun, Michael. *Toastmaster's International Guide to Successful Speaking*. Dearborn Trade Pub, 1996.

Talks

Adichie, Chimamanda. "The danger of a single story." Filmed 2009 at TED Edinburgh.

Bolte Taylor, Jill. "My stroke of insight." Filmed 2008 at TED Monterey.

Bergells, Laura "Speech Pace." Filmed 2018.

Brown, Brené. "The Power of Vulnerability." Filmed 2010 at TEDxHouston.

Hari, Johann. "Everything you think you know about addiction is wrong." Filmed 2015 at TEDGlobal London.

Hicks, Abraham. "The key to effortless manifestation." Filmed 2009 at San Diego.

Kelly, Diane. "What we didn't know about male anatomy." Filmed 2012 at TEDx Washington DC.

Robinson, Ken. "Do schools kill creativity?" Filmed 2006 at TED Monterey.

Sinek, Simon. "How great leaders inspire action." Filmed 2010 at TEDxPugetSound.

Treasure, Julian. "How to speak so that people want to listen." Filmed 2013 at TED Edinburgh.

Zichermann, Gabe. "Gamification: The Power of Videogames & Children." Filmed 2010 at TEDxYouth Brussels.

Zichermann, Gabe. "How to Win at Losing: A Failosophy for Innovation." Filmed 2020 at TEDx Frankfurt.

Other Resources

Astley, Rick. "Never Gonna Give You Up." 1987. https://www.youtube.com /watch?v=iik25wqIuFo.

Kawasaki, Guy. "How to Kick Butt on a Panel." 2006. https://guykawasaki.com /how_to_kick_but/.

Kawasaki, Guy. "How to Be a Great Moderator." 2006. https://guykawasaki.com /how_to_be_a_gre/

Kawasaki, Guy. "Pitch Decks." 2015. https://guykawasaki.com/the-only-10-slides -you-need-in-your-pitch/.

Lincoln, Abraham. "The Gettysburg Address." 1863. https://www.britannica.com /event/Gettysburg-Address.

Robinson, Ken. "Do schools kill creativity?" Filmed 2006 at TED Monterey.

Tam, Janelle. "How to Build a Great Series A Pitch and Deck." https://www.ycombina tor.com/library/8d-how-to-build-a-great-series-a-pitch-and-deck.

Index

About the Author

Gabe Zichermann is an entrepreneur, author, investor, and leader of people. His four books, hundreds of speeches, and dozens of workshops on gamification and behavioral design have fundamentally altered the future of Silicon Valley and how it designs technology products and workplace processes by making them more fun and engaging. Companies such as Apple, Google, Facebook, Microsoft, and Amazon have adopted Gabe's theories and practices, leading to significant revenue increases over time.

Widely recognized for his ability to digest complex problems and processes and turn them into easily accessible, engaging, and game-changing communication that cuts through the noise, Gabe is a frequent keynote speaker who is routinely rated as an audience (and organizer) favorite. He also runs an exclusive speaker coaching practice that has helped hundreds of successful entrepreneurs, executives, and celebrities communicate beautifully in all settings.

Gabe is a polyglot with a culinary streak. Originally from Canada, he's visited more than 105 countries as a speaker and adventurer. Now a resident of sunny Los Angeles, Zichermann has recently co-founded a keto ice cream company called Two Spoons Creamery with his ex, proving complexity can be deliciously transformative if it's well packaged.